LUTHER

Luther

A PROFILE

Edited by H. G. Koenigsberger

WORLD PROFILES
General Editor: Aïda DiPace Donald

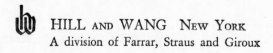

HILL AND WANG NEW YORK
A division of Farrar, Straus and Giroux

ISBN (CLOTHBOUND EDITION): 0–8090–6702–1
ISBN (PAPERBACK EDITION): 0–8090–1403–3
LIBRARY OF CONGRESS CATALOG CARD NUMBER: 76–184946
FIRST EDITION, 1973
PUBLISHED SIMULTANEOUSLY IN CANADA BY DOUBLEDAY CANADA LTD.,
TORONTO
PRINTED IN THE UNITED STATES OF AMERICA
1 2 3 4 5 6 7 8 9 10

To Dorothy

Contents

Introduction

FOUR HUNDRED YEARS AFTER THE EVENT, Martin
Luther's defiance of emperor and pope, at the Diet of Worms
on 20 April 1521, still stands as one of the great dramatic moments in the history of the human mind. But what did it signify?
Was it a declaration of freedom of the human mind in the face
of venerable tradition grown tyrannical, or was it only the affirmation of a private obstinacy raised to spurious universality by its
theatrical setting and the irrelevant political aims of most of those
present? For centuries the Reformation was regarded as the most
important spiritual and intellectual event in modern European
history. It was so for Leopold von Ranke and, probably, still for
Gerhard Ritter. In the sense that it could be seen as the contemporary intellectualization of the breakthrough of capitalism
and the bourgeoisie, it was similarly regarded even by Friedrich
Engels. And if we are now more skeptical of being able to evaluate the importance of the Reformation in quite such a definitive

way *sub specie aeternitatis,* the very fact of its enormous impact on the sensibilities of so many generations will assure it of continued interest and study.

The figure of Martin Luther remains central; of this there can be no doubt. But he was not central in all historical phenomena which are usually lumped together under the term Reformation. The sudden surfacing of a veritable babel of religious voices, each one preached and followed with a burning conviction of its sole truth, should make us hesitate to ascribe too much influence on the minds of contemporaries of any one set of theological doctrines, even of Luther's doctrine of justification by faith. To the great mass of those who had no taste for religious change or who were shielded from contact with its propaganda —that is, the majority of Christians—the reformers were simply heretics. In Spain there is still a widespread belief that Martino Lutero, like most great saints and villains, was a Spaniard and that the one really unforgivable thing he did was to marry a nun. One story runs that Martino Lutero, toward the end of his life, repented of his great sins and vainly sought absolution. Finally he came to a holy hermit in the sierras. The hermit was not a priest and had no power to grant absolution, but he was sympathetic and advised Martino Lutero to wait with the crowd on the railway bridge over the river for the train in which the local bishop would come to town that very afternoon. As soon as the bishop leaned out of the window to bless the crowd, Lutero was to tumble into the river. The bishop, seeing a man falling to his death, would immediately pronounce an absolution. Everything went as planned, except that the bishop shouted: "My son, I absolve you from all your sins, unless you are Martino Lutero." [1]

To good Catholics—laymen and clergy alike—in fact, to all except a few theologians who specialized in such matters, the specific doctrines of the reformers and their mutual hostilities remained utterly unimportant, for it simply made no sense to choose to be a heretic. This was, basically, the attitude of Cardinal Cajetan when he summoned Luther before him in 1519,[2] just

1. This story is told by R. Tyler, *The Emperor Charles the Fifth* (London, 1956), p. 125*n*. The views about Luther's nationality and marriage I have heard myself.

2. See pp. 18–19.

as it was still, in the early years of the twentieth century, that of the Catholic archivist Heinrich Denifle when he set out to prove, in several immensely erudite volumes, that Luther's religious beliefs were only a cloak for, or a rationalization of, his sexual urges.[3]

It can, moreover, be argued that the unity of the church and of Christendom, the "seamless garment of Christ" which Luther and the other reformers were accused of having willfully rent asunder, was already so tattered that it probably would have fallen to pieces in any case. For this unity was not an inevitable and eternal condition, necessarily springing from the church's own universalist claims; rather, it was the result of quite specific and transitory, even though long-term, historical conditions. These conditions were functional: the usefulness—not only religious but also intellectual, political, and administrative—of having both a universal faith and a universal organization which claimed to embody this faith. By the beginning of the sixteenth century, this usefulness had all but disappeared in the eyes of the European monarchies and the national churches they had come to control. Louis XII of France summoned the anti-papal council of Pisa. Ferdinand of Aragon (known as Ferdinand the Catholic) threatened to withdraw all his realms from ecclesiastical obedience to the pope in 1508, that is, twenty-five years before Henry VIII actually did so. In none of these cases was religion the reason for the break (or threatened break) with Rome, nor was religion the motive for Gustavus Vasa's actions in Sweden. Since Charles V and Philip II actually waged war against the pope, it is clear that the Roman church would have collapsed as a universal church in Europe even without a religious problem. Paradoxically, it was the Reformation that, by reaction, may well have saved the unity of the church in at least the greater part of Europe.[4]

Nevertheless, the Reformation was more than just a heresy and it was more than the breakup of the unity of the old church. It was precisely what most Catholics were unwilling to concede:

3. H. S. Denifle, *Luther und Lutherthum in der ersten Entwicklung,* 2 vols. (Mainz, 1903); *Ergänzungen,* 2 vols. (Mainz, 1905–1906). French translation by J. Paquier, *Luther et le luthéranisme,* 4 vols. (Paris, 1910–1913).

4. I have argued this thesis at greater length in "The Unity of the Church and the Reformation," *Journal of Interdisciplinary History,* Vol. 1, No. 3 (Spring 1971), 1971.

a profound change in religious sensibilities, a change which has affected not only the religious beliefs but the whole intellectual, artistic, and, perhaps even economic and social life of almost half of Europe and most of North America up to the present time. These changes cannot be thought of without Luther. It was Luther who had the courage—moral, intellectual, and physical—to challenge the established powers of his day, knowing that previous similar efforts had almost invariably ended in disaster to the challenger. Once Luther had been successful in making his challenge, it became relatively easy for others to imitate his example. Perhaps even more important, it was Luther's very personal religious convictions and his unsurpassed ability to express them which found echoes among thousands who had been left unmoved by Erasmus and the Christian humanists. The "evangelical" churches, from Saxony and Hesse to Denmark and Sweden, developed very much as "Lutheran" churches in spite of their mutual differences and the elderly reformer's own disclaimers.

No serious scholar, Protestant or Catholic, any longer doubts that Luther's motivation and purpose were essentially religious. The modern study of Luther's theology, initiated some fifty or sixty years ago in Scandinavia and then taken up in Germany, England, France, and America, has clarified much of Luther's thought that was previously obscure or half-buried in the sands of sectarian polemics. Most of this work, even when it is written in a rather didactic style, is noncontroversial except in matters of technical detail. Even Erik Erikson's psychoanalysis of the young Luther has generated much less hostility from professional Luther scholars than one might have expected. Characteristically, the most violent controversy among theologians (and, to the nonspecialist, the most entertaining) has not been concerned with Luther's beliefs at all but rather with one of his actions: did he (or did he not) nail the ninety-five theses on the church door at Wittenberg on October 31, 1517? This day and action in Lutheran tradition is equivalent to July 14, 1789, in French republican tradition.[5]

Much work still remains to be done on the mass of Luther's

5. E. Iserloh, *The Theses Were Not Posted: Luther Between Reform and Reformation,* translated by J. Wicks (London, 1968).

writings. As Gerhard Ebeling says, there is "no parallel in the whole of history in which a spiritual upheaval of such proportions can be studied with anything approaching the same fullness of original sources." [6] Without this fullness of sources, Erikson's analysis would certainly not have been possible. But it is unlikely that we will find any more important theological surprises. The most interesting historiographical problems about Luther now seem to me to lie less in his personality and in the nature of his religious beliefs than in the impact of both these on his contemporaries.

"For a little while Luther, this first revolutionary individualist, saved the Saviour from the tiaras and the ceremonies, the hierarchies and the thought-police, and put him back where he arose: in each man's soul." Thus Erikson[7] and, indeed, the whole Protestant tradition. Here was certainly one of the reasons why Luther received such widespread support between 1517 and 1521. But it was not the only reason for the extraordinary tide of anti-Roman feeling that swept Germany just before the Diet of Worms. Ranke, convinced Lutheran that he was, seems to have had some doubts as to whether it was even the most important reason, and he caught himself almost wishing that Luther had chosen to lead a national rather than a religious movement.[8]

From the very beginning of his theological controversies—from the posting of the ninety-five theses—Luther could not escape from the political implications of his religious beliefs, and these beliefs themselves were largely crystallized by political pressures. Not justification by faith; but this concept alone need not have caused a breach with Rome. Luther himself did not at first think that it would or should; besides, the church, in its long and turbulent history, had managed to absorb other, perhaps equally indigestible, theological doctrines. It was the financial and political implications of Luther's attack on the sale of indulgences that brought a hostile reaction from his opponents, and this reaction and counterattack, in its turn, drove him to formulate the ecclesiastical consequences of his theological beliefs: the rejection

6. See p. 178.
7. See p. 119.
8. See p. 40.

of the authority of popes and councils, and the denial of the sacramental powers of the priesthood.

By 1525, when Luther wrote his violent diatribes against the
rebellious peasants, all the contradictions between his religious
intentions and the diverse aims of those who had seen him as
their champion had become tragically apparent. It is easy enough
to see that Luther did not betray the peasants. What he had
preached had nothing to do with social oppression and could never
be a justification for rebellion; he had always been perfectly consistent on this point.[9] The peasants' revolt was the more wicked
because they justified it by appealing to the Word of God, thus
doing the Devil's work: "trying to cook and brew the two kingdoms [the heavenly and the earthly] into one another." [10]

It is easy to be ironical and to see, as Lucien Febvre said, a
"Gargantuan humor" in "Luther facing the chaos of battle shouts
and incendiary confusion, his eyes raised to heaven, Dr. Martin
Luther puffing out his cheeks and piping with all his soul his own
little tune on a Christian flageolet." [11] But is it enough to recognize Luther's sincerity and consistency and to refrain from cheap
irony in order fully to understand the German Reformation and
the German spirit? [12] Luther was anxious to keep the two kingdoms separate. Very well. But then his actions and the advice he
gave to others must be judged within the context of the earthly
kingdom (coram hominibus) and by the light of that natural
reason, which, he admitted, was a gift of God even to the pagans.[13]
On this level, Luther may be justified in condemning rebellion
and in exhorting the princes to defeat it. If he had done that and
had denounced the peasants for misappropriating God's Word for
their secular actions, nothing more need be said. But Luther did
much more. He compared the peasants to mad dogs and then used
this metaphor to justify their indiscriminate slaughter. He exhorted the princes to become the butchers of their subjects and
promised them heavenly glory for their pains. The mercy of God,

9. See pp. 141–142.
10. See p. 132.
11. See pp. 61–62.
12. See p. 62.
13. See p. 138.

no doubt, would separate the innocent and the merely misled from those truly deserving punishment for rebellion—in afterlife. It is no excuse that Luther also condemned the princes, that he did so throughout his life, and often with great heat. There remains the stark fact that calling a duke a dirty name will annoy him but not otherwise cause him much harm, whereas calling a peasant a mad dog and urging soldiers to kill him will deliberately provoke a massacre

The princes probably did not need Luther's blessing to engage in their blood sports, but his words were not without influence. Luther's contemporaries esteemed the quality of mercy in earthly matters. Luther's complete lack of it was, and still is, revolting. It shows a moral obtuseness of which the Erasmians, so often criticized for their alleged theological shallowness, were never guilty.

Luther's attitude toward the peasants' revolt was an extreme case even for him, but his growing willingness to advocate the use of force against the Anabaptist preachers and the Jews[14] indicated a basic streak of callousness in his character. No disclaimer that he was not attempting to preach "Lutheranism" but only the true word of the Gospels can fully hide his unwillingness to consider the moral problems inherent in the political consequences of his religious actions. This is also true of his refusal to reach a compromise and reconciliation with his opponents. Gerhard Ritter saw this very clearly in Luther's attitude toward Zwingli[15] but not, it seems to me, in Luther's hostility toward Melanchthon's peace efforts at the Diet of Augsburg in 1530. It may be true that Melanchthon came "close to the borderline where he would have betrayed the gospel in his Erasmic offers of reconciliation."[16] But how could Luther (and Gerhard Ritter) be so certain that "all the offers of compromise on the part of his opponents were nothing but lies and deceit"?[17] We know in fact that both Charles V himself and many of the Catholic theologians were honestly, even passionately, anxious for compromise and reconciliation. The

14. See pp. 92–93.
15. See pp. 87–89.
16. See p. 95.
17. See p. 95.

chances for its acceptance by the papacy were certainly not good, but they were not impossible. A successful outcome of the talks at Augsburg would have enormously strengthened the position of the irenic reformers in Rome. It was Erasmus, in anxious correspondence with both sides at Augsburg, who saw more clearly than the Protestant and Catholic purists the benefits to Christendom of reconciliation. Religious war, Erasmus felt, must be avoided at all costs, not only because it was horrible in itself but because it would ultimately make Christian belief contemptible.

Luther would never have accepted these arguments. The Word of God was not a matter of sweet reasonableness but of thunder. The dreadful Old Testament epithets of Jehovah were ever ready in Luther's polemical armory, together with the exhortation that it was not for man to dispute—or even to understand—God's purpose outside the saving power of Christ crucified. Not for nothing did Luther regard his tract against free will—his definitive parting of the ways with Erasmus—as one of the very few of his writings that he hoped might be preserved. These are not beliefs which the modern historian should judge or dispute. What he can and must judge is Luther's habit of justifying and even encouraging some of the most appalling actions of his contemporaries on the basis of these beliefs.

To make such judgments is not to deny Luther's greatness. In the depths of his religious penetration, in his command—even creation—of a whole language, he has had few equals in European history. Luther's moral and physical courage, his devotion to music, his innumerable acts of kindness to many of his own contemporaries remain as admirable now as they were to those who first fell under the spell of his personality. It is the juxtaposition of these qualities with his self-righteousness and his moral callousness toward those whom he judged the enemies of God's Word which is perhaps the most fascinating and, as yet, least explored aspect of Luther's character.

To anyone studying Luther it soon becomes apparent that Luther himself was a very much better and more interesting writer than most of his commentators, theological analysts, and biographers. This book does not include material from Luther's

works, but his works are readily available; moreover, all the
authors represented in this book have quoted extensively from his
writings.

I have started this "Profile" with a long, though still con-
densed, passage from Ranke's *History of the Reformation in
Germany.* Even in this rather indifferent translation it is, perhaps, still the best narrative of Luther's early life and of the
political circumstances of his breach with Rome, written from a
German Protestant point of view. To balance this, the period of
Luther's life from the Diet of Worms to the Peasants' War is
treated by Lucien Febvre, a French Catholic historian of the
last generation. While not unsympathetic, Febvre is much more
critical of Luther than Ranke. Another perspective is presented
with a passage on Luther from Friedrich Engels's *The Peasant
War in Germany,* which is still the best concise Marxist interpretation. Later Marxist writers are often more subtle and more
knowledgeable than Engels, but most of them are also duller and
they do not basically advance his argument. Luther's later career
is described by Gerhard Ritter, a distinguished exponent of more
recent Protestant German historical scholarship.

The remaining chapters are intended to present different aspects of Luther's personality and beliefs. Erik Erikson attempts,
certainly not for the first time, but more ingeniously than the
majority of his predecessors, a psychological analysis of Luther.
Gordon Rupp, Lennart Pinomaa, and Brian Gerrish analyze
Luther's theological doctrines that are most important for the
general historian in understanding the reformer. Bengt Hägglund
investigates how far Luther's doctrine of justification by faith
was foreshadowed by the fourteenth-century mystic Johannes
Tauler, whom he greatly admired, and by the fifteenth-century
scholastic theologian Gabriel Biel, whom he studied intensively.
Gerhard Ebeling discusses Luther's career as a professor and
writer and some of the historiographical problems connected with
this topic. Heinrich Bornkamm writes of Luther's translation of
the Bible.

From an overabundance of material, I have tried to choose
those chapters and articles that dealt most directly and clearly
with the problems I wanted to present, while offering some variety

in the nationality of the contributors, for the international character of contemporary Luther studies is one of its outstanding characteristics. There was no difficulty in finding adequate English translations. However, in presenting the topic of Luther as a musician, most of what I found was either very technical or not very good. This was especially true for the literature on this subject written in English, and hardly anything has been translated from other languages. Therefore, I translated a passage myself from the standard German textbook on Protestant church music.[18]

18. The passage is from the first edition of Friedrich Blume's *Die evangelische Kirchenmusik*. The corresponding chapters in the second edition, although much fuller, are not as well written, and what is new in them is of interest only to musicological specialists.

Martin Luther
1483–1546

MARTIN LUTHER WAS BORN AT EISLEBEN in Thuringia on 10 November 1483. His father, Hans Luther, was descended from free peasants but, as a younger son, decided to become a copper miner. In 1484 the family moved to the mining town of Mansfeld where Hans Luther gradually achieved moderate prosperity. Martin's later memories of his childhood, however, were of poverty and a strict, even harsh, upbringing. He went to school, first at Mansfeld and, later, at the neighboring towns of Magdeburg and Eisenach. In 1501 he entered the University of Erfurt and for several years studied Scholastic philosophy. Hans Luther hoped that his obviously gifted son would make a brilliant career as a lawyer. But in the summer of 1505 Martin was caught in a thunderstorm and, in sudden fear for his life, he vowed to become a monk. He entered the monastery of the Augustinian Eremites at Erfurt, took monastic vows, and was ordained a priest in 1507. In 1508 he began to lecture at the recently founded University of Wittenberg in electoral Saxony. Two years later, he visited Rome on business of his order. Much later, he was to ascribe a traumatic impact on his religious sensibilities to his experience of the worldliness and ostentation of Rome. In 1511 Luther was appointed a professor at Wittenberg. Some time between 1513 and 1519 Luther had his famous "tower experience" (*Turmerlebnis*), the moment of religious breakthrough in which he resolved his feeling of unbearable tension between the justice of God and his awareness of his own utter sinfulness: man's justification by faith. Most, though not all, experts now tend to date this experience earlier rather than later, but it has also been argued that the "tower experience" was a rather conventional metaphor in the later Middle Ages.

In 1517 Luther published his Ninety-five Theses attacking the sale of indulgences. This action made him immediately famous throughout Germany and even beyond. In the increasingly bitter theological controversies that followed, Luther refused obedience to the papal legate, Cardinal Cajetan, and began to direct his attacks against the papacy. In 1520 he published his three Reformation pamphlets, the *Address to the Christian Nobility of the German Nation, The Babylonian Captivity of the Church,* and *The Liberty of a Christian Man.* These had an enormous impact in Germany. Pope Leo X issued a bull condemning Luther's heresies and Luther publicly burned the bull. Thereupon the pope excommunicated Luther and the emperor Charles V cited him to appear before the Diet of Worms in 1521. There, Luther publicly and dramatically refused to recant. In order to assure Luther's safety, the elector of Saxony had him taken to the castle Wartburg, where he began his translation of the Bible. In 1522 Luther returned to Wittenberg to preach against the radical reformers and image-breakers. During the Peasants' War in Germany (1524–1525) he supported the princes against the rebellious peasants and lost much of his popular support. In 1525 Luther married the former nun, Katharina von Bora, and they had six children. At the instance of the landgrave of Hesse, he met with Zwingli at Marburg in 1529, but failed to reach agreement with the Swiss reformer on the all-important interpretation of the Eucharist.

Luther spent the rest of his life teaching, preaching, and, much against his own inclination, organizing a new reformed church. He continued to write voluminously: theological treatises, works of religious instruction (the most important of which were the *Greater Catechism* and *Smaller Catechism,* published in 1529), as well as hymns and chorales. His *Table Talk,* which provides many insights into his character and opinions on practically every subject, was collected by his students and friends and later published. He had little control over the growing political polarization of the confessional parties, and his occasional interventions in politics, such as his approval of the landgrave of Hesse's bigamy, often had unfortunate results. He died at Eisleben on 18 February 1546. A few weeks later, the outbreak of the Schmalkaldic War, between the emperor and the Lutheran princes and towns of Germany, began a century of religious wars in Europe.

Abbreviations

W., W.A., or L.W.W.A.	Luther's Works (*Weimarer Ausgabe*), cited by volume, page number, and sometimes also by line
W.A.Br. or Letters	Luther's Letters (*Briefwechsel, Weimarer Ausgabe*)
Tr.	Luther's Table Talk (*Tischreden, Weimarer Ausgabe*)
W.A. D.B.	Luther's Bible (*Deutsche Bibel, Weimarer Ausgabe*)
Dok.	Otto Scheel, *Dokumente zu Luthers Entwicklung* (Tübingen, 1929)
Bonn Ed.	*Luthers Werke in Auswahl,* ed. O. Clemen (Bonn, 1912)
W.M.L.	*Works of Martin Luther,* 6 vols. (Philadelphia, 1943)

LUTHER

LEOPOLD VON RANKE

The Beginning of the Reformation

"I AM A PEASANT'S SON," says Luther; "my father, grandfather, and ancestors were genuine peasants; afterwards, my father removed to Mansfeld, and became a miner; that is my native place." Luther's family was from Möhra, a village on the very summit of the Thuringian forest, not far from the spot celebrated for the first preaching of Christianity by Boniface; it is probable that Luther's forefathers had for centuries been settled on their hide of land (*Hufe*) as was the custom with those Thuringian peasants, one brother among whom always inherited the estate, while the others sought a subsistence in other ways. Condemned by such a destiny to seek a home and hearth for himself, Hans Luther was led to the mines at Mansfeld, where he

From Leopold von Ranke, *History of the Reformation in Germany,* edited by R. A. Johnson and translated by S. Austin (London: Routledge & Kegan Paul; New York: E. P. Dutton, 1905), pages 143–242. Reprinted with permission of the publishers.

earned his bread by the sweat of his brow, while his wife, Margaret, often fetched wood from the forest on her back. Such were the parents of Martin Luther. He was born at Eisleben, where his sturdy mother had walked to the yearly fair; he grew up in the mountain air of Mansfeld.

The habits and manners of that time were generally harsh and rude, and so was his education. Luther relates that his mother once scourged him till the blood came on account of one miserable nut; that his father had punished him so severely that it was with great difficulty that he could get over the child's terror and alienation; at school he was flogged fifteen times in one forenoon. He had to earn his bread by singing hymns before the doors of houses, and New Year's carols in the villages. . . .

From his fifteenth year his condition was somewhat better. In Eisenach, where he was sent to the high school, he found a home in the house of some relations of his mother; thence he went to the University of Erfurt, where his father, whose industry, frugality, and success had placed him in easier circumstances, made him a liberal allowance: his hope was that his son would be a lawyer, marry well, and do him honor.

But in this weary life the restraints of childhood are soon succeeded by troubles and perplexities. The spirit feels itself freed from the bonds of the school, and is not yet distracted by the wants and cares of daily life; it boldly turns to the highest problems, such as the relation of man to God and of God to the world, and while eagerly rushing on to the solution of them, it falls into the most distressing state of doubt. We might be almost tempted to think that the Eternal Source of all life appeared to the youthful Luther only in the light of the inexorable judge and avenger, who punishes sin (of which Luther had from nature an awful and vivid feeling) with the torments of hell, and can only be propitiated by penance, mortification, and painful service. As he was returning from his father's house in Mansfeld to Erfurt, in the month of July, 1505, he was overtaken in a field near Stotternheim by one of those fearful tempests that slowly gather on the mountains and at length suddenly burst over the whole horizon. Luther was already depressed by the unexpected death of an intimate friend. There are moments in which the agitated desponding heart is completely crushed by one overwhelming incident, even of the natural world. Luther, traversing his solitary path, saw in the tempest the God of wrath and vengeance; the lightning struck some object near him; in his terror he made a vow to St. Anne that if he escaped, he would enter a convent. He passed one more evening with his friends, enjoying the pleasures of wine, music, and song; it was the last in which he indulged himself; he hastened to fulfill his vow and entered the Augustinian Convent at Erfurt.

But he was little likely to find serenity there; imprisoned, in all the buoyant energy of youth, within the narrow gates and in the low and gloomy cell, with no prospect but a few feet of garden within the cloisters, and condemned to perform the lowest offices. At first he devoted himself to the duties of a novice with all the ardor of a determined will. "If ever a monk got to heaven by monkish life and practices I resolved that I would enter there," were his words. But though he conformed to the hard duty of obedience, he was soon a prey to the most painful disquiet. Sometimes he studied day and night, to the neglect of his canonical hours, which he then passed his nights in retrieving with penitent zeal. Sometimes he went out into some neighboring village, carrying with him his midday repast, preached to the shepherds and plowmen, and then refreshed himself with their rustic music; after which he went home, and, shutting himself up for days in his cell, would see no one. All his former doubts and secret perplexities returned from time to time with redoubled force.

In the course of his study of the Scriptures, he fell upon texts that struck terror into his soul; one of these was "Save me in thy righteousness and thy truth." "I thought," said he, "that righteousness was the fierce wrath of God, wherewith he punishes sinners." Certain passages in the Epistles of St. Paul haunted him for days. The doctrine of grace was not indeed unknown to him, but the dogma that sin was at once taken away by it produced upon him, who was but too conscious of his sins, rather a sense of rejection—a feeling of deep depression—than of hope. He says it made his heart bleed—it made him despair of God. "Oh, my sins, my sins, my sins!" he writes to Staupitz,[1] who was not a

---

1. Luther relates this in his sermon of St. John's day, 1516. V. E. Löscher, *Volständige Reformationsakta und Dokumenta,* Vol. 1 (Leipzig, 1720), p. 258. [ed.]

little astonished when he received the confession of so sorrowful a penitent and found that he had no sinful acts to acknowledge. His anguish was the longing of the creature after the purity of the Creator, to whom it feels itself profoundly and intimately allied, yet from whom it is severed by an immeasurable gulf: a feeling that Luther nourished by incessant solitary brooding, and which had taken the more painful and complete possession of him because no penance had power to appease it, no doctrine truly touched it, no confessor would hear of it. There were moments when this anxious melancholy arose with fearful might from the mysterious abysses of his soul, waved its dusky pinions over his head, and felled him to the earth. On one occasion when he had been invisible for several days, some friends broke into his cell and found him lying senseless on the ground. They knew their friend; with tender precaution they struck some chords on a stringed instrument they had brought with them; the inward strife of the perplexed spirit was allayed by the well-known remedy; it was restored to harmony and awakened to healthful consciousness.

But the eternal laws of the universe seem to require that so deep and earnest a longing of the soul after God should at length be appeased with the fullness of conviction.

The first who, if he could not administer comfort to Luther in his desperate condition, at least let fall a ray of light upon his thick darkness was an old Augustine friar who with fatherly admonitions pointed his attention to the first and simplest truth of Christianity—the forgiveness of sins through faith in the Redeemer; and to the assertion of St. Paul (Romans 3) that man is justified without works, by faith alone: doctrines that he might indeed have heard before but, obscured as they were by school subtleties and a ceremonial worship, had never rightly understood. They now first made a full and profound impression on him. He meditated especially on the saying "The just shall live by faith." He read St. Augustine's commentary on this passage. "Then was I glad," says he, "for I learned and saw that God's righteousness is his mercy, by which he accounts and holds us justified; thus I reconciled justice with justification, and felt assured that I was in the true faith." This was exactly the conviction of which his mind stood in need: it was manifest to him that the same eternal grace from which the whole race of man is sprung mercifully brings back erring souls to itself and enlightens them with the fullness of its own light; that an example and irrefragable assurance of this is given us in the person of Christ: he gradually emerged from the gloomy idea of a divine justice only to be propitiated by the rigors of penance. He was like a man who after long wanderings has at length found the right path, and feeling more certain of it at every step, walks boldly and hopefully onward.

Such was Luther's state when he was removed to Wittenberg by his provincial (A.D. 1508). The philosophical lectures he was obliged to deliver sharpened his desire to penetrate the mysteries of theology, "the kernel of the nut," as he calls it, "the heart of the wheat." He studied St. Paul's Epistles, St. Augustine against the Pelagians, and, lastly, Tauler's sermons: he troubled himself little with literature foreign to this subject; he cared only to strengthen and work out the convictions he had gained.

A few years later we find him in the most extraordinary frame of mind during a journey he took for the affairs of his order to Rome. As soon as he descried the towers of the city from a distance, he threw himself on the ground, raised his hands, and exclaimed, "Hail to thee, O holy Rome!" On his arrival there was no exercise in use among the most pious pilgrims that he did not perform with earnest and deliberate devotion, undeterred by the levity of other priests; he said he was almost tempted to wish that his parents were dead, so that he might have been able certainly to deliver them from the fire of purgatory by these privileged observances. Yet, at the same time, he felt how little such practices were in accordance with the consolatory doctrine that he had found in the Epistle to the Romans and in St. Augustine. While climbing the Scala Santa on his knees in order to obtain the plenary indulgence attached to that painful and laborious work of piety, he heard a reproving voice continually crying within him, "The just shall live by faith."

After his return in 1512, he became Doctor of the Holy Scripture, and from year to year enlarged his sphere of activity. He lectured at the university on both the Old and New Testament;

he preached at the Augustine church, and performed the duties of
the priest of the parochial church of the town during his illness;
in 1516, Staupitz appointed him administrator of the order during
his absence on a journey, and we trace him visiting all the monasteries in the province, appointing or displacing priors, receiving
or removing monks. While laboring to introduce a profounder
spirit of piety, he did not overlook the smallest economical details; and besides all this, he had to manage his own crowded and
extremely poor convent. Some things, written in the years 1515
and 1516, enable us to understand the state and workings of his
mind during that period. Mystical and scholastic ideas had still
great influence over him. In the first words of his on religious
subjects in the German language that we possess—a sketch of a
sermon dated November, 1515—he applies, in somewhat coarse
terms, the symbolical language of the Song of Songs to the oper-
ations of the Holy Ghost, which acts on the spirit through the
flesh, and also to the inward harmony of the Holy Scriptures. In
another, dated December of the same year, he endeavors to explain the mystery of the Trinity by the Aristotelian theory of
being, motion, and rest. Meanwhile his thoughts were already
turned to a grand and general reform of the church. In a speech
that appears to have been intended to be uttered by the provost
of Lietzkau at the Lateran council, he sets forth that the corruption of the world was to be ascribed to the priests, who delivered to the people too many maxims and fables of human
invention, and not the pure Word of God. For, he said, the word
of life alone is able to work out the regeneration of man. It is well
worthy of remark that, even then, Luther looked for the salvation
of the world far less to an amendment of life, which was only
secondary in his eyes, than to a revival of the true doctrines: and
there was none with the importance of which he was so penetrated
and filled as with that of justification by faith. He continually
insists on the absolute necessity of a man denying himself and
fleeing for refuge under the wings of Christ; he seizes every
opportunity of repeating the saying of St. Augustine—that faith
obtains what the law enjoins. We see that Luther was not yet
completely at one with himself; that he still cherished opinions
fundamentally at variance with each other; but all his writings

breathe a powerful mind, a youthful courage, still restrained within the bounds of modesty and reverence for authority, though ready to overleap them. . . .

If it be asked wherein he discovered the mediating power between divine perfection and human sinfulness, we find that it was solely in the mystery of the redemption and the revealed word; mercy on the one side and faith on the other. These opinions led him to doubt many of the main dogmas of the church. He did not yet deny the efficacy of absolution, but no later than the year 1516, he was perplexed by doubt about how man could obtain grace by such means: the desire of the soul was not appeased by it, nor was love infused; those effects could be produced only by the enlightenment of the mind and the kindling of the will by the immediate operation of the Eternal Spirit; for, he added, he could conceive of religion only as residing in the inmost depth of the heart. He doubted whether all those outward succors for which it was usual to invoke the saints ought to be ascribed to them.

Such were the doctrines, such the great general direction of mind immediately connected with the opinions implanted by Pollich[2] and Staupitz, which Luther disseminated among the Augustine friars of his convent and his province, and, above all, among the members of the university. For a time Jodocus Trutvetter of Eisenach[3] sustained the established opinions, but after his death in the year 1513, Luther was the master spirit that ruled the schools. His colleagues, Peter Lupinus and Andreas Carlstadt, who for a time withstood his influence, at length declared themselves overcome and convinced by the arguments of Augustine and the doctrines of the Holy Scripture, which had made so deep an impression on him; they were almost more zealous than Luther himself. A totally different direction was thus given to the University of Wittenberg from that in which the other seats of learning continued to move. Theology itself, mainly indeed in consequence of its own internal development, made similar claims to

2. Martin Pollich (died 1513). Personal physician of the elector Frederick the Wise. He induced the elector to found the new University of Wittenberg, and became its first rector. [ed.]

3. Jodocus Trutvetter (died 1519). Professor of philosophy at Erfurt where Luther attended his lectures on logic. [ed.]

those asserted by general literature. In Wittenberg arose opposition to the theologians of the old and the new way, the nominalists and the realists, and more especially to the reigning Thomistic doctrines of the Dominicans; men turned to the Scriptures and the Fathers of the church, as Erasmus (though rather as a conscientious critic than an enthusiastic religionist) had recommended. In a short time there were no hearers for the lectures given in the old spirit.

Such was the state of things in Wittenberg when the preachers of papal indulgences[4] appeared in the country about the Elbe, armed with powers such as had never been heard of before, but which Pope Leo X did not scruple, under the circumstances in which he found himself, to grant. For no fear whatever was now entertained at Rome of any important division in the church.

In the place of the council of Pisa,[5] one had been convoked at the Lateran, in which devotion to the see of Rome and the doctrine of its omnipotence reigned unalloyed and undisputed. . . .

The position which the pope, now absolute lord of Florence and master of Siena, occupied, the powerful alliances he had contracted with the other powers of Europe, and the views his family[6] entertained on the rest of Italy, rendered it absolutely indispensable for him, in spite of the prodigality of a government that knew no restraint, to be well supplied with money. He seized every occasion of extracting extraordinary revenues from the church.

The Lateran council was induced, immediately before its dissolution (15 March 1517), to grant the pope a tenth of all church property throughout Christendom. Three different commissions for the sale of indulgences traversed Germany and the northern states at the same moment.

4. Indulgences were the remission of temporal punishments, or penalties imposed by the church, for the commission of sins. In the Middle Ages, the practice had arisen of commuting such penalties into money payments. Many theologians also held that a treasury of spiritual merit, accumulated by Christ and the saints, could be dispensed by the church for the reduction of the time a soul had to spend in purgatory. The preachers of the papal indulgences in 1517 claimed that such a reduction could be obtained in return for a money payment. [ed.]

5. An abortive anti-papal council, summoned by Louis XII of France in 1511. [ed.]

6. The Medici, whose rule in Florence had been restored in 1512, after eighteen years of exile. [ed.]

These expedients were, it is true, resorted to under various pretexts. The tenths were, it was said, to be expended in a Turkish war, which was soon to be declared; the produce of indulgences was for the building of St. Peter's Church, where the bones of the martyrs lay exposed to the inclemency of the elements. But people had ceased to believe in these pretenses.

Devoted as the Lateran council was to the pope, the proposition was carried by only two or three votes; an extremely large minority objected to the tenths, that it was impossible to think of a Turkish war at present. Who could be a more zealous Catholic than Cardinal Ximenes, who then governed Spain? Yet even in the year 1513, he had opposed the attempt to introduce the sale of indulgences into that country; he made vehement professions of devotion to the pope, but he added, as to the tenths, it must first be seen how they were to be applied. . . .

The only means of resistance to these impositions was therefore to be sought in the powers of the state, which were just now gradually acquiring stability, as we see by the example of Ximenes in Spain; or in England, where the decision of the Lateran council could not have reached the government at the time when it forced the papal collectors to take an oath that they would send neither money nor bills of exchange to Rome. But who was there capable of protecting the interests of Germany? The Council of Regency no longer existed; the emperor was compelled by his uncertain political relations (especially with France) to keep up a good understanding with the pope. One of the most considerable princes of the empire, the archchancellor of Germany, Elector Albert of Mainz, born Margrave of Brandenburg, had the same interests as the pope—a part of the proceeds were to go into his own exchequer. . . .

In the year 1514 the chapter elected Margrave Albert for no other reason than that he promised not to press heavily on the diocese for the expenses of the pallium. But neither was he able to defray them from his own resources. The expedient devised was that he should borrow 30,000 gulden from the house of Fugger of Augsburg and detain one-half of the money raised by indulgences to repay it. This financial operation was perfectly open and undisguised. Agents of the house of Fugger traveled about with the preachers of indulgences. Albert had authorized them to take half of all the money received on the spot, "in payment of the sum due to them." . . .

And it is important to examine what were the advantages thus obtained.

The plenary indulgence for all, the alleged object of which was to contribute to the completion of the Vatican Basilica, restored the possessor to the grace of God and completely exempted him from the punishment of purgatory. But there were three other favors to be obtained by further contributions: the right of choosing a father confessor who could grant absolution in reserved cases and commute vows that had been taken into other good works; participation in all prayers, fasts, pilgrimages, and whatever good works were performed in the church militant; lastly, the release of the souls of the departed out of purgatory. In order to obtain plenary indulgence, it was necessary not only to confess, but to feel contrition; the three others could be obtained without contrition or confession—by money alone. . . .

Never indeed was the union of secular objects with spiritual omnipotence more strikingly displayed than in the epoch we are now considering. There is a fantastic sublimity and grandeur in this conception of the church as a community comprehending heaven and earth, the living and the dead, in which all the penalties incurred by individuals were removed by the merit and the grace of the collective body. What a conception of the power and dignity of a human being is implied in the belief that the pope could employ this accumulated treasure of merits in behalf of one or another at his pleasure! The doctrine that the power of the pope extended to that intermediate state between heaven and earth, called purgatory, was the growth of modern times. The pope appears in the character of the great dispenser of all punishment and all mercy. And this most poetical, sublime idea he now dragged in the dust for a miserable sum of money, which he applied to the political or domestic wants of the moment. Mountebank itinerant commissioners, who were very fond of reckoning how much they had already raised for the papal court, while they retained a considerable portion of it for themselves and lived a life of ease and luxury, outstripped their powers with blasphemous eloquence. They thought themselves armed against every attack, so long as they could menace their opponents with the tremendous punishments of the church.

But a man was now found who dared to confront them.

While Luther's whole soul was more and more profoundly imbued with the doctrine of salvation by faith, which he zealously diffused not only in the cloister and the university, but in his character of parish priest of Wittenberg, there appeared in his neighborhood an announcement of a totally opposite character, grounded on the merest external compromise with conscience, and resting on those ecclesiastical theories that he, with his colleagues, disciples, and friends, so strenuously combated. In the neighboring town of Jüterbock, the multitude flocked together around the Dominican friar John Tetzel, a man distinguished above all the other pope's commissioners for shamelessness of tongue. . . . Among the buyers of indulgences were also some people from Wittenberg; Luther saw himself directly attacked in his cure of souls. . . .

On the vigil of All Saints, on which the parochial church was accustomed to distribute the treasure of indulgences attached to its relics—on 31 October 1517—Luther nailed on its gates ninety-five propositions—"a disputation for the purpose of explaining the power of indulgences."

We must recollect that the doctrine of the treasure of the church, on which that of indulgences rested, was from the very first regarded as at complete variance with the sacrament of the power of the keys. The dispensation of indulgences rested on the overflowing merits of the church: all that was required on the one side was sufficient authority: on the other, a mark or token of connection with the church—any act done for her honor or advantage. The sacrament of the keys, on the contrary, was exclusively derived from the merits of Christ; for that, sacerdotal ordination was necessary on the one side, and, on the other, contrition and penance. In the former case the measure of grace was at the pleasure of the dispenser; in the latter, it must be determined by the relations between the sin and the penitence. In this controversy, Thomas Aquinas had declared himself for the doctrine of the treasure of the church and the validity of the indulgences that she dispensed: he expressly teaches that no priest is necessary—a mere legate can dispense them, even in return for temporal services, so far as these were subservient to a spiritual purpose. In this opinion he was followed by his school.

The same controversy was revived, after the lapse of ages, by Luther, but he espoused the contrary side. Not that he altogether denied the treasures of the church, but he declared that this doctrine was not sufficiently clear and, above all, he contested the right of the pope to dispense them. For he ascribed only an inward efficacy to this mysterious community of the church. He maintained that all her members had a share in her good works, even without a pope's brief; that his power extended over purgatory only insofar as the intercessions of the church were in his hand, but the question must first be determined whether God would hear these intercessions: he held that the granting of indulgences of any kind whatsoever without repentance was directly contrary to the Christian doctrine. He denied, article by article, the authority given to the dealers in indulgences in their instructions. On the other hand, he traced the doctrine of absolution to that of the authority of the keys. In this authority, which Christ delegated to St. Peter, lay the power of the pope to remit sin. It also extended to all penances and cases of conscience, but of course to no punishments but those imposed for the purpose of satisfaction; even then, their whole efficacy depended on whether the sinner felt contrition, which he himself was not able to determine, much less another for him. If he had true contrition, complete forgiveness was granted him; if he had it not, no brief of indulgence could avail him: for the pope's absolution had no value in and for itself, but only insofar as it was a mark of Divine favor.

It is evident that this attack did not originate in a scheme of faith new to the church, but in the very center of the Scholastic notions; according to which the fundamental idea of the papacy—viz., that the priesthood, and more especially the successors of St. Peter, were representatives and vice-gerents of Christ—was still firmly adhered to, though the doctrine of the union of all the powers of the church in the person of the pope was just as decidedly controverted. . . .

Let us not forget to remark, however, that as the abuse complained of had a double character, religious and political, or financial, so also political events came in aid of the opposition emanating from religious ideas.

Frederick of Saxony had been present when the Council of Regency prescribed to Cardinal Raimund very strict conditions for the indulgence then proclaimed (A.D. 1501); he had kept the money accruing from it in his own dominions in his possession, with the determination not to part with it until an expedition against the infidels, which was then contemplated, should be actually undertaken; the pope and, on the pope's concession, the emperor had demanded it of him in vain: he held it for what it really was—a tax levied on his subjects; and after all the projects of a war against the Turks had come to nothing, he had at length applied the money to his university. Nor was he now inclined to consent to a similar scheme of taxation. His neighbor, Elector Joachim of Brandenburg, readily submitted to it; he commanded his states to throw no obstacles in the way of Tetzel or his subcommissioners, but his compliance was clearly only the result of the consideration that one-half of the amount would go to his brother. For this very reason, however, Elector Frederick made the stronger resistance. . . . and declared that Albert should not pay for his pallium out of the pockets of the Saxons. The sale of indulgences at Jüterbock and the resort of his subjects thither was not less offensive to him on financial grounds than to Luther on spiritual. . . .

There was, as we have already observed, no one who represented the interests of Germany in the matter. There were innumerable persons who saw through the abuse of religion, but no one who dared to call it by its right name and openly to denounce and resist it. But the alliance between the monk of Wittenberg and the sovereign of Saxony was formed; no treaty was negotiated; they had never seen each other; yet they were bound together by an instinctive, mutual understanding. The intrepid monk attacked the enemy; the prince did not promise him his aid—he did not even encourage him; he let things take their course. . . .

Luther's daring assault was the shock that awakened Germany from her slumber. That a man should arise who had the courage to undertake the perilous struggle was a source of universal satisfaction and, as it were, tranquilized the public conscience. The most powerful interests were involved in it—that of sincere and profound piety against the most purely external means of obtaining pardon of sins; that of literature against fanatical persecutors, of whom Tetzel was one; the renovated theology against the dogmatic learning of the schools, which lent itself to all these abuses; the temporal power against the spiritual, whose usurpations it sought to curb; lastly, the nation against the rapacity of Rome.

But since each of these interests had its antagonist, the resistance could not be much less vehement than the support. A numerous body of natural adversaries arose.

The University of Frankfurt on the Oder, like that of Wittenberg, was an offshoot of Leipzig, only founded at a later date and belonging to the opposite party. Determined opponents to all innovation had found appointments there. Conrad Koch, surnamed Wimpina, an old enemy of Pollich, who had often had a literary skirmish with him, had acquired an influence there similar to that possessed by Pollich at Wittenberg. Johann Tetzel now addressed himself to Wimpina, and with his assistance (for he was ambitious of being a doctor as well as his Augustine adversary) published two theses, on one of which he intended to hold a disputation for the degree of licentiate, on the other, for that of doctor; both were directed against Luther. In the first he attempted to defend the doctrine of indulgences by means of a new distinction between expiatory and saving punishment. The pope, he said, could remit the former, though not the latter. In the second thesis he extolled most highly the power of the pope, who had the exclusive right of settling the interpretation of Scripture and deciding on articles of faith; he denounced Luther, not indeed by name, but with sufficient distinctness, as a heretic, even a stiff-necked heretic. This now resounded from pulpit and chair. . . . Luther left none of these attacks unanswered, and in every one of his polemical writings he gained ground. Other questions soon found their way into the controversy. . . . The whole theological world of Germany was thrown into the most violent agitation.

But already a voice from Rome was heard through the loud disputes of excited Germany. Silvester Mazzolini of Prierio, master of the sacred palace, a Dominican, who had given out a very equivocal and cautious opinion concerning the necessity of repentance and the sinfulness of lying, but had defended the system of teaching practiced by his order with inflexible zeal—who, in Reuchlin's controversy, had been the only member of the commission that had prevented it from coming to a decision favorable to that eminent scholar—now deemed himself called upon to take up arms against this new and far more formidable assailant. . . . He thought Luther sufficiently confuted by the mere citation of the opinions of his master, St. Thomas. An attack emanating from Rome made some impression even upon Luther: feeble and easy to confute as Silvester's writing appeared to him, he now paused; he did not wish to have the Curia his open and direct foe. On May 30 he sent an explanation of his propositions to the pope himself and seized this occasion of endeavoring to render his opinions and conduct generally intelligible to the Holy Father. He did not as yet go so far as to appeal purely and exclusively to the Scriptures; on the contrary, he declared that he submitted to the authority of the Fathers who were recognized by the church and even to that of the papal decrees. But he could not consider himself bound to accept the opinions of Thomas Aquinas as articles of faith since his works were not yet sanctioned by the church. "I may err," he exclaims, "but a heretic I will not be, let my enemies rage and rail as they will."

Affairs, however, already began to wear the most threatening aspect at Rome.

The papal fiscal, Mario Perusco . . . commenced criminal proceedings against Luther; in the tribunal that was appointed the same Silvester who had thrown down the gauntlet to the accused on the literary ground was the only theologian. There was not much mercy to be expected.

There is no question that German influences were also at work here. Elector Albert, who instantly felt that the attack from Wittenberg was directed in part against himself, had referred Tetzel to Wimpina; the consequence of this was that Frederick was attacked in Tetzel's theses (indirectly indeed, but with the utmost bitterness) as a prince who had the power to check the heretical wickedness and did not—who shielded heretics from their rightful judge. . . .

Such was the state of the spiritual power in Germany. As yet, a secession or revolt from the pope was not thought of; as yet, his power was universally acknowledged, but indignation and resistance rose up against him from all the depths of the national feeling and the national will. Already had his sworn defenders sustained a defeat—already some of the foundations of the edifice of dogma, on which his power rested, tottered; the intense desire of the nation to consolidate itself into a certain unity took a direction hostile to the authority of the Court of Rome. An opposition had arisen which still appeared insignificant, but which found vigorous support in the temper of the nation and in the favor of a powerful prince of the empire. . . .

CAJETAN AND MILTITZ

It had more than once appeared probable that the Lutheran controversy would be brought to a peaceful termination; to this both sides were inclined.

During the Diet of Augsburg, Elector Frederick prevailed on himself to pay a visit to the papal legate and to invite his mediation. I do not find that the latter had any special commission from Rome to this effect, but his general powers gave him full liberty to accept such an office. He promised the elector to listen to the monk whenever he should appear before him, and to dismiss him with paternal kindness.

The business of the meeting was already ended when Luther . . . set out to present himself before the cardinal. He traveled indeed in a most lowly guise; the cowl he wore was borrowed, and he wandered on, craving hospitality from convent to convent, ill, and sometimes exhausted even to fainting. He often said afterward that if the cardinal had treated him kindly, he might easily have induced him to keep silence. When he came into his presence he fell down at his feet.

Unhappily, however, this legate, Thomas de Vio of Gaeta (Cajetan), was not only a representative of the Curia, but a most zealous Thomist. . . . Luther, therefore, was already extremely odious to him as a nominalist, as an impugner of the theological despotism of St. Thomas, and as leader of an active opposition party in a newly created university. At first he replied to Luther's humility with the official fatherly condescension of a spiritual superior. But the natural antagonism between them soon broke out. The cardinal was not disposed to be satisfied with mere silence, nor would he permit the matter to come to a disputation, as Luther proposed; he thought he had demonstrated the monk's error to him in a few

words and demanded a recantation. This awakened in Luther a
feeling of that complete contrariety of opinions and systems that
acknowledges no subordination, whether spiritual or temporal. It
appeared to him that the cardinal did not even understand his idea
of faith, far less confute it: a conversation arose in which Luther
displayed more reading, more distinctness and depth of view than
the legate had given him credit for; speculations of so extraordinary a kind had never come before him; the deep-set glittering
eyes, fixed upon his, inspired him with a sort of horror; at length
he exclaimed that Luther must either recant or never venture into
his sight again.

It was the Dominican system that here, clad in purple, repulsed
its antagonist. Luther, though furnished with a safe-conduct from
the emperor, thought himself no longer secure from violence; he
drew up an appeal to the pope, praying him to inquire into the
matter, and took to flight. His going corresponded with his coming. Escaping through a secret gate that his Augsburg friends
opened for him by night, mounted on a horse procured for him
by his provincial, Staupitz, habited in his cowl, and without any
proper riding garments, he rode, accompanied by a mounted guide,
eight long German miles the first day; on alighting, he fell half
dead from fatigue by the side of his horse on the straw. But he was
happily out of the immediate jurisdiction of the legate.

Cajetan's accusations soon followed him to Saxony. He conjured
the elector not to stain the glory of his house for the sake of a
heretical friar; if he did not choose to send him to Rome, at least
to get rid of him out of his country; he declared that Rome would
never allow this affair to drop. But he could no longer produce
any impression; his indiscreet and violent conduct had robbed him
of all credit with Frederick. The university wrote to their prince
that they only knew that Luther showed all due reverence for the
church and even for the pope; were there wickedness in the man,
they would be the first to notice it. This corporation was irritated
that the legate should treat one of its members as a heretic before
any sentence had been pronounced. Thus seconded, Frederick replied to the legate that it had not yet been shown by any of the
numerous learned men in his own states, or those contiguous, that
Luther was a heretic, and refused to banish him.

Luther, however, did not conceal from himself that the sentence pronounced by Rome might very probably be unfavorable to him. He hastened to secure himself against this as far as possible by a fresh appeal to the general council that was just about to be called.

But the conduct of the cardinal did not obtain the approbation of Rome. That court was not disposed to alienate so considerable and respected a sovereign as Frederick, who had just acquired twofold weight by his conduct at the election, and with whom it had probably rested to raise the king of France to the imperial throne, as the pope had desired. Leo therefore now made an attempt to bring the discussion concerning Luther to an amicable conclusion. He determined to send the elector the golden rose, a mark of the apostolical favor, for which that prince had always been very anxious. In order to draw the loosened ties closer between them, he likewise dispatched a native of Saxony, and agent of the elector at Rome, to him as nuncio.

Karl von Miltitz unquestionably showed great address in the manner in which he set about the affair.

On his arrival in Germany he abstained from visiting the legate, who indeed had lost all influence and now showed a sullen resentment against the elector; even on the journey, Miltitz contracted an intimacy with one of Frederick's privy councilors, Degenhard Pfeffinger. He did not scruple among friends over the convivial table, or even in inns and taverns to join in the complaints that were made in Germany of the Curia and of the abuses of the church—even to confirm them by anecdotes of what he had himself witnessed. But he assured his hearers that he knew the pope and had influence with him, and that Leo did not approve these things. He pronounced the most entire and distinct disapprobation of the scandalous proceedings of the vendors of indulgences; and in short the reputation that preceded him was such that Tetzel did not dare to present himself before him.

On the other hand, the prince, toward whom he maintained the demeanor of a subject and servant, and Luther himself, whom he treated very indulgently, conceived great confidence in him. Without much trouble, he succeeded in bringing about that degree of approximation between himself and the anti-Dominican party, which was absolutely necessary to the success of his negotiation.

On 3 January 1519, he had an interview with Luther at Altenburg. The nuncio represented to the monk the evils that arose from his vehemence and the great breach that he would thus make in the church; he implored him with tears to lay these things to heart. Luther promised to remedy, by a public explanation of his doctrine, whatever mischief he might have done. On the other hand, the nuncio gave up the idea of bringing Luther to a recantation. They came to an agreement that the matter should be referred to a German bishop and that, meanwhile, both parties should be bound to observe silence. So, thought Luther, the controversy would die away. They embraced and parted. . . .

But at this very moment, when external peace at least was restored and when it was still possible that the anticipated struggles between differences of opinion and education could be confined within the region of school learning, there arose a contest touching those important doctrines whereon the church and the state are founded, and thus began the war that has never been ended. It must be admitted that Luther was not the person who caused its outbreak.

DISPUTATION AT LEIPZIG

During the diet of 1518, Eck had appeared in Augsburg, dissatisfied that his polemical writings had as yet procured him neither emolument nor honor; he had called on Luther and had agreed with him, in a perfectly amicable manner, publicly to fight out an old controversy that he had with Dr. Carlstadt in Wittenberg concerning grace and free will. Luther had readily offered his mediation in order, as he says, to give the lie to the opinion that theologians cannot differ without hostility. Carlstadt consented to dispute with Eck in Erfurt or Leipzig, upon which Eck immediately published a prospectus of the disputation and made it known as widely as possible.

Luther's astonishment was extreme when he saw in this prospectus certain opinions announced as the subject of the debate, of which he was far more the champion than Carlstadt. He concluded this was an act of bad faith and duplicity, which he was called upon openly to resist: the agreement he had just reached with Miltitz seemed to him broken; he was determined to take up the gauntlet.

It was of vast importance that Eck had annexed to the dogmatic controversy a proposition as to the origin of the prerogatives of the papacy. At a moment when anti-papal opinions were so decidedly triumphant throughout the nation, he had the clumsy servility to stir a question, always of very difficult and dubious solution, yet on which the whole system of the church and state depended and, when once agitated, was certain to occupy universal attention; he ventured to irritate an adversary who knew no reservations, who was accustomed to defend his opinions to the utmost, and who had already the voice of the nation on his side. In reference to a former assertion of Luther's, which had attracted little attention, Eck pro-pounded the maxim that the primacy of the pope of Rome was derived from Christ himself and from the times of St. Peter; not, as his opponent had hinted, from those of Constantine and Syl-vester. The consequences of this gross imprudence were soon ap-parent. Luther, who began to study the original documents of the papal law, the decretals, and often in the course of this study felt his Christian convictions wounded, answered with a much bolder assertion, namely, that the primacy of Rome had been first estab-lished by the decretals of the later popes in the last four centuries (he meant, perhaps, since Gregory VII) and that the primitive church knew nothing of it. . . .

It was settled that, together with various other important points of doctrine on the mysteries of faith, the question whether the papacy was established by God or whether it was instituted by man, and consequently might be abolished by man (for that is in fact the point at issue in the two doctrines), was to be argued in a public disputation at a great university in the face of all Ger-many; that this question, the very one in which all political and ecclesiastical interests met as in a point, was to be thus discussed in a period of ferment and of ardent innovation.

At the very moment when the electors assembled at Frankfurt to choose an emperor (June, 1519), the theologians met to perform an act of no less importance.

Eck arrived first from Ingolstadt. Johann Mayr von Eck was unquestionably one of the most eminent scholars of his time—a reputation which he had spared no pains to acquire. . . . He was one of those learned men who held that the great questions which had occupied men's minds were essentially settled. . . . He regarded a disputation with the eye of a practiced fencer, as the arena of unfailing victory; his only wish was to find new adversaries on whom to try his weapons. He therefore seized with avidity on an opportunity of extending his fame in North Germany. He was now seen in the midst of the Leipzig professors (who welcomed him as an ally against their neighboring rival and enemy), taking part in the procession of the Corpus Christi, dressed in his priestly garments and with an air of great devotion. . . .

On June 24 the Wittenbergers arrived; the professers in low open wagons on rollers or solid wooden wheels (*Rollwagen*), Carlstadt first, then Luther and Melanchthon, and some young licentiates and bachelors; with them was Duke Barnim of Pomerania, who was then studying in Wittenberg and held the dignity of rector; around them, on foot, some hundreds of zealous students armed with halberds, battle-axes, and spears. It was observed that the Leipzigers did not come out to meet them, as was the custom and the courtesy of those times. . . . On June 27, the action was commenced with a mass and invocation of the Holy Ghost.

Carlstadt had insisted on his right of opening the debate, but he acquired little glory from it. He brought books, out of which he read passages, then hunted for others, then read again; the objections his opponent advanced one day, he answered the next. How different a *disputator* was Johann Eck! His knowledge was all at his command, ready for use at the moment; . . . his memory and address dazzled his hearers. In the matter itself—the explanation of the doctrine of grace and free will—no progress was, of course, made; . . . the most important points were scarcely touched upon; and the whole affair was sometimes so tedious that the hall was emptied.

The interest was, therefore, the more intense when, at length, on Monday July 4, at seven in the morning, Luther arose: the antagonist whom Eck most ardently desired to meet, and whose rising fame he hoped to crush by a brilliant victory. Luther was of middle size, at that time so thin as to be mere skin and bone; he possessed neither the thundering organ, the ready memory stored with various knowledge, nor the skill and dexterity acquired in the gladiatorial exercises of the schools that distinguished his opponent. But he, too, stood in the prime of manhood and in the fullness of his strength: he was in his thirty-sixth year; his voice was melodious and clear; he was perfectly versed in the Bible, and its aptest sentences presented themselves unbidden to his mind; above all, he inspired an irresistible conviction that he sought the truth. He was always cheerful at home and a joyous, jocose companion at table; he even, on this grave occasion, ascended the platform with a nosegay in his hand; but when there, he displayed the intrepid and self-forgetting earnestness arising from the depths of a conviction until now unfathomed, even by himself. He drew forth new thoughts and placed them in the fire of battle with a determination that knew no fear and no personal regards. His features bore the traces of the storms that had passed over his soul and of the courage with which he was prepared to encounter those that yet awaited him; his whole aspect breathed profound thought, joyousness of temper, and confidence in the future. The battle immediately commenced on the question of the authority of the papacy which, at once intelligible and important, riveted universal attention. Two sons of German peasants (for Eck, too, was the son of a peasant—Michel Mayr, who was for many years Ammann[7] of Eck, as Luther's father was town councilor of Mansfeld) represented the two great tendencies of opinion that divided the world then and divide it now; the future condition of the church and the state mainly hung on the issue of their conflict—on the success of the one in attack and of the other in defense.

It was immediately obvious that Luther could not maintain his assertion that the pope's primacy dated only from the last four centuries: he soon found himself forced from this position by ancient documents, and the more so as no criticism had as yet shaken the authenticity of the false decretals.[8] But his attack on the doctrine that the primacy of the pope (whom he still persisted in regarding as the ecumenical bishop) was founded on Scripture and by divine right was far more formidable. Christ's words "Thou art Peter, feed My sheep," which have always been cited in

7. Title of local magistrate. Transl.
8. The false decretals, or decretals of Pseudo-Isidore, were a ninth-century collection of partially forged documents purporting to establish the independence of the church from interference by the state. [ed.]

this controversy, were brought forward. Luther labored to support the already well-known explanation of them, at variance with that of the Curia, by other passages that record similar commissions given to the Apostles. Eck quoted passages from the Fathers in support of his opinions, to which Luther opposed others from the same source. As soon as they got into these more recondite regions, Luther's superiority became incontestable. One of his main arguments was that the Greeks had never acknowledged the pope and yet had not been pronounced heretics; the Greek church had stood, was standing, and would stand without the pope; it belonged to Christ as much as the Roman. Eck did not hesitate at once to declare that the Christian and the Roman church were one; that the churches of Greece and Asia had fallen away, not only from the pope, but from the Christian faith—they were unquestionably heretics; in the whole circuit of the Turkish empire, for example, there was not one soul that could be saved, with the exception of the few who adhered to the pope of Rome. "How," said Luther, "would you pronounce damnation on the whole Greek church, which has produced the most eminent Fathers and so many thousand saints, of whom not one had even heard of a Roman primate? Would Gregory of Nazianzen, would the great Basil, not be saved? Or would the pope and his satellites drive them out of heaven?" These expressions prove how greatly the omnipotence and exclusive validity of the forms of the Latin church, and the identity with Christianity that she claimed, were shaken by the fact that, beyond her pale, the ancient Greek church, which she had herself acknowledged, stood in all the venerable authority of her great teachers. It was now Eck's turn to be hard pressed: he repeated that there had been many heretics in the Greek church and that he alluded to them, not to the Fathers—a miserable evasion, which did not in the least touch the assertion of his adversary. Eck felt this and hastened back to the domain of the Latin church. He particularly insisted that Luther's opinion—that the primacy of Rome was of human institution and not of divine right—was an error of the poor brethren of Lyons, of Wycliffe, and of Huss, but had been condemned by the popes and especially by the general councils where the spirit of God lived and recently at that of Constance. This new fact was as indisputable as the former. Eck was

not satisfied with Luther's declaration that he had nothing to do
with the Bohemians, moreover that he condemned their schism,
and that he would not be answered out of the Collectanea of inqui-
sitors, but out of the Scriptures. The question had now arrived at
its most critical and important moment. Did Luther acknowledge
the direct influence of the Divine Spirit over the Latin church and
the binding force of the decrees of her councils, or did he not?
Did he inwardly adhere to her, or did he not? We must recollect
that we are here not far from the frontier of Bohemia; in a land
which, in consequence of the anathema pronounced in Constance,
had experienced all the horrors of a long and desolating war and
had placed its glory in the resistance it had offered to the Hussites;
at a university founded in opposition to the spirit and doctrine of
John Huss; in the face of princes, lords, and commoners whose
fathers had fallen in this struggle; it was said that delegates from
the Bohemians, who had anticipated the turn this conflict must
take, were also present. Luther saw the danger of his position.
Should he really reject the prevailing notion of the exclusive power
of the Roman church to secure salvation; oppose a council by
which John Huss had been condemned to the flames, and perhaps
draw down a like fate upon himself? Or should he deny that
higher and more comprehensive idea of a Christian church that he
had conceived, and in which his whole soul lived and moved?
Luther did not waver for a moment. He had the boldness to affirm
that among the articles on which the council of Constance
grounded its condemnation of John Huss, some were fundamentally Christian and evangelical. The assertion was received with
universal astonishment. Duke George, who was present, put his
hands to his sides and shaking his head, uttered aloud his wonted
curse, "A plague upon it!" Eck now gathered fresh courage. It was
hardly possible, he said, that Luther could censure a council since
his Grace the Elector had expressly forbidden any attack upon
councils. Luther reminded him that the council of Constance had
not condemned all the articles of Huss as heretical, and specified
some that were likewise to be found in St. Augustine. Eck replied
that all were rejected; the sense in which these particular articles
were understood was to be deemed heretical, for a council could
not err. Luther answered that no council could create a new article

of faith; how then could it be maintained that no council whatever was subject to error? "Reverend father," replied Eck, "if you believe that a council regularly convoked can err, you are to me as a heathen and a publican." . . .

The main result of the meeting was that Luther no longer acknowledged the authority of the Roman church in matters of faith. At first he had attacked only the instructions given to the preachers of indulgences and the rules of the later Schoolmen, but had expressly retained the decretals of the popes; then he had rejected these, but with appeal to the decision of a council; he now emancipated himself from this last remaining human authority also; he recognized none but that of the Scriptures. . . .

BULL OF LEO X

We must bear in mind that the advocates of the old opinions were not satisfied with opposing Luther with all the authority they possessed (for example, the Dominican universities of Louvain and Cologne pronounced a solemn condemnation of his works), but sought to prove themselves the strictest and most faithful allies of the Roman see. . . . In February, 1520, Eck . . . completed a treatise on the primacy in which he promised triumphantly and clearly to confute Luther's assertion "that it is not of Divine right," and also to set forth various other rare and notable things, collected with great labor, partly from manuscripts that he had most diligently collated. . . . Nor is his work by any means devoid of learning and talent; it is an armory of very various weapons, but it affords the most distinct evidence of the importance of this controversy to [historical] science, independent of all theological considerations, and of the profound darkness in which all true and critical history still lay buried. . . . Among his favorite documents are the decretals of the elder popes, from which much certainly is derived that we should not otherwise be inclined to believe; the only misfortune is that they are altogether forgeries. . . .

It is important to have a distinct idea of the actual state of things. With these claims of an absolute power, including all other earthly powers, were connected not only dogmatic theology as elaborated in the schools, but this gigantic fiction, this falsification of history, resting on innumerable forged documents, which, if not overthrown, as it subsequently was (and we must add chiefly by truly learned men of the Catholic Church itself), would have made all authentic and well-founded history impossible—the human mind would never have arrived at the true knowledge of ancient times or at the consciousness of the stages [the human mind] itself had passed through. The newly awakened spirit of the German nation seized at once upon this entire system and labored energetically to open new paths in every direction of human thought and action—politics, religion, science, and letters. Equal zeal was displayed on the other side in maintaining the old system entire. As soon as Eck had finished his book, he hastened to Rome to present it to the pope and to invoke the severest exercise of the ecclesiastical authority against his opponents.

It was asserted at that time that Eck was in fact sent to Rome by the house of Fugger, which was alarmed at the prospect of losing the profit arising from the money exchanges between Rome and Germany. It is at least certain that the doctor had some intimate connection with those eminent merchants. It was in their behalf that he defended usury in his disputation at Bologna.[9]

But his chief aid was derived from the judgment pronounced against the new opinions by Cologne and Louvain. Cardinals Campeggi and Vio, who were well acquainted with Germany, gave him all the support in their power. His book was fully calculated to place the imminence of the danger before their eyes. A commission of seven or eight zealous theologians was appointed, of which Giovan Pietro Carafa, Aleander, and probably also Silvestro Mazzolini and Eck, himself, were members; their judgment could not be, for one moment, doubtful; already, in the beginning of May, the draft of the bull by which Luther was condemned was prepared. . . . At length on June 16 the bull was completed. Forty-one propositions from Luther's writings were declared false, dan-

---

9. *Literæ cujusdam e Roma.* From the Pirkheimer papers in Riederer, *Nachrichten zur Kirchen Gelehrten und Büchergeschichte,* i., p. 178. As a letter, this document certainly inspires me with some suspicion; at all events, however, it is of the same date and expresses the opinion of a well-informed contemporary. Welser also says (*Augspurgische Chroniken, ander theil,* p. 275) that that disputation had been held "at the cost of Jacob Fugger and his partners."

gerous, scandalous, or absolutely heretical, and the damnatory decrees of the universities of Louvain and Cologne as learned, true, and even holy. Christ was invoked to protect his vineyard, the management of which he had, at his ascension, entrusted to St. Peter. St. Peter was besought to take the cause of the Church of Rome, the mistress of the faith, under his care. Luther, if he did not recant within the sixty days allowed him, was to be considered a stubborn heretic and to be hewn off, as a sere and withered branch, from Christendom. All Christian authorities were exhorted to seize his person and to deliver him into the hands of the pope.

It appears that no doubt of the complete success of this measure was entertained in Rome. Two vigorous champions who had a personal interest in the matter, Aleander and John Eck himself, were entrusted with its execution. In Germany there was no need of a royal *placet;*[10] the commissioners had their hands completely free.

How proud and elated was Eck on reappearing in Germany with the new title of papal prothonotary and nuncio. He instantly hastened to the scene of the conflict, and in the month of September caused the bull to be fixed up in public places in Meissen, Merseburg, and Brandenburg. Meanwhile, Aleander descended the Rhine for the same purpose.

It is said, and with perfect truth, that they did not everywhere meet with the best reception, but the arms they wielded were still extremely terrible. Eck had received the unheard-of permission to denounce any of the adherents of Luther at his pleasure when he published the bull; a permission which, it will readily be believed, he did not allow to pass unused. Among others he had named Adelmann of Adelmannsfeld, his brother canon at Eichstädt, with whom he had once nearly come to blows at dinner concerning the questions of the day. In pursuance of the bull the bishop of Augsburg now set on foot proceedings against Adelmann, who was compelled to purge himself of the Lutheran heresy by oath and vow. Eck had not scrupled also to denounce two eminent and respected members of the council or senate of Nuremberg— Spengler and Pirkheimer; the intercessions of the city, of the bishop of Bamberg, even of the dukes of Bavaria, were of no avail;

10. Sentence or approval. [ed.]

they were forced to bow before Eck, who made them feel the whole weight of the authority of one commissioned by the see of Rome. . . . Luther's works were first burned in Mainz. Aleander's exultation at this was raised to a pitch of insane insolence. He let fall expressions like those of Mazzolini—that the pope could depose king and emperor; that he could say to the emperor, "Thou art a tanner" (*"Du bist ein Gerber"*); he would soon, he said, settle the business of a few miserable grammarians, and even that Duke Frederick[11] would be dealt with by some means or other.

But though this storm raged far and wide, it passed harmless over the spot it was destined to destroy. Wittenberg was unscathed; Eck indeed had instructions, if Luther did not submit, to execute on him the menaces of the bull with the aid of the surrounding princes and bishops. He had been authorized to punish as a heretic the literary adversary whom he was unable to overcome; a commission against which the natural instinct of morality so strongly revolted that it more than once endangered Eck's personal safety, and which, moreover, it was found impossible to execute. The bishop of Brandenburg had not the power, even if he had the will, to exercise the rights of an ordinary in Wittenberg; the university was protected by its exemptions and, on receiving the bull from Eck, it resolved not to publish it. . . .

The only question now was what the elector of Saxony, who had just gone to meet the emperor on his arrival at the Rhine, would say. Aleander met him in Cologne and instantly delivered the bull to him. But he received a very ungracious answer. The elector was indignant that the pope, notwithstanding his request that the affair might be tried in Germany, notwithstanding the commission sent to the archbishop of Treves, had pronounced sentence in Rome at the instigation of a declared and personally irritated enemy who had then come himself to publish, in the sovereign's absence, a bull which, if executed, would ruin the university and must inevitably cause the greatest disorder in the excited country. But, besides this, he was convinced that injustice was done to Luther. Erasmus had already said to him at Cologne that Luther's sole crime was that he attacked the pope's crown and the monks' bellies. This was likewise the prince's opinion; it was easy to read in his face how

11. Of Saxony. [ed.]

much these words pleased him. His personal dignity was insulted, his sense of justice outraged; he determined not to yield to the pope. He reiterated his old demand that Luther should be heard by his equals, learned and pious judges, in a place of safety; he would hear nothing of the bull. This, too, was the opinion of his court, his brother, and his nephew, the future successor to the throne, even of the whole country.

For it was in the nature of things that the partial and ill-considered proceedings of the see of Rome should awaken all antipathies. We may safely affirm that it was the bull that first occasioned the whole mass of public indignation to burst forth.

CRISIS OF SECESSION

During the early months of the year 1520, Luther had remained comparatively passive and had only declared himself against auricular confession and against the administration of the Lord's Supper in one kind, or defended the propositions he had advanced at Leipzig; but when the tidings of Eck's success at Rome and of the impending excommunication reached him, at first as a vague rumor, but daily acquiring consistency and strength, his ardor for spiritual combat awoke; the convictions that had meanwhile been ripening in him burst forth; "At length," he exclaimed, "the mysteries of Antichrist must be unveiled." In the course of June, just as the bull of excommunication had been issued at Rome, he wrote his *Address to the Christian Nobility of the German Nation,* which was, as his friends justly observed, the signal for a decisive attack. The two nuncios, with their bulls and instructions, were met by this book, which was published in August at Wittenberg. It consists of a few sheets, the matter of which, however, was destined to affect the history of the world and the development of the human mind—at once preparative and prophetic. How loud had been the complaints uttered in all countries at this time of the abuses of the Curia and the misconduct of the clergy! Had Luther done nothing more, it would have signified little, but he brought into application a great principle that had taken firm hold on his mind since Melanchthon's disputation; he denied the *character indelibilis* conferred by ordination and thus shook the whole groundwork of the separation and privileges of the clergy. He came to the conclusion that in regard to spiritual capacity all Christians are equal; this is the meaning of his somewhat abrupt expression that "all Christians are priests." Hence followed two consequences: first, that the priesthood can be nothing but a function, "no otherwise separate or superior in dignity," said he, "than that the clergy must handle the Word of God and the Sacraments; that is their work and office"; but also that they must be subject to the sovereign power, which has another office to perform, "which holds the sword and the rod in its hand wherewith to punish the wicked and to protect the good." These few words run counter to the whole idea of the papacy as conceived in the Middle Ages; on the other hand, they furnish a new basis to the secular power, for which they vindicate the scriptural idea of sovereignty, and they include in themselves the sum of a new and grand social movement, which was destined by its character to be prolonged through centuries. Yet Luther was not of the opinion that the pope should be overthrown. He would have him remain neither, of course, as lord paramount of the emperor nor as possessor of all spiritual power, but with well-defined, limited functions, the most important of which would be to settle the differences between primates and archbishops and to urge them to the fulfillment of their duties. He would retain cardinals also, but only as many as should be necessary—about twelve—and they should not monopolize the best livings throughout the world. The national churches should be as independent as possible; in Germany, especially, there should be a primate with his own jurisdiction and his chanceries of grace and justice, before which the appeals of the German bishops should be brought; for the bishops, too, should enjoy greater independence. Luther strongly censured the interference that the see of Rome had recently been guilty of in the diocese of Strasbourg. The bishops should be freed from the oppressive oaths with which they were bound to the pope; convents might still be suffered to exist, but in smaller number and under certain strict limitations; the inferior clergy should be free to marry. It is not necessary to enumerate all the changes that were connected with these in his mind; his meaning and purpose are clear. It could not be said that he wished to break up the unity of Latin Christendom or completely destroy the constitution of the church. Within the bounds of their vocation, he acknowledged the independence, even the authority of the clergy, but to this vocation he wished to recall them, and at the same time to nationalize them and render them less dependent on the daily interference of Rome. This wish, indeed, he shared with every class of the community.

This was, however, only one point of his attack—the mere signal for the battle that followed soon after in all its violence. In October, 1520, appeared the treatise on *The Babylonian Captivity of the Church*; for Luther regarded the gradual establishment of the Latin dogmas and usages, which had been effected by the cooperation of the schools and the hierarchy, in the light of a power conferred on the church. He attacked them in the very center of their existence—in the doctrine of the sacraments—and, in the first place, in the most important of these, the Eucharist. We should do him injustice were we to look for a thoroughly elaborated theory on this subject; he only pointed out the contradictions that subsisted between the original institution and the prevailing doctrine. He opposed the refusal of the cup, not because he did not believe that the bread contained the whole sacrament, but because nobody ought to attempt to make the smallest change in the original institutions of Christ. He did not, however, counsel the resumption of the cup by force; he only combated the arguments with which it had been attempted to justify the refusal of it from Scripture and zealously traced out the vestiges of the pure and primitive practice. He then treated of the doctrine of transubstantiation. The reader will recollect that Peter Lombard had not ventured to maintain the transformation of the substance of the bread. Later theologians did not hesitate to do this; they taught that the *accidens* alone remained—a theory they supported by a pretended Aristotelian definition of subject and accident. This was the point taken up by Luther. The objections raised by Peter of Ailly to this hypothesis had, at a former period, made a great impression upon him, but he now also thought it dishonest to introduce into Scripture anything that was not found in it and that its words were to be taken in their plainest and most precise meaning; he no longer acknowledged the force of the argument that the Church of Rome had sanctioned this hypothesis since she was that same Thomist Aristotelian church with which he was engaged in a mortal struggle. Moreover, he believed himself able to prove that Aristotle had not even been understood on this point by St. Thomas. But a yet more important doctrine, as affecting the practical views of Luther, was that the celebration of the sacrament was a meritorious work—a sacrifice. This dogma was connected with the mysterious notion of the identity of Christ with the Church of Rome, which Luther now entirely rejected. He found nothing of it in the Scripture; here he read only of the promise of redemption connected with the visible sign or token and with the faith; nor could he forgive the Schoolmen for treating only of the sign and passing over in silence the promise and the faith. How could any man maintain that it was a good work—a sacrifice—to remember a promise? That the performance of this act of remembrance could be profitable to another, and that other absent, was one of the most false and dangerous doctrines. In combating these dogmas, he does not conceal from himself the consequences—that the authority of countless writings must be overthrown, the whole system of ceremonies and external practices altered, but he looks this necessity boldly in the face; he regards himself as the advocate of the Scripture, which was of higher significance and deserved more careful reverence than all the thoughts of men or angels. He said he only proclaimed the Word in order to save his own soul; the world might then look to it whether it would follow that Word or not. He would no longer adhere to the doctrine of the seven sacraments. Thomas Aquinas delights to show how their order corresponds with the incidents of the natural and social life of man—baptism with his birth; confirmation with his growth; the eucharist with the nutriment of his body; penance with the medicine of his diseases; extreme unction with his entire cure; how ordination sanctified public business; marriage, natural procreation. But these images were not calculated to make any impression on Luther; he only inquired what was to be clearly read in the Scriptures; what was the immediate relation between a rite and faith and redemption; he rejected, almost with the same arguments as those to be found in the confession of the Moravian brethren, four of the sacraments, and adhered only to baptism, the Lord's Supper, and penance. The others could not even be derived from the see of Rome; they were the product of the schools, to which, indeed, Rome was indebted for all she possessed and, hence, there was a great difference between the papacy of a thousand years ago and that of the present day.

The hostile systems of opinion on the destiny and duties of man and on the plan of the universe now stood confronted in all their might. While the papal see proclaimed anew in every bull all the privileges that it had acquired during the gradual construction of its spiritual-temporal state in the Middle Ages and the principles of faith connected with them, the idea of a new ecclesiastical constitution according to which the priesthood should be brought back to a merely spiritual office, and of a system of faith emancipated from all the doctrines of the schools and deduced from the original principles of its first apostles—an idea conceived by one or two teachers in a university and emanating from a little town in Germany—arose and took up its station as antagonist of the time-hallowed authority. This the pope hoped to stifle in its birth. What if he could have looked down that long vista of ages through which the conflict between them was destined to endure!

We have already observed that the pope's bull did not touch Wittenberg. Luther had even the audacity to denounce the pope as a suppressor of the Divine Word, for which he substituted his own opinions—even as a stubborn heretic. Carlstadt also raised his voice against the fierce Florentine lion, who had never wished any good to Germany and who now condemned the truest doctrines, contrary to laws Divine and human, without even having granted the defenders of them a hearing. The whole university rallied more and more firmly around its hero, who had in fact given it existence and importance. When the intelligence arrived that in some places the authorities had begun to execute the bull and to burn Luther's books, the monk felt himself sufficiently strong to revenge this arbitrary act on the pope's writings. On 10 December 1520, the academic youth,[12] summoned by a formal proclamation posted on a blackboard, assembled in unwonted numbers before the Elster

12. According to Andreas Sennert, *Athenæ: itemque Inscriptiones Witteber-genses* (Wittenberg, 1678), pp. 58 and 59, the names in the university books amounted in the year 1512 to 208; in 1513 to 151; in 1514 to 213; in 1515 to 218; in 1516 to 162; in 1517 to 232; in the year 1518 the number of the students entered already rose to 273; in 1519 to 458; in 1520 to 578.

Gate of Wittenberg; a pile of wood was collected, to which a
Master of Arts of the university set fire; in the full feeling of the
orthodoxy of his secession, the mighty Augustine, clad in his cowl,
advanced to the fire holding in his hand the pope's bull and
decretals: "Because thou hast vexed the Lord's saints," exclaimed
he, "mayest thou be consumed in eternal fire!" and threw it into the
flames. Never was rebellion more resolutely proclaimed. "Highly
needful were it," said Luther another day, "that the pope [that is,
the papacy] with all his doctrines and abominations should be
burnt."

The attention of the whole nation was now necessarily drawn
to this open resistance. What had first procured for Luther the
general sympathy of the thinking and serious-minded among his
contemporaries was his theological writings. By the union of profound thought and sound common sense which distinguishes
them, the lofty earnestness which they breathe, their consolatory
and elevating spirit, they had produced a universal effect. "That
know I," says Lazarus Spengler[13] in the letter that was imputed
to him as a crime, "that all my life long no doctrine or sermon
has taken so strong hold on my reason.". . . The collections of
letters of that time afford abundant proof of the interest that the
religious publications—for example, the exposition of the Lord's
Prayer or the new edition of the German Theology—excited; societies of friends were formed for the purpose of communicating
them to each other, of getting them reprinted and then distributed
by messengers sent about with these books, and no others, in order
that the attention of the buyers might not be diverted; preachers
recommended them from the pulpit.

The boldness of this attack, so formidable and so immediately
connected with the deepest feelings of religion, was another cause
of popular interest. Some . . . disapproved the turn it had taken,
but its temerity only served to heighten the admiration and the
sympathy of the majority; all the elements of opposition naturally
congregated around a doctrine which afforded them that of which
they stood most in need—justification in their resistance on religious grounds. Even Aleander remarked that a great proportion
of jurists declared themselves against the ecclesiastical law. . . . It

13. Lazarus Spengler (1479–1534), secretary of Nuremberg. [ed.]

was not, however, the jurists alone but even the clergy whom Aleander found wavering, especially the inferior clergy who severely felt the pressure of the hierarchical power; he was of opinion that throughout Germany they approved Luther's doctrines. Nor did it escape him that the religious orders too were infected; among the Augustines this arose from the influence of the later vicars and partiality for a brother of their own order; with others, from hatred of the tyranny of the Dominicans. It was also inevitable that in the heart of many a reluctant inmate of a cloister, the events now passing would awaken the wish and the hope of shaking off his fetters. The schools of the humanists belonged of course to this party; no dissension had as yet broken out among them, and the literary public regarded Luther's cause as their own. Already two attempts had been made to interest the unlearned in the movement. Hutten[14] understood perfectly the advantage he possessed in writing German: "I wrote Latin," he says, "formerly, which not every one understands; now I call upon my fatherland." The whole catalogue of the sins of the Roman Curia, which he had often insisted upon, he now exhibited to the nation in the new light thrown upon it by Luther, in German verses.[15] He indulged the hope that deliverance was at hand, nor did he conceal that if things came to the worst, it was to the swords and spears of brave men that he trusted; by them would the vengeance of God be executed. The most remarkable projects began to be broached— some particularly regarding the relation of the German church to Rome—as that no man should for the future possess an ecclesiastical dignity who could not preach to the people in the German tongue; that the prerogatives of the papal months, accesses, regresses, reservations, and, of course, annates[16] should be abolished;

14. Ulrich von Hutten (1488–1523), imperial knight, humanist, and German patriot. [ed.]

15. *Klage und Vermanung gegen die ungeistlichen Geistlichen.*

16. Papal months: January, March, May, July, September, and November. If a church benefice fell vacant during one of these months, the pope had the right to appoint to it.

Accesses: the right of someone who is not permitted to hold a church benefice (for instance, if he is too young) to have another person hold it in his place until such time as he is permitted to hold it himself.

Regresses: the revocation of a previous renunciation of a church benefice.

that no sentence of excommunication issued by Rome should have any validity in Germany; that no brief should have any force until a German council had pronounced whether it was to be obeyed or not; the bishops of the country were always to hold in check the papal power. Others added proposals for a radical reform in details: that the number of holy days should be diminished, the curates regularly paid, fit and decorous preachers appointed, fasts observed only on a few days in the year, and the peculiar habits of the several orders laid aside; a yearly assembly of bishops should watch over the general affairs of the German church. The idea even arose that a Christian spirit and life would, by God's special ordinance, spread from the German nation over the whole world, as once from out Judaea. Thereunto, it was said, the seeds of all good had sprung up unobserved: "A subtle sense, acute thought, masterly skill in all handicrafts, knowledge of all writings and tongues, the useful art of printing, desire for evangelical doctrine, delight in truth and honesty." To this end, too, had Germany remained obedient to the Roman emperor.

All hopes now rested on Charles V, who was at this moment ascending the Rhine. Those who opposed the new opinions wished him the wisdom of Solomon and of Daniel, "who at as early an age were enlightened by God";[17] they even thought the state of things so desperate that, if not changed by a serious and thorough reformation, the last day must quickly come. The partisans of innovation approached him with the boldest suggestions. He was asked to dismiss the gray friar, his confessor, who boasted that he ruled him and the empire; to govern with the counsels of temporal electors and princes; to entrust public business not to clerks and financiers, but to the nobles, who now sent their sons to study; to appoint Hutten and Erasmus members of his council; and to put an end to the abuses of Rome and to the mendicant orders in Germany. Then would he have the voice of the nation for him; he would no longer stand in need of pope or cardinal but, on the contrary, they would receive confirmation from him. "Then," said

---

Reservations: benefices whose provision was specifically reserved to the pope.

Annates: the first year's income of a benefice or church office which the papacy claimed from newly appointed holders of the benefice.

17. Charles V was born on February 24, 1500. [ed.]

one, "will the strong Germans arise with body and goods and go with thee to Rome and make all Italy subject to thee; then wilt thou be a mighty king. If thou wilt settle God's quarrel, he will settle thine."

"Day and night," exclaimed Hutten to him, "will I serve thee without fee or reward; many a proud hero will I stir to help thee; thou shalt be the captain, the beginner, and the finisher; thy command alone is wanting." [18]

Diet of Worms. a.d. 1521

. . . In Germany, however, the emperor could accomplish nothing without the approbation of the empire; and in submitting the draft of the mandate alluded to before to the Estates, he had added, "that if they knew of anything better, he was ready to hear it." This gave rise to very warm discussions in the imperial council. "The monk," said the Frankfurt deputy, "makes plenty of work. Some would gladly crucify him, and I fear he will hardly escape them; only they must take care that he does not rise again on the third day." The same doubt and fear that condemnation by a party would produce no permanent effect prevailed in the Estates. The emperor had intended to publish the edict without further trial, according to the advice of Aleander, who declared that the sentence of condemnation already pronounced was sufficient; Doctor Eck, too, sent in a little memorial full of flatteries and admonitions to the same effect. It was the same question that had been discussed in the Curia, but the Estates of Germany were not so obsequious as the jurists of Rome. They begged the emperor to reflect what an impression would be made on the common people, in whose minds Luther's preaching had awakened various thoughts, fantasies, and wishes, if he were sentenced by so severe a mandate, without even being called to take his trial. They urged the necessity of granting him a safe-conduct and summoning him to appear and defend himself. But a new question arose. On what basis was this trial to be conducted? The Estates distinguished between two branches of Luther's opinions: the one relating to church govern-

18. Compare Napoleon's expression of astonishment that Charles V did not champion the Protestant cause, for, had he done so, he would have had all Germany at his feet.

ment and discipline, which they were for handling indulgently, even if he refused to recant (and they seized this occasion for once more strongly impressing on the emperor the complaints of the nation against the see of Rome); the other, against the doctrine and the faith "which they, their fathers, and fathers' fathers had always held." Should he also persist in these and refuse to recant, they declared themselves ready to assent to the imperial mandate and to maintain the established faith without further disputation. Such were the views with which Luther was summoned to Worms. . . . An imperial herald was sent to conduct him.

With regard to the opposition to the temporal interference of Rome, the Estates were essentially of the same opinion as Luther. As the emperor was bound even by his capitulation to restore and maintain the Concordat and the ecclesiastical liberties of the nation, which had been continually violated to an insufferable extent, the lesser committee was now employed in drawing up a complete statement of the grievances of the nation against the see of Rome. Their manner of proceeding was this: each prince delivered in a list of the grievances of which he had more particularly to complain, and every charge alleged by more than one was received and recorded. Already it was feared that the spiritual princes would draw back, but the councilors of the temporal were determined in that case to carry the matter on to the end alone. A statement of grievances was produced which reminds us of the writings of Hutten and the *Address to the Christian Nobility,* so strong was the censure of the papal see generally and, above all, of the government of Pope Leo X. It is filled with the cunning and malignant devices, the roguery and cheating that prevailed at the Court of Rome. The Curia was also directly accused, in practice, of simony. If Luther had done nothing more than attack the abuses of the Curia, he could never have been deserted by the Estates; the opinion he had expressed on this subject was the general one, and was indeed their own. Probably the emperor himself would not have been able to withstand it; his Father confessor had threatened him with the chastisements of heaven if he did not reform the church.

We feel almost tempted to wish that Luther had remained for the present satisfied with this. The nation, engaged under his conduct in a common struggle against the temporal sway of the Church of Rome, would have become for the first time strongly united and completely conscious of its own unity. But the answer to this is that the strength of a mind like his would have been broken had it been fettered by any consideration not purely religious. Luther had been incited not by the wants of the nation, but by his own religious convictions, without which he would never have done anything, and which had indeed led him further than would have been either necessary or expedient in a political struggle.

Some still hoped, however, that he would recall one step—that he would at least not persist in his last most offensive expressions, which occurred in *The Babylonian Captivity of the Church*. This was in particular the opinion of the emperor's confessor. He did not regard the papal anathema as an insuperable obstacle to an amicable adjustment. . . . At first he proposed to the elector of Saxony [that he] nominate two or three councilors with whom he could consult as to the means of arranging the affair . . . , [but] the silent, reserved prince, who repelled all attempts at intimacy or sympathy from others, and who was in fact the only human being that had any influence over Luther, was absolutely unapproachable: it was impossible to obtain from him even a private audience. The confessor, therefore, addressed himself to other friends of Luther. He went to the Ebernburg to visit Sickingen, who had just then reentered the emperor's service and was esteemed one of Luther's most distinguished patrons, in the hope of obtaining his mediation. . . . It is obvious that Luther's opposition to the pope promised to be a doubly powerful instrument of the imperial policy, if the government did not find itself compelled absolutely to condemn him on account of his open schism and could keep the matter pending before a court of arbitration. Sickingen sent an invitation to Luther to visit him in passing by.

For Luther was already on his way from Wittenberg to Worms. He preached once on the road, and in the evening when he arrived at his inn, amused himself with playing the lute; he took no interest whatever in politics, and his mind was elevated far above all subjects of mere personal interest, whether regarding himself or others. At various places on the road he had to pass through might be seen posted up the decretal condemning his books, so that when they arrived at Weimar the herald asked him whether he would go on. He replied that he would rely on the emperor's safe-conduct. Then came Sickingen's invitation. He replied: if the emperor's confessor had anything to say to him, he could say it in Worms. Even at the last station, a councilor of his sovereign sent him word that he had better not come, for that he might share the fate of Huss. "Huss," replied Luther, "was burnt, but not the truth with him: I will go, though as many devils took aim at me as there are tiles on the roofs of the houses." Thus he reached Worms, on 18 April 1521, one Tuesday about noon, just as people sat at dinner. When the watchman on the church tower blew his trumpet, everybody crowded into the streets to see the monk. He sat in the open wagon (*Rollwagen*), which the council of Wittenberg had lent him for the journey, in the cowl of his order; before him rode the herald, with his tabard embroidered with the imperial eagle hung over his arm. Thus they passed through the wondering, gaping crowd, regarded by some with sympathy, by all with various and unquiet emotions. Luther looked down upon the assembled multitude and his daring courage rose to the height of firm confidence: he said, "God will be with me." In this state of mind he alighted.

The very next day toward evening he was conducted into the assembly of the empire. The young emperor, the six electors (among whom was his own master), a body of spiritual and temporal princes before whom their subjects bowed the knee, numerous chiefs celebrated for deeds in war and peace, worshipful delegates of cities, friends and foes were there, awaiting the entrance of the monk. The sight of this majestic and splendid assemblage seemed for a moment to dazzle him. He spoke in a feeble and almost inaudible voice. Many thought he was frightened. Being asked whether he would defend his books (the titles of which were read aloud) collectively or consent to recant, he replied that he begged for time to consider; he claimed, as we have seen, the benefit of the forms and customs of the empire.

The following day he appeared again before the diet. It was late before he was admitted; torches were already lighted; the assembly was perhaps more numerous than the day before; the press of people so great that the princes hardly found seats; the interest in the decisive moment, more intense. Luther now exhibited not a trace of embarrassment. The same question as before being repeated to him, he answered with a firm, distinct voice and with an air of joyful serenity. He divided his works into books of Christian doctrine, writings against the abuses of the see of Rome, and controversial writings. To be compelled to retract the first, he said, would be unheard of, since even the papal bull had acknowledged that they contained much that was good; the second would afford the Romanists a pretext for the entire subjugation of Germany; the third would only give his adversaries new courage to resist the truth—an answer which was more directed against the erroneous form in which the questions had been arranged than against the views with which the Estates had entered on the trial. The official of Treves put the matter in a more tangible shape by advising Luther not to give a total and unqualified refusal to the proposal to retract. Had Arius, he said, retracted some points, his good books would not have been destroyed together with the bad. In his (Luther's) case, too, means would be found to rescue some of his books from the flames if he would recant what had been condemned by the council of Constance and what he had repeated in defiance of that condemnation. The official insisted more on the infallibility of councils than on that of the pope.

But Luther now believed as little in the one as in the other; he replied that even a council might err. This the official denied. Luther repeated that he would prove that this might happen and that it had happened. The official could not, of course, go into the inquiry in that assembly. He asked again definitively whether Luther meant to defend all his works as orthodox or to retract any part. He announced to him that if he utterly refused to recant, the empire would know how to deal with a heretic. Luther had expected that a disputation or confutation, or some attempt at demonstrating his errors, awaited him in Worms; when therefore he found himself at once treated as a false teacher, there arose in his mind during the conversation the full consciousness of a conviction dependent on no act of the will, founded on God's Word, regardless of and untroubled by pope or council: threats alarmed him not; the universal sympathy, the warm breathings of which he felt around him, had first given him strength and courage: his feeling was, as he said at going out, that had he a thousand heads he would let them all be struck off sooner than recant. He repeated now, as he had done before, that, unless it were demonstrated to him by texts from the Holy Scripture that he was in error, he could not and would not recant since his conscience was captive to God's Word. "Here I stand," exclaimed he, "I can do no otherwise; God help me. Amen."

It is remarkable how different was the impression that Luther made upon those present. The Spaniards of high rank, who had always spoken of him with aversion and contempt, who had been seen to take a book of Luther's or Hutten's from a bookstall, tear it in pieces, and trample it in the mire, thought the monk imbecile. A Venetian, who was otherwise perfectly impartial, remarked that Luther showed himself neither very learned nor remarkably wise, nor even irreproachable in his life, and that he had not answered to the expectations conceived of him. It is easy to imagine what was Aleander's judgment of him. But even the emperor had received a similar impression: "That man," said he, "will never make a heretic of me." The next day (April 19) he announced to the Estates of the empire in a declaration written in French and with his own hand, his determination to maintain the faith that had been held by his predecessors, orthodox emperors and Catholic kings. In that word he included all that had been established by councils, and especially that of Constance. To this he would devote his whole power, body and soul. After the expressions of obstinacy that they had yesterday heard from Luther, the emperor felt remorse that he had spared him so long and would now proceed against him as against an avowed heretic. He called upon the princes to act in the same spirit, according to their duty and their promises.

Luther had, on the contrary, completely satisfied his own countrymen. The hardy warriors were delighted with his undaunted courage; the veteran George of Frundsberg clapped him on the shoulder encouragingly as he went in; the brave Erich of Brunswick sent him a silver tankard of Eimbeck beer through all the press of the assembly. At going out, a voice was heard to exclaim, "Blessed is the mother of such a man!" Even the cautious and thoughtful Frederick was satisfied with his professor. . . . From this time, the princes rivaled each other in the frequency of their visits to him. "If you be right, Sir Doctor," said Landgrave Philip of Hessen, after a few jocose words, which Luther gently rebuked with a smile, "may God help you." Luther had already been told that if his enemies burned him, they must burn all the German princes with him. Their latent sympathy was aroused and set in motion by the emperor's peremptory manifesto, so foreign to all the forms of the empire. A paper was found in his apartments on which were written the words: "Woe to the land whose king is a child!" A declaration of open hostility was fixed on the town hall, on the part of four hundred allied knights against the Romanists, and especially against the archbishop of Mainz, for trampling underfoot honor and Divine justice. They had sworn not to abandon the upright Luther. "I am ill at writing," said the author of this proclamation, "but I mean a great mischief, with 8,000 foot soldiers at my back. *Bundschuh, Bundschuh, Bundschuh!*" [19] This seemed to announce a combination between the knights and the peasants to protect Luther against his enemies. In fact, the courtiers did not feel perfectly at ease when they saw themselves thus unarmed and defenseless in the midst of a warlike nation, in a state of violent excitement, and agitated by conflicting passions.

19. The war cry of the league of the peasants of the Upper Rhine in 1501–1502.

LUCIEN FEBVRE

The Crisis of 1521–1525

T HE TRADITIONAL HISTORY OF MARTIN LUTHER
had one great merit—its simplicity. It was not encumbered
with subtleties. Luther had become hardened to abuse. Isolated
at the Wartburg, he had lost the direction of the movement.
Fanatics had thrown all into confusion, so much so that, in
order to keep his vessel afloat, Luther had been forced to steer a
somewhat irregular course.

"Contradiction" is the word used by friendly critics; his enemies
said he was "lying." A harsh word, the latter, one not in the
vocabulary of historians. But the former also is a word that is less
than pleasant, not to be applied without the modification of one
or two preliminary observations.

From Lucien Febvre, *Martin Luther: A Destiny,* translated by R. Tapley.
Copyright © 1929, Renewed 1957 by E. P. Dutton & Co., Inc., pages 229–63.
Reprinted with permission of the publisher.

"We do not construct forms without selection and arrangement," wrote André Gide recently, relating personal recollections. "But the most troublesome problem arises from the necessity of describing as successive states those that interweave or are simultaneous." An astute observation. How often do we historians neglect this lesson, as if there were nothing of artifice in this "strictly objective" chronology of which we are so proud when, having given numerical sequence to Luther's intellectual discoveries, we call them out one after the other, systematically, like a good cashier behind his wicket. . . .

In the second place—but this follows naturally—we should not think of the reformer as sharing the fate of the architect who is forced to alter his plans to suit the whim of his clients. The history of Luther's relations with his contemporaries will naturally appear a little more complicated to us than to our fathers. To make of Luther a man who, confronted with opposition, immediately sloughs off his personality as a serpent its skin and, at the cost of a sweeping disavowal, regains his ascendancy over the masses, is to belittle at the same time both Luther and his contemporaries. He was not capable of doubling with such careless abruptness, nor they of following him with such docility. Between him and them, there were many mutual exchanges, actions, and reactions. The following notes will make this clear.

I

Impatient under the handicap of his isolation, and eager to learn more of events than his too brief letters conveyed, Luther stole away from the Wartburg and made a secret visit to Wittenberg between 4 and 9 December 1521. He reimbued all with confidence and hope, and then reascended to the cloud country and his castle of the birds. His soul at peace, his spirit again serene, he announced his determination to reside there again until Easter. But three months had not elapsed when suddenly, on 1 March 1522, he again left his retreat. Garbed in his Junker costume, as appears from the testimony of two young Swiss who saw him one night at the Black Bear in Jena, he made all speed to his beloved Wittenberg. He was not to return to the Wartburg.

While he was traveling, on March 5, he sent from Borna, near Leipzig, a famous letter to the elector of Saxony.[1] A long but pithy communication, essential to the understanding of a Luther —terse, imperious, proud, marvelous in the freedom and ease of its sure strokes, with something at the same time tender, benevolent, and exalted—in short a heroic utterance, one of those rare documents that four centuries have not succeeded in tarnishing. In it anyone can see plainly how Luther felt in his soul when, in that trying spring of 1522, he came posting down to the troubled cities and the rumor-ridden countryside.

First, briefly, he reminded the prince that when he went to the Wartburg, it had been in his, the elector's, interests. "I made a great concession to Your Highness in secluding myself for a year. The Devil knows it was not from fear I did it! He saw into my heart when I went to Worms and knows that if I had thought there were more demons there than tiles on the roofs I would even so have thrown myself eagerly into their midst." Always the same regret, the same uneasiness, this looking back upon a past that, heroic as it was, left Luther disappointed, troubled, a prey to uneasiness. And now when he was renouncing the shelter that Frederick had contrived, his first thought was still for the elector. Would he suppose that Luther, by his sudden decision, was planning to compromise him, force him to modify his tactics, to declare that he would not enforce the edict of Worms? It was necessary to repel this possible suspicion; the fugitive from the Wartburg set about it with energy. "By no means is it my intention to solicit your protection. . . . No matter whether or not I knew that Your Grace had the power and the intention to protect me I would come to Wittenberg." In a word, he placed himself "under a much higher protection than that of an elector"; and since God watched over all, he had no need of human intervention. "Here he who has the greatest faith can give the greatest protection. But since, in my opinion, Your Grace is still very feeble in the faith, I cannot believe you to be the man capable of defending and liberating me." Frederick had nothing to do but let events take their natural course. And Luther

1. W. A. Br. 2, 455.

firmly outlined for him his duty: "This is how Your Grace should comport himself before men: bow to authority as becomes a Prince Elector. Let His Imperial Majesty rule over your cities and countryside, persons and chattels, in compliance with the laws of the empire. Do not resist, do not oppose, do not place the slightest obstacle in the way of authority if it wishes to seize me or put me to death. For no one can break or flout authority, no one but He who established it." And Luther concluded: "If they come to seek me, or if they have me sought out, events will shape themselves without worry, inconvenience, or demands of any sort upon Your Grace. For Christ has not taught me to be a Christian to the risk and peril of others."

Those are words both noble and sincere. It was not an imaginary danger that Luther was braving. Frederick knew it and, on the eve of Luther's departure, advised him to remain in the Wartburg or at least to await the outcome of the Diet of Nuremberg, announced for March, 1522, in the course of which many ugly threats would be directed against both the priest and his noble protector. These were brave and hardy words, therefore, which Luther uttered from the depths of his heart. And, coming as they did on the very eve of his return to the conflict, how well they display his character!

To risk life, to go forth alone, unarmed except with dreams, to advance under fire, to stand so far in the forefront of the fighting that even at the moment of the first instinctive recoil, produced by the sudden shock of imminent danger, retreat is already out of the question and one simple, inevitable outcome appears to be indicated, namely, death: these are things that millions and millions have done and are capable of doing. With a clear sense of what he was and what he could do, Martin Luther, like them, was offering himself as a martyr—like them, who were only disciples, servants of the ideal, not creators.

But what stringent necessity impelled the reformer, in March, 1522, to disregard the wishes of the Elector Frederick and return in such haste to Wittenberg?

Since May, 1520, there had been disturbances in Zwickau, a little town in Saxony to the north of the Erzgebirge and the Hus-

site country. A fanatical priest, Thomas Müntzer, with the help
of the craftsmen, especially the clothiers, had attempted to establish there a "kingdom of Christ," a kingdom without a king, without a magistrate, without ecclesiastical or temporal authority,
without any law, any church, any cult; the free subjects of which,
relying only on the Scriptures, were supposed to experience the
blessings of communism whose utopian glamour has a special
power over simple minds. The Zwickau magistrate took fright and
adopted harsh measures. Müntzer fled. His lieutenants followed
his example. And on 27 December 1521, the three of them—
Nicholas Storch the fuller, Thomas Drechsel, and Marcus Thomae
—took refuge . . . at Wittenberg. This was three weeks after
Luther had returned to the Wartburg from his first trip to
Wittenberg.

As soon as they were settled in the town, the three apostles
began to fulfill their mission as men of God, especially favored
with grace and direct revelations. Soon the strangeness of their
doctrines, their fanatical assurance, their mingled respect and scorn
for Luther—a timorous reformer useful only as affording the true
prophets a springboard of a reasoned doctrine for their leap into
the absolute—their diatribes against knowledge as tending to produce inequalities, their advocacy of manual labor, their incite-
ments to image-breaking, since the images tended to foster in
the depths of the people's souls the leaven of old beliefs and super-
stitions, inherited and handed down by women, healers, and vi-
sionaries, of whom we shall never know anything exact, although
we can scarcely exaggerate their hold upon the people of this
period—all this served the fugitives from Zwickau, the "Cyg-
naean prophets," to gain in a few weeks an alarming hold on the
Wittenberg citizens. Among the first to hear and be suddenly
fired with the new grace was Carlstadt; the adhesion of such a
scholar and, in the modern phrase, such a typical specimen of
the intelligentsia was immensely valuable to these untutored
illuminati.

The prophets soon proceeded to action. Rushing upon the
churches they pillaged them brutally. Was it not written: "Thou
shalt not make unto thyself any graven images"? The disease
spread. Nobody attempted to oppose Storch and his acolytes.

Melanchthon did not know what to do. The perfect assurance of the newcomers baffled this timid fellow, always fearful of letting the spirit of God pass by on the other side without his recognizing it in time to extend his greeting. So he turned to Luther who, alone in this chaos, was capable of putting things and people in their proper places—he alone, with his lucidity of a true prophet.

Luther did not even hesitate, but set out at once. For fear of being superseded, supplanted in the favor of the people by rivals, by enemies? What nonsense! It was merely that Luther believed it his duty to appear at once wherever Melanchthon and the Christian flock of which he had charge should summon him. Because, too, a conviction actuated him: these prophets were certainly not of God; therefore they must be of the Devil—at least Satan was using them in his battle with truth; so he must expose and unmask them. Because, finally, there were many who advocated harsh measures against these men whom the magistrates of Zwickau had already prosecuted, and this Luther could not endure. That was his first care: no bloodshed, no tortures! On 17 January 1522, he wrote to Spalatin: "I should not like to have them imprisoned, especially by those who are asking it of us. Without spilling blood or drawing the sword, let it not be doubted that we shall gently extinguish these two firebrands. For your part, guard carefully against our Prince's soiling his hands with the blood of these new prophets!" His faith in the Word inspired these lines. For, had not God actually made *him* the herald and interpreter of this Word? Was it not a strict obligation on him to impose it as an obstruction to Satan's nefarious enterprises? What mattered the expediencies of the elector, his wish to placate the emperor, his political forethought? On March 6, Luther arrived at Wittenberg. The day before, from Borna, he had written his famous letter to Frederick. Three days later, on Sunday the ninth, he entered the pulpit. He preached on eight successive days.

For eight days he preached, with simplicity, force, perfect clarity, a singular moderation withal, and a surpassing sense of values and of justice. Men, women, savants, and common people: all

could feast freely, fully, and eagerly, and could commune with a
spirit formed to charm and to dominate. In Luther they again
found the hero type, *their* hero in fact. He was built in the
physical mold of a hero and leader, with a trace of the common
people, a firm stance, a deep chest that resounded under the
blows of his fists. But his eyes, deep-set beneath a prominent over-
hanging forehead, gleamed with strange darting flames, and his
speech pulsated with those quickening vibrations by which,
through the centuries, the bells pealing high in their belfries have
aroused men to action.

So, in one week, all hearts were recaptured; even the most
violent were calmed by this self-assured force. He had proved his
claim: the Word as he preached it was sovereign. And then, since
others elsewhere were upset and were straying from the fold, he
departed. People saw him, listened to him, came under his spell
in Altenburg, Borna, in Zwickau itself, and in Erfurt also, and
Weimar. Everywhere the same success—crowds completely dominated by the masterful display of moderation and force. The
splendid idealism that animated Luther impressed all as something unique in its power to conquer and rule. Each journey
meant a victory.

II

On the morrow, however, it was all to be done again. To win
a crowd and to sway it exactly as one wished was child's play
for an orator in full possession of his powers. But there were the
little parties and coteries, by whatever name they chose to call
themselves, with their slow, insidious, irresistible influence.

No sooner was Luther away than enemies attacked him for
his mildness, his halfway measures; in the natural course it
would soon be his *treason*. And the tragic element in the situation was that Luther himself, his example, his own revolt furnished these men, who disputed with him his leadership, am-
munition against him; by overthrowing him they declared they
would mount to a higher plane. Mystical individualists, eager
solely to plunge and lave their souls in the abysses of the invisible

and enjoy in the depths of their consciousness, without benefit of the church or of creeds or preceptors, the morbid intoxication of this solitary gratification; fanatical Anabaptists in quest of a kingdom of God embracing only the elect, men fired with the Holy Spirit and entitled to revel with perfect equality in the delights of an unrestricted communism—they all seemed to say, holding out to Luther a mirror stamped with their own reflection: "Behold! This is you—you with all your self-assurance. How can you blame us? What we are saying you have said before us, except that, more logical and more courageous too, we proceed to the logical conclusion. You sit fainthearted by the side of the road and shrug your shoulders as you watch us pass." This was specious reasoning. Luther soon had an opportunity to estimate its success.

On 24 August 1522, when he went to Orlamünde, a domain of Carlstadt, to refute his old associate, the people gathered ominously in front of the house of the alderman who had received him and later around his carriage, hurling insults. "Go to all the devils," they shouted, "and may you break your neck before you leave!" At the same time several artisans, a shoemaker especially, impromptu controversialists, baited him with absurd citations. The scene had a most violent effect on Luther, more especially as several days before, at Jena, he had joined issue with Carlstadt himself, and the contest had been sharp. As Luther had been preaching against what he called "the spirit of Allstädt," the seditious and violent spirit of the image breakers and vandals, the acrid Carlstadt, not without some bravado, had come to the Black Bear to confront his adversary. It was a strange scene, ending in a challenge, a challenge that the two theologians —Carlstadt stiff and hostile, Luther affecting an ironical composure that his words belied—exchanged in due form before the witnesses. Luther drew a florin from his purse and handed it to his adversary. The latter, showing it to the bystanders, said: "My dear brethren, this is called Arrogo. It signifies that I have the right to write against Dr. Luther. You are all my witnesses!" And, depositing in his purse the coin wrapped in a piece of paper, he touched Luther's hand. The latter drank a draught to his health. Carlstadt pledged him in return. They exchanged several words of mock politeness, then with a last handclasp went their separate ways.[2]

A man of action, a reformer, the Luther of tradition in short, would at this point, confronted by such resistance, have collected his thoughts, revolved all the aspects of the problem in his luminous mind, have made his choice, determined his position, and acted. It was late without doubt, but not too late to play the game.

On one side there was a strong group of Catholic princes who were threatening Luther, persecuting his followers, and ferreting out his writings. They were swayed by their devotion to tradition. Also by a dread of the troubles they feared were about to burst upon them. The princes were not alone in this fear. Influential burghers in the cities, literate men too, who had supported Luther when he was in agreement with their Erasmus—such men as Willibald Pirkheimer, the Nuremberg patrician, a friend of Albrecht Dürer—when they saw the storm gather, experienced fatigue, disillusion, alarm, and made an instant retreat.

On the other side were the extremists who accused Luther of not following his ideas to their logical conclusions. And what fault did they find precisely? He retained too many, far too many, of the rites, practices, and sacraments of Catholicism; also he refrained from seeking like them and with them to establish the kingdom of Christ on earth; he approved of the divine right of princes; in brief, he was lukewarm about the political and social revolution whose dawn they were already joyfully hailing.

Between the two was the little army of the faithful. They trusted Luther but yet were uneasy and felt, many of them, that their leader was making them mark time too long. When Luther spoke, they of course fell completely under his spell. They let themselves be lulled and intoxicated by his beautiful and honest optimism, by the generosity of a heart overflowing with love. And then, when he stopped speaking, they again withdrew into the shadow in silence. Why all this hesitation in building an entirely new church to replace the old one they had quit at his bidding—

2. The gift of the gold coin could be interpreted as an old German custom signifying friendship, but also, more mundanely and ironically, as an invitation to Carlstadt to buy paper and go ahead with his controversy with Luther. [ed.]

a great shining, spacious, modern affair, his church, their church, with a beautiful, smoothly running organization, a well-ordered ritual, with well-defined dogmas and uniform liturgy?

In truth the game could play itself. A man of action would have played it. How? According to his own temperament. There were many solutions. One could burn all the bridges, erect as a bulwark a church firmly grounded in good German soil, a haven for everybody, a perfect protection against reactions and revolutions. Or one might, on the other hand, put one's self at the head of the movement and smash the extremists by using them for shock troops; one might ride the crest of a powerful wave that would sweep all away and would leave to the victor a land swept free and with plenty of elbow room in which to pursue the business of reconstruction. A chance for a man of action, one who courts exposure. But Luther—? Luther did not even see that there was a need for action.

Let us dismiss explanations that do not explain. Doubtless Luther belonged, by virtue of his origin, to the petty bourgeoisie and held narrow views. His long monastic retirement had made him introspective, unlike those politicians and jurists against whom he fostered an instinctive dislike. He knew nothing of the world about him, of political, economic, and social problems. When he pretended in the *Address to the Christian Nobility* to offer solutions to certain questions, he made it quite plain, almost stated in so many words, that he knew nothing of them. In fact, in 1524 as in 1520, these questions, as far as he was concerned, were nonexistent.

Luther was a herald of the Word. To spread this Word, as the Lord had shown it to him and commanded him to publish it, was his mission on earth, his true and only mission. But, he thought, the Word has nothing whatever to do with the problems of the age. The gospel is not concerned with temporal affairs, or with knowing whether justice reigns on this earth, or what should be done to make it reign. To suffer rather, to toil, to resign one's self to injustice, and to carry the cross is to be a Christian; such is his lot on earth, and he should accept it with a humble heart, or he is not a good Christian.

We must not expect, then, to find in Luther the impulse to

bring justice into earthly affairs; it was no more to be expected
of the Luther of 1523 than of the earlier Luther of the great
writings of 1520. He was living in the world, certainly, like any
other man. He was a German, thrust into a German society,
subject to mundane laws, affected by numerous institutions. As
such he could have his ideas, true or false, on the statecraft of
princes, the condition of the peasants, or the activities of the bank-
ers. He had them—of a sort, in fact, to strike consternation now
and then to the heart of one reading the *Table Talk*. But that is
of small moment. Martin Luther was not concerned with the
kingdom of the earth. He reposed his faith in the blood of Christ;
he cared for nothing else. As for building a Lutheran Church
with strictly defined dogmas and regularly ordained rites and
ceremonies, Luther had not changed in 1523 and 1524 on that
point either. A Lutheran Church? How often, at this time, did
he protest against the thing itself and even the name! "You do
not believe in Luther but in Christ alone. Leave Luther out of it,
whether he be scoundrel or saint. I have never known Luther,
nor do I wish to know him. What I am preaching is not him,
but Christ. The Devil take Luther, if he can; we need only Christ
and His peace!" He went on persistently pointing out the dangers
of uniformity. "It does not seem to me prudent to call a council
and establish a common ritual. One church need not ape another
in these external matters; why should it be hampered by the
decrees of a council, which soon become laws and fetters upon our
souls?" Churches should be free to copy each other or to please
themselves in their practices, as long as spiritual unity is preserved, "the unity of Faith and the Word."

It was even useless to try to obtain from Luther rulings on
the use of images, on lay participation in both sacraments, on confession—burning questions all, and fruitful of endless division.
To those who insisted upon his opinion, he replied in only one
word: "Trifles, irrelevant details." He says distinctly in his letter
of December 15, 1524, to the Christians of Strasbourg that the
great mistake, or rather one of the mistakes, of Carlstadt was
encouraging people to think that Christianity consisted essentially
in breaking images, abolishing sacraments, condemning baptism.
Smoke and vapor, exclaimed Luther (*Rauch und Dampf*)! And

elsewhere: "Paul says [I Corinthians 8:4]: 'We know that an idol is nothing in the world.' If idols are nothing, then why, for this nothing, should one bind and torment Christian consciences?" Furthermore, twenty times Luther states: "Confession is all right when it is voluntary and not forced." Or again: mass is neither a sacrifice nor a good work; it represents nevertheless "a manifestation of religion and a blessing of God." Here we recognize the man who, in 1523, said without any beating about the bush: "If people wish to remain in the convents, whether because of their age, their bellies, . . . or their consciences, let us not turn them out. For we must remember that it is everybody's blindness and error that has reduced them to their state; they have been taught nothing that would enable them to fend for themselves." And it was Luther moreover who, in the autumn of 1524 (the afternoon of October 9, to be exact), insisted upon wearing his Augustinian robe, no doubt in defiance and in derision of the pope, but also, as he wrote, to lend countenance to the weak.

He was pushed, hauled, and challenged—the Luther of this period. All they got out of him was further rumination of the solutions he had earlier evolved, reexamination of old questions, deeper thought that should have the effect of confirming him in his disinclination to act and of fortifying him with more arguments. Obstinate persistence, indeed, wrested from him several plans for a religious organization, but these were sketchy and provisional. And how could they be anything else? Since the incomparable treasure of belief in Christ comprised man's complete and sole happiness, any outward observances could serve only to interfere with the free communion between God and the faithful. In 1523, Luther consented to express his views on the organization of a sect. He published in December of the same year his *Formula Missae et Communionis* for the church of Wittenberg. He began work on a German mass. In January, 1526, the *Deutsche Messe und Ordnung Gottesdiensts* appeared. All this, while it bore scant relation to coherence and logic, was a manifestation of that conscientiousness with which Luther treated all questions. Compromises! People should treat them as they do old shoes: when they are worn out, throw them away.

Even now, so far as he was concerned personally, Luther would prefer not to publish anything of the sort. The true believers worship God in spirit and in truth. To the humble and the ignorant, however, he made this reluctant concession. A prudent concession, moreover: he did not assume the responsibility of organizing, administering, and conducting the business of the visible church to which the "ritualists" had been begging him to give concrete form. All this Luther persisted in leaving to the state. Which shows clearly enough how unimportant and secondary he deemed it.

But how about the state, politics, the princes? Luther had already expressed himself on these burning questions in his *Treue Vermahung* of 1521. Since people insisted, since the Anabaptists for their part were treating the question in a spirit of intransigent violence, since Germany was threatened with clouds so dark and menacing that the most blind and indifferent had to notice them gathering on the blackened horizon, he would recapitulate in his treatise *On Earthly Authority,* December, 1522, what he had stated before, but with more force, more detail and exactitude.

One cannot attribute any great regard for princes to the man who had addressed the Elector Frederick in such terms as appear above, the man who avoided, as a bore and a nuisance, occasions for seeing and talking with men like Frederick. Insofar as was becoming in a Christian and preacher of the Word, he despised these worldly powers; he was not silent before the people with regard to any of their vices, extortions, or even crimes. He foretold the troubles in store for them. "The people are stirred everywhere, and their eyes have been opened," he wrote on 19 March 1522. "They no longer will, or can, be oppressed by force. It is the Lord who is directing all this and hiding these imminent threats and dangers from the eyes of the princes. He will accomplish His ends through their blindness and violence; I seem to see Germany weltering in blood!" The days were long gone when princes hunted down men like wild beasts. But what now? Was it right to rebel against these wicked and cruel despots, these evil tyrants who oppressed Christian folk? That would be folly and impiety. God intended these miserable princes to be such. If it was the design of Providence, they would be brought to book. If not, all human efforts to resist them were worse than foolish: they were blasphemous.

The princes were scourges, but they were God's scourges. They were bullies, torments, and butchers, but God had ordained them to subject the lawless and induce through fear a reign of external peace and order in a depraved society. "Our Lord is a mighty monarch," writes Luther in the tone of those eloquent orators who proclaim the emptiness of all earthly greatness; "He has use for noble, illustrious, and rich butchers—princes, in other words." So, these haughty and vexatious personages were necessary and legitimate, and, whatever their faults, they should be respected—in the temporal order at least, the only one in which the princes were princes and in which good people were subject to them, in a spirit of resignation and charity, because they remembered always that irresponsible minority—criminals, unprincipled men, evildoers—who make dungeons and shackles necessary. In the spiritual order, however, all Christians were equal in the presence of their God. Princes could make no claim to prerogatives there, nor presume to legislate on points of faith or to state what Christians should or should not believe. Their subjects, however, on the other hand, must expect this spirit of mercy and charity to flourish only in the kingdom of Christ; in the earthly kingdom it was not charity, mercy, and grace that prevailed in all things, but anger, stern justice, and human authority founded on reason.

Thus Luther, faithful to his old ideas, kept maintaining the sharp opposition between spiritual life and material life. He continued to treat human beings as strange compounds, partly Christian and partly secular: the secular man was subject to domination, submissive to princes, obedient to laws; the Christian was free of all dominations, enfranchised, a true priest and king. It was an ingenious solution, at least on paper; there the frontiers of the two kingdoms could be traced without difficulty. But once a crisis arose that would throw into violent conflict these Christian sentiments and secular obligations, was this subtle distinction likely to stand the test? In the summer of 1524 the peasants of Swabia assumed the responsibility of putting it to the proof.

III

The Peasants' War furnished the occasion for Martin Luther's great renunciation. At least, so tradition says. But did it, or did it not? We do not need to tell what the uprising of 1524–1525 was, how many other revolts had preceded it, or what men, of very diverse origins and tendencies, took part in the character of leaders or men of action. But it was quite natural that Luther's position should have been of interest to both sides from the start. On the one hand, he was naturally regarded as the author and instigator of sedition; his doctrines, his preaching, his baneful example had provoked it; and if there was need to repress the rebels, it was still more necessary to punish the agent of Satan who, having sowed the wind over peaceable Germany, was now reaping the tempest. The others, no less naturally, hailed Luther as the official champion of the oppressed, the born patron of the rebels, the natural foe of all tyranny. And besides, were not they, the peasants, the true champions of the gospel against the princes? At the head of their articles did they not claim the right to elect pastors[3] who, translating clearly the Holy Word and preaching it without adulteration, would put them in the way of prayerfully seeking and enjoying the true faith? Let us not be surprised that, late in April, 1525, Luther finally intervened and published his famous *Exhortation to Peace with Reference to the Twelve Articles of the Peasants of Swabia, and also Against the Spirit of Murder and Brigandage of Other Aroused Peasantry.*[4]

Its plan is clear; its thesis simple. A short introduction, then two separate discussions, the one with the princes, the other, much longer, with the peasants; in conclusion, a few phrases of exhortation to both parties. But what is its purpose? To determine the justice or injustice of the peasants' demands? In a fashion. But mainly to deal with a point of religion.

The peasants said: "We are neither rebels nor revolutionists, but the messengers of the gospel. That which we demand, the gospel

---

3. This was Article I of the famous Twelve Articles of the Peasants.
4. *Ermahnung zum Frieden auf die zwölf Artikel der Bauerschaft in Schwaben,* W., 18, 279–334.

justifies us in demanding." That pretension is the only one that Luther attacks, but with what incomparable violence, passion, and fury! To the princes his words are few and vague: those who prohibit the preaching of the gospel are in the wrong, as are those who oppress their people with too heavy burdens. They should strive to assuage the passions that they had aroused and to treat the peasants "as a man in his right mind treats people who are drunk or out of their senses." This would be both expedient and just in the humane sense of the word; authority was not instituted in order that subjects might serve for the gratification of their masters' caprices. But once he had finished this mild discourse in the conditional tense, how clearly and sonorously Martin Luther speaks as he launches upon his crushing harangue to the peasants! To claim the support of the gospel? What monstrous nonsense! Let them burn him, torture him, tear him into pieces—as long as there remains a breath in his body he will shout the truth: the gospel does not justify, but condemns revolt. All revolt.

They said, the peasants: "We are in the right; they are in the wrong. We are oppressed and they are unjust." That may be. Luther goes further and says, I believe it. And then? "Neither oppression nor injustice excuses revolt." The gospel teaches: "Resist not evil; but whosoever shall smite thee on thy right cheek, turn to him the other also." Has he, Luther, ever drawn the sword or preached revolt? No, only obedience. And that is why God has protected his life and favored the spread of his doctrine in spite of the pope and the princes. Those who "would follow their natural promptings and not submit to their wrongs" are pagans. Christians do not fight with sword and arquebus. Their arms are the cross and patience. And if the authority that oppresses them is really unjust they should have no fear, for God will make the tyrant do penance for his injustice. In the meantime they must restrain themselves, obey, and suffer in silence.

That is the doctrine of the *Exhortation to Peace*. And certainly it is easy to be ironical, easy to point out the Gargantuan humor of this singular contrast: in the midst of the tumult and the cries of hate, Luther facing the chaos of battle shouts and incendiary confusion, his eyes raised to heaven, Dr. Martin Luther puffing out his cheeks and piping with all his soul his own little tune on a Christian flageolet, as if he could see and hear nothing but himself. A matter of temperament. But there is one thing nobody can say: he was not, in this delicate situation, inventing insincere arguments.

His doctrine? It was not born of expediency or shaped by a peasants' revolt. Had it not already inspired the letter to Frederick of 5 March 1522? "Only He who has instituted it with his own hands can destroy and ruin Authority; so it follows that if there is any revolt, it is against God!" Does not such a view animate from beginning to end the treatise of 1522 *On Earthly Authority*: Christ's kingdom on the one hand, the kingdom of this world on the other, and in this kingdom absolute obedience to its kings, even if their orders are unjust. For the proverb has truly said: he who strikes blows is in the wrong, and no man can be judge in his own case. No, in truth, Luther invented nothing new, in 1525, when he exhorted the serfs to be resigned and the peasants to humble themselves. And when he added: "The only liberty for which you should care is spiritual liberty; the only rights you can legitimately demand are those that pertain to your spiritual life," these formulas, though they sound ridiculous in the extreme when addressed to simple folk driven to desperation and fighting like beasts for their lives, are such as Luther, the real Luther— the Luther of Leipzig, of Worms, and of the Wartburg—may well cling to implacably for the sake of his own integrity.

Yes, it is easy to be ironical. But is the French spirit of malice or the scorn of an anti-Lutheran a proper guide to an understanding of Luther and, through him, of the German Reformation, and also, incidentally, of one of the most striking manifestations in history of the German spirit?

Michelet thought not, for he wrote in his *Mémoires de Luther* (and with special reference to the *Exhortation*): "Nowhere else, perhaps, did Luther achieve such heights." No doubt, at the time when he was assembling his documents, the historian found himself particularly moved by the torrential force, the terrific ardor of the religious emotion that mastered, transported, overwhelmed, and carried away the reformer so that speech here gushed forth from his heart to spread over the world like the waves on a beach, first eddies and then the irresistible force of the incoming tide—an event explaining exactly what needed to be explained: the fact of Luther's success, of his power over men, the mysterious and vital radiance of his personality. But there is another thing. The capital importance of the crisis of 1525 is that it enables us to tear away all veils and see and measure for the first time, in the clear light of fact, the important historical consequences of the words and actions of a Martin Luther.

Certainly the historians are right who, sensible of the facts, note how the attitude of Luther at this date shocked and dismayed the peasants, the revolutionists, all those who had carried far beyond the limits Luther contemplated the movement that the fearless Augustinian had begun. They are right to insist on one fact: after launching his *Exhortation* and thundering this doctrinal condemnation of the revolt, which he softened a bit at the end by appealing to arbitration, Luther took care to hold his peace; he remained calm and compassionate outside the fray. During the spring of 1525 the peasants' revolt continued to spread. Everywhere towns were pillaged, castles were seized, abbeys sacked. In Thuringia, Thomas Müntzer established a species of communism; his appeals, to the sinister refrain *"Dran, dran!"* ("Up and at them!"), sounded like a tocsin; he implored his followers not to let the hot blood on their swords grow cool. But the princes, little by little, became organized. On 15 May 1525, at Frankenhausen, Müntzer's army was defeated; its leader was captured and put to death. On May 18, at Lupfenstein, the duke Anton[5] crushed the Rustauds (rustics), then seized Saverne. In June the Franconian rebels were cut to pieces at Adolzfurt. Reprisals began; they were terrible. In a ravaged Germany encumbered with smoking ruins, where the horrible specter of famine hovered over the wasted fields and the empty barns, the princes, as one of them said, played at bowls in their turn with the heads of the peasants.

And Luther, the Luther who in December, 1522, in the treatise *On Earthly Authority,* had declared with so much energy: the judge should be stern, power should be implacable, repression

5. Antoine, duke of Lorraine, 1508-1544.

should be carried without false sentimentality to the point of cruelty, for mercy has nothing to do with secular life; the Luther who in 1524, in his paper *Against the Celestial Prophets,* had stated his opinion with such perfect clarity: *Herr Omnes?* the only way to make him do what he ought to do "is to constrain him by law and the sword to a semblance of piety, as one holds wild beasts by chains and cages";[6] the Luther who in the same work wrote, arguing the right of the prince to expel Carlstadt: "Now I think thus: the country belongs to the princes and not to Carlstadt, who is only a lodger and owns nothing . . . "; this Luther was not the man to change his opinions in view of peasant excesses and the countless disturbances of 1525. When we know in addition of the efforts made to involve him, the objections, the accusations, and direct reproaches, which cut him to the quick and incited him, in a spirit of bravado, to an even fiercer intransigency, we shall not be surprised that finally, in May, 1525, when the princes had scored their first successes and reprisals had begun, he again took up his pen and indited "against the plundering and murderous peasant bands" a little book of a sanguinary sternness and violence.

His letters meanwhile breathed only anger. . . . "My sentiment is clear," he wrote to Amsdorf, May 30, 1525, just as the fortunes of war had changed, "better the death of all the peasants than of the princes and magistrates." . . . And this man who was banished from Worms and placed under the solemn ban of the empire declares without beating about the bush: "A man who is convicted of the crime of rebellion is under the ban of God and the emperor, and every Christian can and should slaughter him and will thus be doing a good deed!" . . . Luther goes almost to the point of forgetting his theology in the words with which he concludes: "We are living in such extraordinary times that a prince can win heaven by spilling blood much more easily than others by praying!"

One can easily divine the consequence of such an attitude and how it isolated Luther, how it turned from him a part, and this

6. *Wider die himmlischen Propheten,* W., XVIII 66; *wie man die wilden Thiere mit Ketten und Kercker hellt.*

the most ardent, of that great mass of humanity whom his utterance had once moved and stirred so profoundly. Certainly it was vain to oppose to his letter of May, that veritable Exhortation to the Butcher, which followed so soon after the choleric *Exhortation to Peace,* such statements as those he launched from the altitude of his pulpit in Wittenberg in 1522 upon his return from the Wartburg: "I condemn only by speech. It is by words we must fight, by words we must conquer, and by words tear down what has been erected by force and violence." Luther replied that he was thinking then only of verbal excesses; but the peasants of 1525 were not mere fanatics—they were rebels in open revolt. Luther had his answer. And yet he could not at this date have helped seeing suddenly, by the light of incendiary fires, how erroneous was the conception, how vain was the hope, as he was one day to concede, on which he had ignorantly based his general ideas about life and the world.

The world is bad, said the Catholic piety. So bad that man is foolish to struggle with it; yet he is so deeply involved in it that, however heroic, however sustained his efforts may be, his innate wickedness will vitiate his acts and set his resolutions at naught. For those who foster within their souls a high ideal of sacrifice and sanctity there is only one recourse: to flee the world. To cut themselves off while still living from other living beings. To lead, apart from the world in cloistered sanctuaries, a life of prayer, mortifications, and renunciation; to offer themselves to God in expiatory sacrifice for their own and others' sins.

Delusion and blasphemy, Luther had cried. The world is the world. The spectacle it presents is one that God Himself designed. And it is He also who has placed us, like actors, in this tragic and miserable setting. Let us not try to escape it. Let us live in the world. Let us fulfill, whether we be princes or merchants, judges, executioners or soldiers, the functions that have been confided to us. Let us accept them for the love of those who benefit by them. But as Christians let us live spiritually in another world: in the kingdom of Christ, where, devoting ourselves to the quest of salvation, we shall practice charity, mercy, the superior virtues that have nothing in common with the finite world, which is given over to passion, violence, and the sword.

Of course we must submit to political, economic, and juridical necessities; submit to oppressive laws, to the scourge of war, the injustices of princes, to all sorts of sacrifices. And of course so powerful a personality as Luther would understand how one's slightest movement is apt to smash everything. He understood this; he knew it. He was therefore the more insistent: "Let us remain peaceful. What does it profit us to break up everything, demolish everything, to build a larger house? Let us yield, at the price of perpetual restraint, to the stern necessities of the secular world. What does it matter, since our soul, the soul of a Christian and believer, escapes freely from its cage? In the subtle ether of the spiritual world, where there are neither laws, nor taxes, nor boundaries, the soul can revel in its power and enjoy a royal freedom. Moving without fear from the summit of the virtues to the abyss of the vices, let it penetrate beyond the realm of impurities and stains to a free enjoyment of spiritual peace. At the end of its experiences, at last, it will enter into direct and immediate communication with the fount of all creative energy, the sovereign creator, God. In the flame that surrounds Him, embracing all those who approach Him with shame at being what they are, with a touching sense of their own unworthiness, with an infinite faith in His mercy, everything melts away and is consumed: sins and vices, misery and weakness, the alloy and the dross. This is the complete liberation and pardon, the entry into that world where, laws abolished, sin burned away, death vanquished, the soul finds itself beyond good and evil. It is salvation by faith.

What certainty, then, for the Christian? God enters into him, penetrates his being and inspires him, makes of his life an uninterrupted succession of fruitful creations and of his heart a source of illimitable love. His works spring from the faith that they nourish, thus completing an unbroken circle. "Faith pours itself out in good works, and by good works is again fortified, as the sun rises till the moment of its setting and returns to its starting place to rise again." In the face of such prospects and such intoxicating bliss, what mattered the cares and the misery of this world?

Luther's eyes were full of these wonderful visions: he announced them to men, to mankind. And it was very beautiful—

this appeal to the spiritual life, to the sovereign liberty of the spirit.

1525—the revolt of the peasants. A sudden lightning flash cleared away the clouds of illusion. And Luther beheld the common man as he really was, his bludgeon in hand, his spear raised, coarse, wretched, and crude. A man who did not accept the walls of his cell, but beat against them with all his rude strength. Promise him the wonderful fruits of Christian liberty? More than foolish. Take part in his efforts, espouse his claims? Never. It was against God's will. And besides—that argument with which Luther had opposed the iconoclasts, "An idol is nothing in the world. Why, then, struggle against it?"—it applied equally to the princes: "What power have they over our souls? None. Why then revolt against a tyranny that has no hold upon our real selves?" No, no association with the rebels. Repress them sternly. Have no scruple about bashing in their insolent faces.

Thus all things would again be made clear. Everything would order itself anew satisfactorily. On one side, the heroes. A few rare geniuses, a few strong personalities accepting with indifference external restraints, submitting without protest or useless resistance to all discomforts and petty annoyances, but knowing within themselves the true liberty, the superhuman happiness of escape from servitude, of holding all law for naught, of conducting the revolt of the free spirit against mechanical necessities. On the other side, the masses, submissive to restraints, experiencing their salutary rigor, possessing, they too, in theory their spiritual liberty, but incapable of benefiting by it, men leading their lives within the confines of a patriarchal state operated and planned for all, which applied to its human chattels the methods of a more or less enlightened despotism.

Contrast this Lutheran society—which is destined in its mediocrity with its pharisaical and timorous moralism to achieve a perfect success in small matters but lapse into an utter passivity and indifference to the great—with the visionary faith animating a few heroic spirits, unencumbered persons or things, whose souls race through the spaces of the infinite, while their bodies remain on earth, wallowing in the common mire. Citizens? Yes, of the celestial city. As to the terrestrial city, they aspire neither to direct it nor improve it. Docile subjects, model robots, they furnish the example of perfect submission to the orders of a prince who finally, riding high above the bowed heads of the universe, holds the unique power that none can contest.

Herein is contained the whole history and the whole philosophy of Lutheran Germany. It was conceived thus in Luther's dreams probably, but at least in his exhortations in the spring of 1525, when his inner tumult drove him to the harshest avowal of his beliefs.

GERHARD RITTER

The Founder
of the Evangelical Churches

F OR MORE THAN TWO DECADES Luther shouldered the
weight of this everyday work—an enormous burden that
continually increased and although often seeming to suppress completely his human feelings, instead brought out all the more
strongly the sharper, more offensive traits of his character. Yet it
was never able to stifle the confidence of his faith, nor the many-
sided richness of his character, the inexhaustible humor and good-
naturedness of this great and childlike soul. "I hope they will not
rob me of my courage and joy," he wrote in the middle of the
peasants' revolt. Of course, as a natural man, he was grieved to be

From Gerhard Ritter, *Luther: His Life and Work*. Copyright © 1959 by
F. Bruckmann K. G. Verlag, Munich. English translation by John Riches,
copyright © 1963 by William Collins Sons & Co. Ltd., London, and Harper
& Row Publishers, Inc., New York, pages 172–209. Reprinted with permission
of the publishers.

the object of universal hatred, for "it is something which is deeply rooted in our nature that we should be pleased when people are favorably disposed toward us." But this did not for a moment distract him from his vocation; he was only plagued by the spirit of his conscience. "All their blood is on my hands. But I can lay it at the door of our Lord God, who ordered me to say that." Again, the way in which he countered the hatred and contempt of men was typical of Luther: with supreme defiance for all the blasphemers and to the overwhelming horror of Melanchthon, he chose this precise moment [1525], which was in fact earlier than he had planned, to embark on marriage with a nun who had run away from her order. So, right at the beginning of this last great period of his life, we find an event that almost suggests symbolically to us what will distinguish the work of these decades from that of all previous ones: the monk and man of God who had been so withdrawn from earthly matters now settles into an earthly life; the Titan, without betraying his ultimate aims, is content to work at first only in small circles—to erect by faithful but outwardly modest work a limited and so more solid building and at the same time a cell of the new communion of saints, after the bold outlines of the first plan [i.e., the reform of the whole church] had proved far too ambitious to be able to find any firm footing in the cracked, volcanic ground of Germany. Faust builds dikes to win back a little firm ground from the eternally fluctuating sea.[1] That Luther found courage at this moment, and indeed time and time again, is—in spite of all the trials and tribulations of this late period of his life—the unforgettable historical achievement of the aging reformer.

The catastrophe of the peasants' revolt did not prevent the continuance of the Reformation and perhaps did not even seriously hold it up, but it gave the movement another character. It did away forever with the confidence that one could achieve a reform of spiritual and secular life all at once. The nation as a whole lost not only its hope in this transformation, but also its chance of internal participation in public life—that tempting prospect in which they had followed and applauded the breaking away of

1. Goethe, *Faust*, Part II, Act 5.

the church from Rome as the beginning of a better period for the Germans. From now on the future of Germany was left entirely in the hands of the victors and oppressors, the German princes and their advisers. If they wished now to continue the struggle with the emperor and the pope, then the people obeyed blindly and apathetically. This was the situation that Luther had to reckon with from now on. But a great division between the parties had occurred. Luther's teaching preserved its purely spiritual, fundamentally unpolitical character; it had withstood the severest test of fire, and now it must carry on in its own way: by the inner transformation of men. The revolutionary fanatics, who had wanted to renew everything all at once at the risk of invoking chaos, were overpowered. Their rash courage was broken forever; they became submerged in the peaceful, suffering movement of the Baptists, who were now subjected to a merciless persecution—not least because they were blamed (in the main unjustly) for the disaster of the peasants' revolt. Everything that was not of the Roman Catholic or Lutheran faith was driven underground into concealment and bigotry; oppressed, harassed, and hunted, they were ineradicable and could boast of thousands of brave martyrs. But Luther's lifework was saved from the whirlpool and could continue to hold up its head in public.

But one of the strings to his bow had been broken; no one who had ears could mistake it. Ever since the "tract on the severe little book against the peasants," there had been mixed with the deep, heartfelt pathos of his voice a new, sharper, and at times clearly disharmonious tone. His polemics were always passionate and terrible, but now they were sometimes malicious and bitter; the contradictions of his opponents not only aroused his anger, they made him impatient and irritable; suddenly one saw a nervous man who was no longer in complete control of himself. Even now his battles were in the grand manner: he was always pursuing some great and pertinent aim; he always rose above the level of petty intrigue, of personal enmities, which surrounded him in Wittenberg right up to the very last days of his old age. But, for the first time, in that "tract" he brings himself to threaten his opponent with external force: "Beware: the sword could strike even you!" One does indeed feel that his faith in the effectiveness of

the mere Word on men is no longer what it was. He does not
doubt the power of the Divine Word, but their good will to accept
it and their ability to follow the better insight. Basically this was
nothing but his old notion of the complete sinfulness of natural
man; but the power of Satan must have seemed greater and
greater to him, the more disappointments he experienced, and the
sad pessimistic attitude of the religious in regard to this sinful
world turned into contempt of mankind. The severe physical ill-
nesses that consumed him more and more, and at times plunged
him into unconsciousness, may have done their share toward making the struggle more difficult, but they could never break the
power of his spirit; the amount of work he produced even in his
worst weeks is almost unbelievable. But this battle, which was
carried on without ceasing for decades and which he alone—for
that was what he felt—had to wage day by day against a whole
world of merciless enemies, gradually embittered him. Throughout
his life he could never allow himself to retire from the forefront
of the battle, where he struggled on with ever increasing vigor.
All his actions show this, not least those of his old age, when we
see him leaving Wittenberg in a furious temper, refusing ever to
return to a town where there were so many enemies and false
friends; and it was at this time that he gradually began to estrange
even the closest of his friends with his overdominating will, while
they in turn at the end no longer dared to tell him of all the set-
backs in the church struggle, for fear of his outbursts of anger.
Always he longed for the peace he had left behind him, and always
his fighting spirit drew him into fresh conflicts.

Indeed, the color and tonality of his manner had changed ap-
preciably. But the theme remained the same. Anyone who thinks
he can find a deep-seated break, a formal contradiction, between
Luther's attitude before and after 1525 has never properly understood the depths of his character. It is true that whereas before he
had put all the emphasis on the preaching of the Word and the
inner transformation of men that this would effect, he now allowed
more room for the gradual, educational effect of church institutions on the masses. What was previously for him of least significance, the creation of external forms and organizations, now came
to assume more importance after so many bitter experiences. His

marriage was the first external sign of this change of view; it was high time to make an end of the separation of the clergy, which was manifest to all. Even in this he was led on step by step by the internal logic of these matters; from the gradual establishment of eternal forms of worship to the formulation of a confession of faith, of a new dogma, which he developed more and more fully and which he had to define more sharply against the spiritualism of the Baptists. Out of the free preaching of the Word there arose a new church. And he had never been of the opinion that men could do without church order. It was precisely because the inner sanctuaries of his faith occupied him so exclusively that it never occurred to him to dispute the divine institution of the church, the necessity of external institutions for the education of men. The Reformation tract *Address to the Christian Nobility,* written at the peak of his activity, shows this clearly. Melanchthon's *Loci communes,* the first Protestant attempt at dogmatic theology, was produced in the year of the Diet of Worms. He did not intend to destroy the old church but to restore it in its pure form. But even the freedom of conscience that he preached was not a mere arbitrariness; it was always bound to the Word of God, and over and above this he was much more attached to many of the traditions of the old church than one could have expected at the height of the battle. Everything he renounced had to be torn away from his soul with great pain and suffering. True, what he effected was a revolution, but at the same time it was a historical development. It was here that we have already seen part of his genius and by no means the least. Everything that in the last decades of his life seems like spiritual obduracy, and even like reaction, is at heart nothing of the kind at all: he is only strengthening his continuity with the Middle Ages, which he had never given up. . . .

Yet, for all that, there had been a transformation in his lifework. At first sight it is disappointing, almost tragic, to see how the stormy, openhearted enthusiasm of the early years gradually changes into dogmatic rigidity—how, in his struggles and disputes with opponents on both sides, the immediate testimony of his living experience of God is withdrawn behind theological definitions and ecclesiastical formulations of doctrine. But the cause of this change was anything but a cooling of his original enthusiasm. It was not determined from within but from without, for he was forced by external pressure to change his role of religious liberator for that of a church Father—to become the canonical authority for a new theological school, so that as a teacher he had to define his conviction on all sides. It was just in the same way that he had previously been forced by external circumstances to develop the revolutionary impetus of his own new understanding of God—step by step with greater clarity and power.

By far the most important task that now lay before him was the refounding from within of an evangelical church. This presupposed above all one thing . . . : the reestablishment of an effective spiritual authority. But where could such an authority be found after the decline of canon law and of all priestly and hierarchical powers of coercion, except in the congregation? For Luther had indeed, even in his address to the nobility, recognized the right of the "common will and command" to judge the doctrine of their clergy and to appoint and dismiss them. But in this congregation he had from the beginning counted on the "Council or Authority," that is, the secular powers in the late medieval sense, as the most important members. He even included the rulers of the state, although only insofar as they subscribed to right doctrine. And on the whole he had more confidence in these secular rulers than in "Messrs. Omnes" from whom he expected wild tumults and the blind destruction of their traditional inheritance rather than the calm reconstruction and clear insight. This did not exclude certain practical attempts to organize the congregation on an ecclesiastical basis: the laity were to take part in the administration of church possessions; indeed, Luther wanted to see the voluntary establishment of a Christian rule of life with "house fathers and house mothers" with certain means of discipline, with a greater and lesser excommunication. But his constant worry in all this was to prevent this new rule of love from becoming a new spiritual compulsion, or even a new canon law. Before he would allow this to happen, he would rather leave the establishment of external order to the secular authorities as a "service of love." Nor would he grant any purely spiritual authority to the "congregation" in the sense of a compulsory rule because of his deep conviction that it was impossible to separate the pure, true Christians from those who merely seemed to be Christians, from the camp followers and the busybodies. He had thought at first of gathering together a small congregation of living witnesses and disciples of the new doctrine around the communion table in the chapel of the Black Cloister, as a core from which the new communion of the saints would gradually develop. He would preach to them himself, while "outside" in the town church his chaplains would preach to the "great mass" as missionary preachers. But this was to be no more than an outward means to an end; and it should in no way lead to a sect-like separation of the "Elect," still less to any special position of privilege for the inner circle in church government. The true church of Christ was for him always the invisible one. For this reason the plans for the systematic development of the Lutheran congregation were never properly put into effect, and Luther contented himself instead with the formula that the church is everywhere to be found where the pure Word is preached and the sacraments are properly celebrated. . . .

But in this way the problem of a new form of spiritual authority was not solved but merely shelved. Could it in fact be solved at all? Or was it for the Lutheran way of thought, which only recognized the "pure Word of God" as the final authority and which feared that any human authority might bring with it the falsification of that Word, basically insoluble? Was it not a paradoxical task that Luther had set his church: to build a community not of this world and yet for this world and in this world—invisible and yet visible—a community not based on outward laws but on the inner conscience, and yet again not a sect, but a national church, an organized community of baptized Christians? Unquestionably there is reflected in these contradictions something of the paradox of Lutheran theological thinking, which in the last resort is a consequence of his ruthless renewal of the paradox of the preaching of primitive Christianity. As a community in love of like-minded men, the new church needed no external order, while as a national church . . . it did; for, as such, it embraced true believers and apparent Christians alike—and Luther had no intention of leaving the affairs of church government in the hands of such a motley crowd. The practical consequences of this were the

endless trials of evangelical church order which, till this day, have
not been overcome but rather (in a largely non-Christian world)
have been considerably increased, and this is particularly true of
the Lutheran Church. Zwingli, the sober, practical, humanistically
minded Swiss, helped himself out of this difficulty by building his
church "goers" from Zurich into a form of Christian community
—a type of theocracy—in which the preachers of the reform were
in fact assured that the majority of the council were dependent on
them, and so were able to bring secular politics for a time completely into the service of the new community of the faithful. This
was a political and so purely temporal solution. Calvin, who attempted the same thing in Geneva, had to withstand a long and
difficult struggle in order to gain a majority in the council. He
had, therefore, to form a militant and purely ecclesiastical organization that could maintain itself and hold sway, even without—
or, indeed, against—the secular authority; a community of chosen,
fanatically convinced adherents that excluded all halfhearted and
weak members or mere hangers-on by excommunicating them,
and which then created its own order and its own means of government according to "biblical norms," in the executive committee
of the presbyters and consistories. But this was not possible without the creation of a new legalism: official church trials of conscience in situations of acute danger with inquisition and consequently trials for heresy, and the erection of a new canon law
which, instead of the old books of canon law, used the Bible in the
New as well as the Old Testament as a lawbook for external
ordinances. Luther rejected both these ways on grounds of the
deepest conviction, and he had to as the preacher of a purely inner
religion that recognized no code of "divine" ordinances and also
no visible community of the Elect. He was left no alternative but
to substitute respect for secular authority for the ecclesiastical authority that he was unable to obtain by the creation of new ordinances; thus, to a very great degree, he entrusted the fate of his
church to the "secular sword."

This step, to modern thinking with its clear-cut distinction between church and state, seems very risky, and its dangers have
been amply experienced by the evangelical church since the eighteenth century. At the time of the Reformation there was scarcely

anything remarkable in it. Already long before the appearance of Luther, the internal collapse of the papal church had made it necessary on all sides (not only in Germany) for the "Christian rulers" to take more and more responsibility for the reform of church life. . . . [Luther] knew nothing of the modern distinction between "state" and "church," as autonomous forms of community independent of each other. He only knew of an admittedly secular, but nevertheless Christian, authority as an estate of Christendom among others. . . . Like every other estate, the authorities are duty-bound to serve the kingdom of God—the prince firstly as a private person . . . but also by virtue of the duty attaching to his estate, as the bearer of his office of government. . . . Luther speaks of this duty of the Christian father of the state in complete agreement with the medieval law code of the princes; only his understanding is more fundamental and radical, and above all (at least after 1522) he suffers from no illusions about the demonic powers of political reality and so discards the traditional servile hypocrisy. The most noble of all the duties of the prince is the care for the salvation of the souls of his subjects by the establishment, preservation, and protection of true Christian doctrine and discipline. Even if the "spiritual government" of the preachers is responsible for making man devout and just for eternal life, not by the power of the sword but by the proclamation of the Word alone, it must nevertheless be complemented by the secular government; for the real Christians who do not need the power of compulsion are always in the minority compared with the great mass of those who are not Christians or who merely seem to be such. So the secular government has the duty of seeing that all those who do not wish to become devout and just for eternal life should be yet compelled by the sword to become devout and just in the eyes of the world. Both spiritual and temporal government are under the same law of God and serve the same highest moral and religious duty.

Luther held fast to those basic insights . . . unerringly in spite of all his many changes of outward approach. . . . One lesson had been made unmistakably clear by the catastrophe of the peasants' revolt, and that was that no time must be lost in building up a new and stable form of church order. In this task Luther could less than ever afford to dispense with the help of the state authorities;

how else could he have saved the few and have built up again the pitiful ruins of the beginnings of a new form of church organization that had been left by the storm of the revolution? In the larger towns it would still be possible to continue with the attempt to build up the new church on the basis of the congregation; in the country all hopes for the success of this plan had been destroyed. These wild, ignorant, religiously indifferent peasants ought not even to be entrusted with the choice of their own pastor. . . . Even the imperial diet recognized (at least, the imperial dismissal of the Diet of Speyer in 1526 could in emergency be interpreted in this way) that the secular heads of state, who alone of all the imperial estates had successfully calmed the storm, were also the only ones in a position to create new forms of church order, even if this was only a temporary measure. They all, north and south, Lutheran and Catholic alike, vied with each other to exploit the favorable situation of the next few years in the sense of the imperial direction from Speyer. While their emperor and pope were at open war with each other, and the imperial mercenaries were engaged in sacking the holy city of Rome, they sought to strengthen their own power by church reforms carried out within the boundaries of their own territories with the use of secular force. The foundation of the German State Churches, which had been prepared since the previous century, was now finally realized and became one of the most important factors in German history. While it formally put the seal on the political divisions of the nation, it also determined the character of church life and political life in the individual states. The Reformation, which was one of the spiritual roots of modern political democracy in Western Europe, also contributed substantially in Germany and in the countries that came under the reforming influence of Lutheranism to the victory—which, admittedly, was inevitable in any case—of absolute monarchy.

However great Luther's historical responsibility for this course of affairs may be, particularly with regard to his role as founder of the Reformation movement, it would not be fair to say that he really determined its further development. As always in history, as soon as a spiritual movement has advanced beyond the battleground of pure ideas and has come into the spheres of political struggles for power and of material avarice, its founder loses all power over it. The force of historical circumstance and the interplay of political interests wins the upper hand. What good was it that the reformer was at pains to make a careful distinction between questions of the ministry of the church and of its external order, between occasional and temporary legal assistance (in the visitations) and the permanent government of the church, between the service of love of the prince as the most respected member of the church and his duties as secular father and lord of the state, if he never spoke at all of the rights of the princes in church government but only of their duties? The constantly growing influence of state bureaucracy on the inner life of the church could not be withstood for long, particularly once Luther had made the decision to undertake, with the help of the officials of the princes, a great visitation of all religious foundations and parishes for the correction of the countless abuses and emergencies that had arisen (1526–1528). This gradually developed into a formal "church police." . . . Even if Luther himself sighed and at times raged over the claims of the government lawyers, his fellow workers, above all Melanchthon, Bugenhagen, and Amsdorf with their theologico-juristic formulations, consciously prepared the way for the state consistories and helped them to create a new evangelical church law (not without considerable leanings toward the old canon law), which had in practice become indispensable. But in this Melanchthon, the humanist, considerably watered down the Lutheran doctrine of the spiritual duties of the rulers greatly in favor of the supreme power of the state. At first, that is, as long as Luther's powerful personality dominated the court of the Wettins, there was little practical danger in the Electorate of Saxony of a misuse of the new church government for the ends of secular power. But beyond the Saxon borders his personal influence was much smaller; and would his successors ever be in a position to withstand the political independence of the German rulers? The reformer himself was soon able to see what course things were taking when the pious and easily led duke was succeeded by the theological dilettante and absolutist John Frederick. His generation and the one that followed took up its responsibilities for true doctrine in a highly personal way and with a zeal that seemed for a moment as if it would turn the complicated and purely dogmatic disputes over the doctrine of the Lord's Supper into the most important issue in German territorial politics. In this development, opposed points of dogma and the territorial interests of the states became entangled in each other in a truly disastrous manner. The more petty the power of the princes, the more petty and malicious became the squabblings of their theologians. The misfortune of the small German states was made even worse by the half-spiritual authority of the German princely courts; and in reverse effect this multiplicity of states succeeded finally in really hardening and exacerbating the theological bickering.

So the historical development of Luther's lifework wandered far from the point where it had begun. In the orthodox court-preachers and theological faculties of this later period, there was nothing to be seen of the coarse, bold defiance of the Luther who had ranted against the German princes as the "biggest fools and the most arrant knaves on earth" because they put obstacles in the way of his preaching—the preaching of the pure Word of God. But did he not himself play a part in accustoming the state authorities to making decisions on purely spiritual matters? Did he not himself set the secular sword in motion in order to destroy his spiritual opponent with it? What could one say if he who had poured so much scorn on the art "of overcoming heretics with fire" himself advised the ruler of his state to prevent the preaching of the Baptists by exile or even by execution? Is this not a gross betrayal of the principle that he had wrung from himself of the freedom of conscience? Indeed it is not—if in the place of our modern relativism of all values, on which our concept of freedom of conscience is based, one substitutes the religiously bound conscience of a medieval man who knows that he is in sure possession of absolute truth—a truth whose possession arbitrates over this life and the next! Here, as everywhere in Luther's thought, the idea of God stands in the forefront and explains associations of ideas that would otherwise remain obscure. If he demanded freedom of conscience, he was not concerned, as we are today, to allow more scope to the human personality with its subjective claims to certainty, its convictions and prejudices; rather, he was concerned with something that excluded this—to clear a way for the working of the Word of God in the hearts of men. Only if the individual comes before his God immediately and with full responsibility for himself, without the sacramental mediation and guidance of the priests, can the mysterious struggle with God be broken off and that blessing of grace be experienced that lies at the center of all Luther's religious thought. But only in this sense, in the sense of the responsibility of every individual before God, could he come to a knowledge of what we call (and in most cases also fundamentally misinterpret) his "autonomous conscience," which in no way means that man is now free to think up his own arbitrary ideas about God and divine things. For man's thinking is just as much subjected to God, and so fundamentally unfree, as is the human will. The *content* of divine revelation was for Luther as sure and as certain as it had been for the old church; it has been laid down once and for all in the Word of God, which Word and its contents one must know and whose interpretation is not in any sense a purely arbitrary matter. Any doubts about this are the works of devilish powers, and the prophet fights for the Lordship of his God when he battles against Satan, who blinds men to God's clear revelation. There is still more: God's purpose of grace, revealed in Christ, is not a mere gift to men: it is our sacred duty to prostrate ourselves to it unconditionally and to accept grace willingly; whoever resists this, whoever makes reservations for the freedom of the human will, blasphemes and brings down God's just wrath upon himself. That there were many interpretations of the revelation was plain for all to see; but that he, the reformer, had with God's help again discovered the true one, and that every other exposition was idolatry and devilish error was for him never in doubt: how else could he have accomplished the gigantic task of standing alone against the whole world? Only a man who has the sure and certain conviction that he is proclaiming nothing but God's will and meaning can withstand such tensions in the soul. All the strangely wild and terrifying aspects of Luther's character in the eyes of modern men, and also the heroic greatness of his historical achievement, are most closely bound up with this conviction.

Yet it is not true to say that the Lutheran belief in revelation led to the same outward constraint of conscience as in the inquisition of the old church. God's spirit blows where it will and we men should not presume to interfere in its work or to compel its activity by outward means. God wills that his Word should be preached, pure and unhindered by false doctrine, and that all men should hear it; for this reason the authorities must employ the true teachers and prevent the false ones from preaching, and insure that their subjects attend the schools and churches. But the working of God's Word in our hearts is not our affair but God's. No one may be forced into a state of mind or a decision of faith; in the last instance everyone stands immediately before God. The unity of the church, which so much preoccupied Luther, was a unity of the spirit and not of external church order—of the Word, not of the hierarchy. The Spirit of God must have a free path, but no blood, no inquisition, no trials for heresy; not the church and still less the secular authorities are responsible for the eternal salvation of the individual soul, but every individual himself, because no one can or may take away his immediate responsibility before God. It is not for the sake of human freedom that the consciences are free, but only for the sake of God; then the individual who turns away may go to the devil on his own responsibility—if only the preaching of God's Word is unhindered.

From these basic concepts we can understand Luther completely. Their interrelatedness was clear from the beginning; there could be no question of any fundamental alteration. Yet he does not always seem to have defined in quite the same way the outer limits of what was to be regarded as immediate Divine truth. A certain basis of dogmatic propositions, as they had been developed up to the Council of Nicaea and formulated in the so-called Apostolic Creed, was for him, as for nearly all his contemporaries, inviolable, and any attack on it would have been tantamount to public blasphemy. . . . But the longer the fight with the Baptists lasted . . . the closer he came to the idea that every deviation from his understanding of Christianity was to be seen as false teaching and idolatry. At the beginning he had been prepared to tolerate such false teachings so long as they did not preach revolt against secular order. . . . After the experience of the peasants' revolt (which he, too, unfairly blamed on the Baptists), he became sterner. . . . Now he wanted to banish public false doctrines even if they were only preached "in corners" by unofficial preachers, and to punish public denial of the basic truths of Christianity and the preaching of revolt even, if circumstances demanded it, with the death penalty. For now the gospel had been preached long enough and had been established on all sides, so that no one could any longer with justice plead ignorance of the true faith. From now on toleration could be afforded only if false doctrines were kept locked in the heart; for no one can or may compel the working of the spirit by external means. Indeed, even this narrowly limited "toleration," which was soon limited even more by the circumscribed zeal and nervousness of the Lutheran rulers and by the narrow-minded mis-understanding of the orthodox followers of Luther, was an enor-mous step forward for those times; even the permission of un-hindered departure for reasons of belief, which became law first in the Protestant territories and then in the whole of Germany, was then felt to be an unheard-of innovation. Nor can it be denied that the freedom from Roman dogma, which Luther won for himself and for his church, was able to be used against his will for the general destruction of dogma: the split in the church, purely as such, had infinitely wider consequences than he had intended or even realized. But Luther was not, and did not want to be, a forerunner of the modern idea of freedom of conscience. On the contrary, the new fire of religious life that he kindled in the world countered most successfully and powerfully the rationalization of religious thought that was even then beginning to spread from Italy.

So we too may perhaps attempt to understand the last great crisis of his spiritual development—his much criticized dispute with Zwingli, his Swiss fellow reformer—in its proper context. It has often been pointed out that in this quarrel, which split the two men, there were more fundamental contradictions at stake than theological formulations for the interpretation of the sacrament of the altar. The Swiss stood opposed to the North German, the secular priest to the monk, the born ecclesiastical statesman to the purely religious prophet, the son of the Renaissance to the founder of the German Reformation. If Luther's education had been purely governed by Scholastic theology, Zwingli had only come into con-tact with theology very late, when he was already in office as a

secular priest. Originally he was exclusively a pupil of the humanists and an enthusiastic admirer of the ancient writers, and
had in these early studies been steeped in the moralism and rationalism of the pre-Christian world of ideas—admittedly as they were
presented in that narrow mixture, which was peculiar to German
and Erasmic humanism, of Christian, Platonic, and Stoic ideas, in
which the ancient world was seen through Christian eyes, but
which was nevertheless entirely foreign to Luther's deepest feelings, which indeed appeared antagonistic to them. For this was
precisely Luther's aim; to restore religious life to its naïve origi-
nality, to free it from the bonds of natural reason and moralizing
legalism that had fettered and crippled it under the domination of
ecclesiastical and Scholastic thought and which now threatened
to become more dangerous than ever in the age of the tame, delicate, and somewhat pale edifying religion of the humanists. That
these radical contrasts in their spiritual outlook should be fired
off over just this question of the Lord's Supper was of course no
mere chance: the sacrament of the altar was the central core of
medieval worship and stood even at the time of the Reformation
(unlike today) right at the center of the evangelical divine service.
On its understanding depended not only the form of all church
services but, in the last instance, the position of the ministry of
the church in relation to the congregation. It was inevitable that
at this point men should begin to differ passionately.

This is not the place to attempt to expound in detail the religious depths of the Lutheran doctrine of the Lord's Supper;
fundamentally Luther was moved here by the same simple but
powerful religious thoughts that we saw in his struggles in the
monastery: the immeasurable omnipotence of God, for which no
miracle is too great, and which alone is active in this sacrament,
while man can do nothing but receive in humility. The Lord's
Supper is seen then not as a self-elevation of the soul in a common
ceremony of remembrance of the congregation's founder, but as
God's gift to the individual believer, the surest and, for the
doubter, indispensable, token of his grace, in which (in a wonderful way) he makes a gift of himself. . . . It is in such a way that
we (to put it into Luther's own words) find consolation in the
sacrament, not merely in a meal of remembrance, "not in the

bread and wine, nor in the body and blood of Christ, but in the
Word, which in the sacrament offers, presents, and gives to me the
body and blood of Christ which was given and shed for me," a
formulation, as one can see, whose religious intention is clear, but
which makes the sacramental process for the first time really enig-
matic.

To Zwingli's clear good sense this was all nothing but a relapse
into the Middle Ages; he could not understand why the man from
Wittenberg should torment himself with so many mysteries. Sufficient for him was the celebration of the pure meal of remembrance,
at which, of course, Christ the founder was present in the spirits of
the celebrants; and this too was testified biblically in Jesus's words
of institution. . . . Behind this stood a different understanding of
man, who is seen not as a self-assured being . . . who needs no
grace or redemption, nor as an eternally tempted one who stands
always in fear and trembling before the omnipotence, the wrath,
and the mysterious elusiveness of God, but rather as a happy,
confident person, sure of God's clear purpose of grace and convinced of the reasonableness of this will and of the justice of the
divine government of the world—which is also clear to the human
reason—and so inspired by a strong confidence in the importance
of human reason. . . . This was the central question of the whole
dispute, although of course it became involved in all sorts of
theologico-metaphysical questions about the omnipresence of God
and the two natures of Christ, which to us (in spite of their very
real importance) seem in some ways purely scholastic. At heart,
however, the dispute reaches right down into the realms of the
purely religious, to the question of the true understanding of
God. For it is obvious that the God whose grace is assured forever by my insight of faith into his being is different from the
hidden God of Luther, if the Lutheran Christian cannot be sure
of his own salvation without the constantly renewed help of the
sacrament. . . .

At least at the beginning it did seem perfectly possible that
[Zwingli and Luther] would be able to reach agreement in nearly
all the disputed points of doctrine except on the interpretation of
the sacrament of the altar. Even if it were not possible to gain
complete agreement on this point, could they not have tolerated

each other's differences over this? Was it so completely necessary to make precisely this issue into the cause of such violent struggles, and on top of everything to do it with the help of Scholastic formulations that previously had not even been mentioned in Luther's own writings? It would be idle to waste too much time on these questions. Only one thing is clear beyond all doubt. Luther was always sensitive to the dangers of this alliance and never to its necessity. Was it personal pride as so many of his best friends asserted then, and as even today many of his admirers admit with resignation? Was it his boundless vigor, which blinded him in the dispute and which ran away with him in extreme situations so that he could not find his way back again? Or was it simply that the aging man lapsed back into the Middle Ages? Indeed his writings against the "sacramentalizers" are among the most terrible of his polemics; and in spite of their deep insight, their manner is in places intolerable. The most powerful conviction in the rightness of one's own conviction cannot justify such excesses; even Calvin later showed how for the sake of the unity of Protestantism certain differences in doctrine may well be tolerated without in any way abandoning one's own teaching. But even the example of Calvin makes it easier for us to understand Luther's position, for he had the greatest horror of the political battle that Calvin directed with such skill. One can understand the course of affairs only in the context of this situation in which Luther and Zwingli faced each other as the leaders of the two main groups of Protestantism.

For a long time it had been shown that it was impossible (as we have already seen) to restrict the gospel to the spheres of a battle purely of ideas. The extent to which countless worldly and particularly political interests depended on it had become clearer from year to year. After the foundation of the State Churches this fact gained its true prominence. And with this the political tension between the two religious parties increased in the same degree. Again and again confessional dispute began to destroy old political relationships: it dissolved the old community of interest between the city states, it reached out over the political borders of Switzerland, softened old feuds between princely houses of an evangelical disposition, broke up political friendships of others, and began slowly to make itself felt in the religion of the European coalition —in short, it created a new political world overloaded with tensions. Luther's gospel, which had been intended to release religion from its entanglement with earthly powers, had now been brought to the stage (this tragic contradiction confronts us again and again) in which, for the first time in the history of Europe since the days of Islam (and in a much more remarkable way than at that time), religion assumed a position of central importance in the political struggles of a whole century. . . . New feuds produced new alliances. North and south of the Main the Estates that remained true to the old faith began to unite; against them stood Philip of Hesse and the elector of Saxony, who were soon joined by other north German princes; in the south, the evangelical imperial cities of Upper Swabia and in Switzerland the friends of Zwingli in the Christian Civic League under the leadership of Zürich stood against the Catholic alliance. Immediately these alliances became of immense actual importance. In the summer of 1529 Charles V had at last managed to safeguard his rear by treaties with the pope and with France, so that he could turn his attentions to fighting the hated German heresy and to asserting the supremacy of the Habsburgs in the empire. The long-awaited change in German fortunes seemed to be imminent; without armed resistance against the emperor and the empire, which was supported by the majority of the Estates, it would be impossible to withstand the forces of reaction any more or to save the work of the Reformation from destruction. If both parties were true to their intentions then there seemed no longer to be any way out; it must inevitably end in a war of religion.

What a prospect for Martin Luther! Where was he being led by his God, with whom he had wrestled in his monastery cell at Erfurt! Was this the end of the way on which he had then unsuspectingly embarked? . . . His true mood in all the political confusion of these years is far better shown by the [words he spoke] at the Coburg in 1530: "When I looked out of the window I saw the stars in the heavens and the whole beautiful vault of God, and could nowhere see any pillar on which the master could have set such a vault; and yet the heavens did not fall down and the vault is still secure." In all the vicissitudes of politics he remained unchangeable; and nothing was further from his thoughts than to support the vault of his heaven on the pillars of earthly might. He could not and would not see that, independently of himself, the fate of his own church had become inextricably entangled with the fate of the German states; that the only choice left now was either to fight with all the tools of political force for the preservation of the new doctrine and its ecclesiastical organization, or else to perish. Wherever possible he had thrown himself against the policy of revolt against the imperial authority—for that was how he saw it—even against the very policy of alliances and military agreements in itself, with the clear foresight that if it was carried to its logical conclusion it would one day lead to "unspeakable murder and misery." "How could one's conscience bear such a thing! The devil would delight in such a game, but may God preserve us from it!" At this point the real greatness of the man who remains true to himself to the last becomes clear, but so also do the limitations of his influence on the world. The only effect of his warnings was to make the politics of the Lutherans internally uncertain, to rob them of their good conscience, and to hamstring their powers of action, without in any way averting the disaster. He is not without his share of the blame for the tragic outcome of the Schmalkaldic war. It is here that we can see most clearly how he differed from Zwingli.

Their meeting in the castle at Marburg (October, 1529) was the meeting of two foreign worlds. Zwingli, the true civic republican in the Swiss manner, with that remarkable mixture of the narrowness of outlook of the small state and international perspective, which attaches itself so easily to politicians of the Swiss confederation, lived and moved in the world of politics, and spun thousands of plans, great and small, for the salvation of the gospel from Rome and the Habsburgs. . . . Luther himself did not indeed see through all the political plans of his opponent, but he could sense clearly enough that there was another spirit abroad there. . . . Was it not inevitable that this man should appear to him as the tempter sent to him from the prince of this world, to drag his work into the immeasurable whirlpool of higher politics and thus into sure destruction? Did not his seductive arts become all the more dangerous, the nearer one came to a theological agreement? Even Luther sensed, as did all the participants, that a storm was gathering in Europe over the young plant of the gospel: even he sensed the magic spell that was drawing all the Protestant Estates, princes, and cities alike into the net of higher politics. Again and again the feeling must have overwhelmed him that he was sitting at the table with the emissary of Satan. . . . Luther would not allow himself to be tricked out of his leadership in any way; he treated the Swiss with all the imperious consciousness of his own religious superiority. A few years later Zwingli's political career ended in disaster and he sealed his fate with his heroic death on the battlefield; his opponent in Wittenberg, however, rejoiced that God had now judged the heretic and blasphemer as He had once judged Thomas Müntzer, and only regretted one thing: that the successful Catholic cantons had not immediately attended to the task of rooting out the heresy that he had sown. He was in no doubt that it had been none other than Satan himself who had been the loser in Switzerland.

Strangely enough, for the time being he was right about all this. Once again peace was preserved in Germany: to all appearance "without human agency," that is to say by virtue of new changes in the eternally uncertain fate of Europe. Zwingli's great plans for defense turned out to be nothing but an empty political bubble, and all the fears of the industrious Melanchthon and all his efforts to exorcise the danger by cleverly thought-out statements of reconciliation at the new Diet of Augsburg in 1530 were in vain.

It was at this point that Magister Philip, as the leading theologian of the Protestant Estates, thought to gain acceptance for his own fainthearted policy of reconciliation, while the exiled Luther, who since 1521 had been under the imperial ban, did not dare to leave Saxony, where he was protected by his elector, and was thus forced to remain in the fortress of Coburg, right on the extreme borders of the Saxon domains. The Lutherans should testify to their true faith, in the sense of the oldest and purest catholic traditions, before the emperor and the empire. And so their "Augsburg Confession" (*Confessio Augustana*), which set out their doctrine of faith in detail in the form of separate theses, and which today still holds as the foundation of dogma of all Lutheran Churches, was made to appear as near to the old faith as possible, and moved

markedly away from the "sacramentalizers." Every possible offer
was made in the discussions in order to come to an agreement and
reconciliation with the representatives of the papal party. In the
last event, of course, it was all in vain. The unification with the
old church failed as it was bound to fail, and yet the Reformation
was again granted almost half a generation to develop undisturbed.
All the enemies of the Habsburgs, now France, now the Turk,
played their part in averting the danger from it, and in the curious
game of European politics there were moments when the papacy,
wedged between France and the Habsburgs, secretly assisted the
opposition of the Lutheran heretics against the Catholic emperor;
moments when the principles of the Renaissance, the politics of
purely secular interests, broke through the system of confessional
differences almost by force. But the process of the souring of all
political life by the party hate of the various confessions could no
longer be withstood. Least of all in Germany, where after the departure of the Swiss, the political unification of all the Protestants
was eventually achieved in the Schmalkaldic League. Saxony assumed the leadership; the confession of faith of its theologians was
taken as a basis for the alliance. But Luther did not play a deter-
minative role in these affairs. The timid spirit of the *Confessio
Augustana* was as foreign to him as was this whole world of political negotiations. He could not prevent it and so he left the
matter to God, to his friends, and to the lawyers, who tried to con-
vince him that opposition to the emperor was not revolution but
a legitimate action in accordance with legal procedure. . . . Among
the members of the league, above all in the Upper German cities,
there now arose a vigorous new breed of theologians, which spiritually already stood on the shoulders of Luther. The perfect example
of this type was Martin Butzer, a much experienced man from
Alsace, a born diplomat and negotiator: the reformer of Strasbourg, the city on the border of the two nations, which was then
of more importance for the course of German history than ever
before or since, and in whose council chamber the strands of political interest from all sides were intertwined. He was the confi-
dant of the Landgrave Philip, the most active of all the Protestant
princes, and the friend of John Calvin, in whom the particular
qualities of these political theologians and theological politicians

were united with a religious life of true original genius and depth. . . .

These were the men to whom the present and the immediate future belonged. Among them Martin Luther looks like a piece of the Middle Ages in another age. He was beset by an increasing feeling of inner loneliness, by sickness, and by a deep resentment at the course of affairs, which ever remained a mystery to him. So he buried himself in the spiritual tasks that had always been dearest to him, and to which, so he himself thought, he was best suited: the translation of the Bible into German, on whose constant revision and correction he spent an immeasurable amount of time and energy, the creation of a new evangelical service, of a new evangelical hymnody, of a new type of church music, and finally in his favorite work of all, the catechism for religious instruction in schools and in the home. He even took pains to continue his academic writing; and as the tutor of his students, as the counselor of countless people and as the Father confessor and pastor in particular of the Protestant princes, he daily accomplished a host of small tasks. The benefit of this work is greatest where Luther was most faithful to his mission. Once only did he seem to betray it, and that was in the unhappy bigamy of the Landgrave Philip of Hesse, in which he confused spiritual and secular law, responsibility before God and before men in a truly disastrous way. The Landgrave, one of the most important princely patrons of the Reformation, appealed in his (alleged) trials of conscience to Luther as his Father confessor, and asked whether he could not take a noble young lady as his second wife in a secret marriage, since she refused to submit to him without a marriage ceremony. He based his appeal on the fact that otherwise (if his proper marriage were to break up) he would be in danger of falling into the sin of extramarital intercourse, and had pointed to the double marriage of the Old Testament. Luther clearly, honestly believed in the trials of conscience of the Landgrave (who in actual fact had committed adultery several times before) and so equally (with a biblical justification) gave his "penitent" dispensation. But it was never more clearly shown how fatal any compromise with sinful reality would be for the religious rigorism that he preached, what calamities would be wrought by any compromise, no matter what

theological sophistries were found to justify it. That Luther then
tried to cover up the step, once it had been taken, for motives that
the world neither could nor would understand, with "a good,
honest lie," only served to make matters worse. It is difficult to say
which was worse: the moral or the directly political damage of
this princely failure: in any case it decisively crippled the Protestant party at the moment when they were most sorely pressed by
the emperor. As a result of his bigamy, the Landgrave came into
contact with the punitive laws of the empire and had to woo the
emperor's favor in order to avoid being deposed, which favor, of
course, could be had only at a high political price: Philip had to
break with his allies in the further negotiations of the imperial Estates over the questions of faith and had to promise the emperor
that he would hinder their alliance with foreign powers. So the
disastrous bigamy led to the first division of the Evangelical party.

In this case, as in others, one can sense clearly the limitations of
Luther's genius. It was not so much lack of worldly wisdom that
caused him to miscalculate so seriously (the worldly wise but all
too active Butzer was even more embarrassed by this match-
making), but, rather, a lack of that calm calculation, that certain
political intuition, without which it is not possible to take successful action in the world of secular affairs. The more difficult
and incomprehensible the tasks were which fell to him as head
of the Reformation movement, the more obvious did this become.
Instead of assuming the confidence and assurance of a long-tried
ruler, we see him becoming more and more passionate in his outbursts, more and more heated in his rage. The tone of his polemics
does not become milder as he grows older, but more and more
violent and uninhibited. Alongside his theological opponents there
now emerged more and more strongly new enemies of the gospel:
Turks, heathens, Jews, Catholic potentates. On many occasions he
worked as an "army preacher"; he considered the war against the
Turks to be a Christian duty—no longer a spiritual exercise, a
crusade, but a secular undertaking for the protection of "Christendom"; and he further considered the Emperor Charles to be the
appointed leader of all the Western powers. He urged the Germans
to throw their last energy into this battle—with a belligerent pa-
triotism that would not allow itself to be outdone by the zeal of

the humanist propagandists. It is most remarkable to note the change in his attitude to the question of the Jews, and it is most characteristic of the old Luther. Before the peasants' revolt, in the period when his hopes were still high, he had still expected that the light of the refurbished gospel would also attract the Jews and lead to countless conversions; for this reason he had urged people to "treat them in a friendly way" and not with "arrogance and contempt." His disappointment now drove him to the extremes of bitterness. In his later writings, particularly in the notorious battle cry *Of the Jews and Their Lies* (1543), which has since become the stock-in-trade of anti-Semitism, he unleashes against them a whole flood of popular hatred and evil rumors about their secret abominations. It is clear that as a foreign people they appeared to him to be repulsive and uncanny. Nevertheless, his attitude was not determined by any racial political points of view (of which he had no knowledge), but by moral and religious considerations: as obstinate liars and enemies of Christ he wanted to impose exceptional laws on them. The authorities were forcefully to prevent their public services by destroying their synagogues and houses (as also happened in the case of heretics) and to restrain them from usury by dispossession and forced labor, indeed at best they should expel them from the land (which did happen in Saxony and Hesse). He did not want to compel them to believe in the Christian faith, "for we must leave that to every individual's conscience"; nor did he give up hope that individual Jews might be converted to Christ and thus escape destruction; but as a whole the Jewish people stood under the wrath of God as a result of their religious obstinacy, and the Christian preacher believed that his rulers (and clearly in no way every private individual) are called to carry out the Divine judgment on the damned. So one sees the reformer at the end of his life assuming more and more the role of the wrathful prophet proclaiming the woes of the evildoers of the world and announcing God's coming vengeance. He even assumes a more threatening tone with the rulers of this world and again and again pours out polemics against such powerful potentates as Duke George of Saxony, the Cardinal Archbishop Albrecht of Mainz, King Henry VIII of England, or "against that Tomfool," the bellicose Henry, Duke of Brunswick. He attained a last extreme of coarseness in his maliciously bitter pamphlet *Against the Papacy at Rome, Founded by the Devil* (1545), with which the last echoes of his life's struggle died away; appended to them was a series of caricatures drawn by Cranach, on the *Ass and Swine of a Pope,* which Luther furnished with some extremely coarse and indeed lewd verses. . . .

Undeniably, all these later polemics bear the highly personal stamp of Luther's own nature and cannot simply be explained and justified by the boorishness of the times. . . . Yet whoever seeks to characterize Luther's later years in the light of this alone has failed to see the riches of his personality. For immediately behind the terrible anger, one finds, to one's constant surprise, the good-natured man who wants to be loved, the poetic spirit with its warm joy in everything beautiful, in all the fresh life in the woods and fields, in the garden and in the house; the intensely musical creator of the chorale, seeking refreshment in singing and playing on the lute, and working on the rewriting of a German mass with astounding zeal and technical skill; and finally the father, friend, and tutor of his children, whom he cares for lovingly and tenderly. . . . Whoever listens to the sharp, unsophisticated yet penetrating conversation of the master at the round table in the Black Cloister at Wittenberg, whoever follows him in his study, in Katie's garden, playing music with his friends, taking counsel with fellow preachers, in the pulpit, in the lecture hall, and at the sickbed, will again and again recognize the greatness of the man in the spontaneity and informality of his actions. Indeed he will not be able to rid himself of the impression that here a great soul was burning itself out in the fetters of triviality. His genius was of the kind that can only breathe freely and stretch out its wings on the heights of great historical developments, in the regions of the great storms, and which in the lowlands of monotonous daily routine, hemmed in by the blank and narrow walls of political realities, beats its wings like a trapped bird trying to escape. But even now there were moments of great historical importance, in which great fundamental decisions had to be taken; then once again he reached up to his full height before us, and in a trice all the others seemed like pitiful accessories beside the one great hero. He was at his most magnificent in the Coburg in 1530. While Melanchthon, nearly overcome by the weight of responsibility, was coming dangerously close to the borderline where he would have betrayed the gospel in his Erasmic offers of reconciliation to the representatives of the old church, Luther alone in his fortress looked up to heaven with a heart sure in the knowledge that God was on his side alone and that all the offers of compromise on the part of his opponents were nothing but lies and deceit. . . .

"The way of the ungodly will perish. But it will endure for a long while yet. So be steadfast!" These are the words that at one time he wrote on the walls of his room in the castle for his own comfort. His steadfastness was rewarded. It happened as he had always prophesied: that all the power of this world could do nothing against the preaching of the pure Word. When, in Augsburg, the representatives of the Protestant estates were allowed to read the evangelical confession of faith to the imperial assembly and to the very same emperor who had once sworn in Worms that he would stake everything—his crown and his life—in the attempt to root out this heresy, Luther had the sure feeling that "the Gospel has been established." Not entirely without the help of the sword, and yet in the majority of cases by peaceful means, one bulwark after another had been wrested from the Catholics in Germany over the last thirty years. Meissen, Saxony, the Electorate of Brandenburg, Anhalt, Pomerania, the Palatinate, Wurtemberg, and Brunswick, and over and above that, many cities in all parts of the empire; even in Bavaria and Austria and other no less spiritual dominions, the evangelical message began to gain ground, and eventually it seemed as if even the Archdiocese of Cologne would become evangelical. No matter how little Martin Luther understood the younger generation, they still flocked to him in large numbers. As he neared the end of his life it seemed as if, given a little more time, all Germany would be won over to the gospel, as he had once hoped in his happiest days. "The reign of the pope has lost its glory; both his eyes have been put out." Of course, he could still hear the roll of the drums recruiting for the imperial regiments, which were being raised for the fight against the heretics, and still hear the Spanish troops delivering the first blows on the Lower Rhine, heralding the outbreak of war. Yet he was allowed to close his eyes (February 18, 1546) just before the disaster broke over Germany, which had so long hung over his life like a dark cloud, and which had passed over so many times before that many had ceased to believe in it. If he had lived to see it, it would have deeply troubled his conscience; yet even this would not have cowed him. He gives his own testimony to this in his *Warning to His Dear Germans:*

> If it should come to an outbreak of war, then my God and Lord Jesus Christ can save me and my people, just as He saved Lot at Sodom and as He saved me in the last revolt when I was more than once in the greatest danger of my body and life. And if He does not wish to save me, then let us give Him praise and thanks. I have lived long enough and well deserve death, beginning at my baptism honestly to avenge my Lord Christ. After my death they will all feel the true Luther for the first time just as if I were now to be murdered in an uprising of the Baptists or the priests. Then I will take a whole crowd of bishops, priests, and monks with me so they can say that Doctor Martin was brought to the grave by a great procession; for he is a great doctor above all bishops, priests, and monks, and so they shall go with him to the grave so that men will sing and tell of it. And if they, the papists, should feel like making a little pilgrimage together to their God of lies and murder in hell, whom they serve with their lies and murders, then I will go to my Lord Jesus Christ, whom I have served in truth and peace.

FRIEDRICH ENGELS

The Marxist Interpretation of Luther

THE MIDDLE AGES HAD DEVELOPED altogether from the raw. They wiped the old civilization, the old philosophy, politics, and jurisprudence off the slate, to begin anew in everything. The only thing they kept from the shattered old world was Christianity and a number of half-ruined towns divested of all civilization. As a consequence, the clergy obtained a monopoly on intellectual education, just as in every primitive stage of development, and education itself became essentially theological. In the hands of the clergy, politics and jurisprudence, much like all other sciences, remained mere branches of theology and were treated in accordance with the principles prevailing in the latter. Church dogmas were also political axioms, and biblical quotations had the

From Friedrich Engels, *The Peasant War in Germany*, translated and edited by Vic Schneierson (Moscow: Progress Publishers, 1965), second revised edition, pages 41–52.

validity of law in any court. Even as a special estate of jurists was taking shape, jurisprudence long remained under the patronage of theology. This domination of theology over the entire realm of intellectual activity was at the same time an inevitable consequence of the fact that the church was the all-embracing synthesis and the most general sanction of the existing feudal domination.

It is clear that under the circumstances all the generally voiced attacks against feudalism, above all the attacks against the church, and all revolutionary social and political doctrines had mostly and simultaneously to be theological heresies. The existing social relations had to be stripped of their halo of sanctity before they could be attacked.

The revolutionary opposition to feudalism was alive all down the Middle Ages. It took the shape of mysticism, open heresy, or armed insurrection, all depending on the conditions of the time. As for mysticism, it is well known how much sixteenth-century reformers depended on it. Müntzer himself was largely indebted to it. The heresies gave expression partly to the reaction of the patriarchal Alpine shepherds against the feudalism advancing upon them (Waldenses), partly to the opposition of the towns that had outgrown feudalism (the Albigenses, Arnold of Brescia, etc.), and partly to direct peasant insurrections (John Ball and, among others, the Hungarian teacher[1] in Picardy). We can here leave aside the patriarchal heresy of the Waldenses and the Swiss insurrection, which was in form and content a reactionary, purely local attempt at stemming the tide of history. In the other two forms of medieval heresy we find the twelfth-century precursors of the great antithesis between the burgher and peasant-plebeian oppositions, which caused the defeat of the Peasants' War. This antithesis is evident all down the later Middle Ages.

The town heresies—and those are the actual official heresies of the Middle Ages—were turned primarily against the clergy, whose wealth and political importance they attacked. Just as the present-day bourgeoisie demands a *gouvernement à bon marché* (cheap government), the medieval burghers chiefly demanded an *église à bon marché* (cheap church). Reactionary in form, like any heresy

1. One of the leaders of the peasant revolt in France in 1251 ("Shepherds'" revolt). [Schneierson]

that sees only degeneration in the further development of church and dogma, the burgher heresy demanded the revival of the simple early Christian church constitution and abolition of exclusive priesthood. This cheap arrangement would eliminate monks, prelates, and the Roman court; in short, all the expensive element of the church. The towns, which were republics by their own rights, albeit under the protection of monarchs, first enunciated in general terms through their attacks upon the papacy that a republic was the normal form of bourgeois rule. Their hostility to some of the dogmas and church laws is explained partly by the foregoing and partly by their living conditions. Their bitter opposition to celibacy, for instance, has never been better explained than by Boccaccio. Arnold of Brescia in Italy and Germany, the Albigenses in southern France, John Wycliffe in England, and Huss and the Calixtines in Bohemia were the principal exponents of this trend. The towns were then already a recognized Estate sufficiently capable of fighting lay feudalism and its privileges either by force of arms or in the Estate assemblies. This explains quite simply why the opposition to feudalism appeared only as opposition to *religious* feudalism.

We also find in southern France and in England and Bohemia that most of the lesser nobility joined the towns in their struggle against the clergy and in their heresies—which is explained by the dependence of the lesser nobility on the towns, and by their common interests as opposed to the princes and prelates. We shall encounter the same thing in the Peasants' War.

The heresy that lent direct expression to peasant and plebeian demands and was almost invariably associated with an insurrection was of a totally different nature. Though it had all the demands of burgher heresy with regard to the clergy, the papacy, and the revival of the early Christian church constitution, it went infinitely further. It demanded the restoration of early Christian equality among members of the community and recognition of this equality also as a prescript for the burgher world. It invoked the "equality of the children of God" to infer civil equality, and partly even equality of property. Equality of nobleman and peasant, of patrician and privileged burgher and the plebeian, abolition of compulsory labor, quitrents, taxes, privileges, and at least the most crying differences in property—those were demands advanced with more or less determination as natural implications of the early Christian doctrine. At the time when feudalism was at its zenith, there was little to choose between this peasant-plebeian heresy of the Albigenses, for example, and the burgher opposition, but in the fourteenth and fifteenth centuries it developed into a clearly defined party opinion and usually took an independent stand alongside the heresy of the burghers. This was the relation of John Ball, preacher of Wat Tyler's rebellion in England, to the Wycliffe movement, and of the Taborites to the Calixtines in Bohemia. The Taborites even showed republican under a theocratic cloak, a view further developed by the plebeians in Germany in the fifteenth and early sixteenth century.

The fanaticism of mystically minded sects, the Flagellants and Lollards, etc., which continued the revolutionary tradition in times of suppression, seized upon this form of heresy.

At that time the plebeians were the only class that stood outside the existing official society. They had no access to either the feudal or the burgher association. They had neither privileges nor property; they did not even have the kind of property the peasant or petty burgher had, which was heavily burdened with taxes. They were unpropertied and rightless in every respect; their living conditions never even brought them into direct contact with the existing institutions, which ignored them completely. They were a living symptom of the decay of the feudal and guild-burgher society, and at the same time the first precursors of the modern bourgeois society.

This explains why the plebeian opposition even then could not stop at fighting only feudalism and the privileged burghers; why, in fantasy at least, it reached beyond the then scarcely dawning modern bourgeois society; why, an absolutely propertyless faction, it questioned the institutions, views, and conceptions common to all societies based on class antagonisms. In this respect, the chiliastic dream-visions of early Christianity offered a very convenient starting point. On the other hand, this sally beyond both the present and even the future could be nothing but violent and fantastic, and of necessity fell back within the narrow limits set by the contemporary situation at the very first practical application of it. The attack on private property and demand for common ownership was bound to resolve into a primitive organization of charity; vague Christian equality could at best resolve into civic "equality before the law" and elimination of all authority would finally culminate in the establishment of republican governments elected by the people. The anticipation of communism, nurtured by the imagination, became in reality an anticipation of modern bourgeois conditions.

This violent anticipation of coming historical developments, easily explained by the living conditions of the plebeians, is first recorded in Germany, with Thomas Müntzer and his party. The Taborites had a kind of chiliastic common ownership, but that was a purely military measure. Only in the teachings of Müntzer did these communist notions express the aspirations of a real fraction of society. He formulated them with a certain definiteness, and they were subsequently observed in every great popular upheaval, until they gradually merged with the modern proletarian movement. It was comparable to the struggles of free peasants in the Middle Ages against increasing feudal domination, which eventually merged with the struggles of serfs and bondsmen for a complete abolition of the feudal system.

While the first of the three large camps, the *conservative Catholic,* embraced all the elements interested in maintaining the existing conditions, i.e., the imperial authorities, the ecclesiastical and a section of the lay princes, the richer nobility, the prelates, and the city patricians, the camp of *Lutheran* reforms, *moderate in the burgher manner,* attracted all the propertied elements of the opposition, the bulk of the lesser nobility, the burghers, and even a portion of the lay princes who hoped to enrich themselves through confiscation of church estates and wanted to seize the opportunity of gaining greater independence from the empire. As to the peasants and plebeians, they formed a *revolutionary* party, whose demands and doctrines were most clearly set out by Müntzer.

Luther and Müntzer each fully represented his party by his doctrine, as well as by his character and actions.

From 1517 to 1525 Luther changed just as much as the present-day German constitutionalists did between 1846 and 1849; and as

every bourgeois party placed for a time at the head of the movement is overwhelmed by the plebeian-proletarian party standing
behind it, so was Luther's.

When in 1517 Luther first opposed the dogmas and statutes of
the Catholic Church his opposition was by no means of a definite
character. Although it did not overstep the demands of the earlier
burgher heresy, it did not, and could not, rule out any trend that
went further. At that early stage all the opposition elements had
to be united, the most resolute revolutionary energy displayed, and
the sum of the existing heresies against the Catholic orthodoxy had
to find a protagonist. In much the same way our liberal bourgeoisie
of 1847 was still revolutionary, called itself socialist and communist,
and clamored for the emancipation of the working class, Luther's
sturdy peasant nature asserted itself in the stormiest fashion in
that first period of his activities. "If the raging madness [of the
Roman churchmen] were to continue, it seems to me no better
counsel and remedy could be found against it than that kings and
princes apply force, arm themselves, attack those evil people who
have poisoned the entire world, and put an end to this game once
and for all, *with arms, not with words.* Since we punish thieves
with the halter, murderers with the sword, and heretics with fire,
why do we not turn on all those evil teachers of perdition, those
popes, cardinals, and bishops, and the entire swarm of the Roman
Sodom *with arms in hand, and wash our hands in their blood?*"

But this revolutionary ardor was short-lived. Luther's lightning
struck home. The entire German people was set in motion. On
the one hand, peasants and plebeians saw the signal to revolt in
his appeals against the clergy and in his sermon of Christian freedom; on the other, he was joined by the moderate burghers and
a large section of the lesser nobility. Even princes were drawn into
the maelstrom. The former believed the day had come to wreak
vengeance upon all their oppressors, the latter only wished to
break the power of the clergy, the dependence upon Rome, to
abolish the Catholic hierarchy, and to enrich themselves on the
confiscation of church property. The parties stood aloof of each
other, and each had its spokesmen. Luther had to choose between
them. He, the protégé of the elector of Saxony, the revered professor of Wittenberg who had become powerful and famous over-

night, the great man with his coterie of servile creatures and flatterers, did not hesitate for a single moment. He dropped the popular elements of the movement and took the side of the burghers, the nobility, and the princes. His appeals for a war of extermination against Rome resounded no more. Luther now preached *peaceful progress* and *passive resistance* (cf., for example, *Address to the Christian Nobility of the German Nation*, 1520, etc.). Invited by Hutten to visit him and Sickingen in the castle of Ebern, where the nobility conspired against the clergy and the princes, Luther replied: "I do not wish the gospel *defended by force and bloodshed*. The world was conquered by the Word, the church is maintained by the Word, the Word will also put the church back into its own, and Antichrist, who gained his own without violence, will fall without violence."

From this tendency, or, to be more exact, from this more definite delineation of Luther's policy, sprang that bartering and haggling over institutions and dogmas to be retained or reformed, that disgusting diplomatizing, conciliating, intriguing, and compromising, which resulted in the Augsburg Confession, the finally importuned articles of a reformed burgher church. It was quite the same kind of petty bargaining as was recently repeated in political form *ad nauseam* at the German national assemblies, conciliatory gatherings, chambers of revision, and Erfurt parliaments. The Philistine nature of the official Reformation was most distinctly evident at these negotiations.

There were good reasons for Luther, henceforth the recognized representative of the burgher reform, to preach lawful progress. The bulk of the towns espoused the cause of moderate reform, the petty nobility became more and more devoted to it, and a section of the princes joined in, while another vacillated. Success was as good as won, at least in a large part of Germany. The remaining regions could not in the long run withstand the pressure of moderate opposition in the event of continued peaceful development. Any violent upheaval, meanwhile, was bound to bring the moderate party into conflict with the extremist plebeian and peasant party, to alienate the princes, the nobility, and many towns from the movement, leaving the alternative of either the burgher party being overshadowed by the peasants and plebeians or the

entire movement being crushed by Catholic restoration. There
have been examples enough lately of how bourgeois parties, after
gaining the slightest victory, seek to steer their way by means of
lawful progress between the Scylla of revolution and the Charybdis
of restoration.

Under the general social and political conditions prevailing at
that time the results of every change were necessarily advantageous
to the princes and inevitably increased their power. Thus it came
about that the more completely the burgher reform fell under the
control of the reformed princes, the more sharply it broke away
from the plebeian and peasant elements. Luther himself became
more and more their vassal, and the people knew perfectly well
what they were doing when they accused him of having become,
as the others, a flunky of the princes, and when they stoned him
in Orlamünde.

When the Peasants' War broke out, Luther tried to strike a
mediatory pose in regions where the nobility and the princes were
mostly Catholic. He resolutely attacked the authorities. He said
they were to blame for the rebellion in view of their oppression;
it was not the peasants, but God himself, who rose against them.
Yet, on the other hand, he said, the revolt was ungodly and contrary to the gospel. In conclusion, he called upon both parties to
yield and reach a peaceful understanding.

But in spite of these well-meaning mediatory offers, the revolt
spread swiftly and even involved Protestant regions dominated by
Lutheran princes, lords, and towns, rapidly outgrowing the "cir-
cumspect" burgher reform. The most determined faction of the
insurgents under Müntzer made its headquarters in Luther's immediate proximity at Thuringia. A few more successes and the
whole of Germany would be in flames, Luther surrounded and
perhaps piked as a traitor, and the burgher reform swept away by
the tide of a peasant-plebeian revolution. There was no more time
for circumspection. All the old animosities were forgotten in the
face of the revolution. Compared with the hordes of peasants, the
servants of the Roman Sodom were innocent lambs, sweet-tem-
pered children of God. Burgher and prince, noble and clergyman,
Luther and the pope, all joined hands "against the murderous and
plundering peasant hordes." "They must be *knocked to pieces,*

strangled and *stabbed, covertly* and *overtly,* by everyone who can, just as one must kill a *mad dog!*" Luther cried. "Therefore, dear sirs, help here, save there, stab, knock, strangle them everyone who can, and should you lose your life, bless you, no better death can you ever attain." There should be no false mercy for the peasant. Whoever hath pity on those whom God pities not, whom He wishes punished and destroyed, belongs among the rebels himself. Later the peasants would learn to thank God when they would have to give up one cow in order to enjoy the other in peace, and the princes would learn through the revolution the spirit of the mob that must be ruled by force only. "The wise man says: *cibus, onus et virga asino.*[2] The peasants must have nothing but chaff. They do not hearken to the Word, and are foolish, so they must hearken to the rod and the gun, and that serves them right. We must pray for them that they obey. Where they do not there should not be much mercy. *Let the guns roar among them,* or else they will do it a thousand times worse."

That was exactly what our late socialist and philanthropic bourgeoisie said when the proletariat claimed its share of the fruits of victory after the March events.[3]

Luther had put a powerful weapon into the hands of the plebeian movement by translating the Bible. Through the Bible he contrasted the feudalized Christianity of his day with the moderate Christianity of the first centuries, and the decaying feudal society with a picture of a society that knew nothing of the ramified and artificial feudal hierarchy. The peasants had made extensive use of this instrument against the princes, the nobility, and the clergy. Now Luther turned it against the peasants, extracting from the Bible such a veritable hymn to the God-ordained authorities as no bootlicker of absolute monarchy had ever been able to extract. Princedom by the grace of God, resigned obedience, even serfdom, were sanctioned with the aid of the Bible. Not the peasant revolt alone, but Luther's own mutiny against religious and lay authority was thereby disavowed; not only the popular movement, but the burgher movement as well, were betrayed to the princes.

2. "Food, pack, and lash to the ass."
3. The revolution of March 1848 in Germany and Austria. [ed.]

ERIK H. ERIKSON

The Search for Identity

RATHER DRAMATIC EVIDENCE EXISTS in Luther's notes on these lectures [on the Psalms] for the fact that while he was working on the Psalms Luther came to formulate those insights later ascribed to his revelation in the tower, the date of which scholars have tried in vain to establish with certainty. As Luther was reviewing in his mind Romans 1:17, the last sentence suddenly assumed a clarity which pervaded his whole being and "opened the door of paradise" to him: "For therein is the righteousness of God revealed from faith to faith: as it is written, *The just shall live by faith*." The power of these words lay in a new perception of the space-time of life and eternity. Luther saw that God's justice is not consigned to a

From Erik H. Erikson, *Young Man Luther*. Copyright © 1958, 1962 by Erik H. Erikson. Reprinted with permission of W. W. Norton & Company, Inc., and Faber and Faber, Ltd., pages 201–18.

future day of judgment based on our record on earth when He will have the "last word." Instead, this justice is in us, in the here and now; for, if we will only perceive it, God has given us faith to live by, and we can perceive it by understanding the Word which is Christ. We will discuss later the circumstances leading to this perception; what interests us first of all is its relation to the lectures on the Psalms.

In a remarkable study published in 1929, Erich Vogelsang demonstrated that the insights previously attributed exclusively to Luther's revelation in the tower, and often ascribed to a much later time, appear fully and dramatically early in these lectures.[1] Whether this means, as Vogelsang claims, that the revelation really "took place" while Luther was occupied with the lectures, that is, late in the year 1513, is a theological controversy in which I will not become involved. My main interest is in the fact that at about the age of thirty—an important age for gifted people with a delayed identity crisis—the wholeness of Luther's theology first emerges from the fragments of his totalistic reevaluations.

Vogelsang's study is remarkable because he weeds out of Luther's text statements which are, in fact, literal quotations from older scholars; Vogelsang thus uncovers the real course and crescendo of Luther's original remarks. Moreover, he studies usually neglected dimensions of the original text, dimensions which are not visible in the monumental Weimar Edition. For instance, there is the "archaeological" dimension—the layers of thought to be seen in the preparatory notes for the lectures, in the transcripts of the lectures, and in later additions written or pasted into the text. Vogelsang studied the kinds of paper and ink used, noted variations in handwriting, and analyzed the fluctuating personal importance attached by Luther himself to various parts of his notes, indicated by underscorings and by marginal marks of self-applause. Vogelsang discovered the path of a spiritual cyclone which cut right through the texts of the lectures on the Psalms: "When Luther, in the *Psalmenkolleg,* faces the task of offering his listeners an *ex professo* interpretation of the passage *in justitia tua libera me* [and deliver me in thy righteousness], this task

1. E. Vogelsang, *Die Anfänge von Luthers Christologie* (Berlin: De Gruyter Co., 1929). [ed.]

confronts him with a quite personal decision, affects him like a clap of thunder, and awakes in him one of the severest temptations, to which he later could think back only with trembling for the duration of his life." [2]

This much was acknowledged by old Luther: "When I first read and sang in the Psalms," he said, "*in iustitia tua libera me,* I was horror-stricken and felt deep hostility toward these words, God's righteousness, God's judgment, God's work. For I knew only that *iustitia dei* meant a harsh judgment. Well, was He supposed to save me by judging me harshly? If so, I was lost forever. But *gottlob,* when I then understood the matter and knew that *iustitia dei* meant the righteousness by which He justifies us through the free gift of Christ's justice, then I understood the *grammatica,* and I truly tasted the Psalms." [3]

Vogelsang finds interesting bibliographical and graphological evidence of Luther's struggle. "In the whole *Dresdener Psalter,*" he writes, "there is no page which bears such direct witness to personal despair as does the *Scholie* to Psalm 30:1 [Psalm 31 in the King James Version]. He who has trained his ear in steady dealings with these lectures here perceives a violence and passion of language scarcely found anywhere else. The decisive words, *in justitia tua libera me,* Luther jumps over in terror and anxiety, which closes his ear to the singularly reassuring passage, 'Into thine hand, I commit my spirit' [Psalm 31:5, King James Version]." [4] . . . Vogelsang continues: "He immediately proceeds with 'Have mercy upon me, O Lord,' [the handwriting here is extremely excited and confused; he adds a great number of underscorings] and prays with trembling conscience in the words of the sixth Psalm [Psalm 7, King James Version]—'*Ex intuitu irae dei.*' And even as the text of the thirty-first Psalm is about to call him out of his temptation with the words '*in te speravi Domine*' ['But I trusted in Thee, O Lord'], he deflects the discussion only more violently back to the words of the sixth Psalm." [5]

Although Vogelsang does not make a point of it, it cannot es-

2. *Ibid.,* p. 32.
3. Tr., V, No. 5247.
4. Vogelsang, pp. 32–33.
5. *Ibid.,* p. 33.

cape us that these psalms are expressions of David's accusations against his and (so he likes to conclude) the Lord's enemies; in them David vacillates between wishing the wrath of God and the mercy of God upon the heads of his enemies. There are other passages in Psalm 31 which Luther ignores besides those which Vogelsang mentioned: "Pull me out of the net that they had laid privily for me: for thou art my strength";[6] and "I have hated them that regard lying vanities: but I trust in the Lord." [7] Luther probably had enemies at the time in Erfurt. But there was an adversary who, "regarding lying vanities," had "privily laid a net" for Martin; had not his father, thwarted in his vain plans for his son, put a curse on his son's spiritual life, predicted his temptations, predicted, in fact, his coming rebellion? In Martin's struggle for justification, involving the emancipation of his obsessive conscience from his jealous father and the liberation of his thought from medieval theology, this new insight into God's pervading justice could not, psychologically speaking, be experienced as a true revelatory solution without some disposition of his smoldering hate. We will come back to this point when we discuss Luther's identification with Christ; for the Psalmist's complaint about his enemies reminds us of the social setting of Christ's passion. He, too, was mockingly challenged to prove his sonhood of God: "He trusted in God; let him deliver him now, if he will have him: for he said, I am the Son of God." [8]

When the lectures on the Psalms reached Psalm 71:2, Luther again faced the phrase "Deliver me in thy righteousness," again preceded (Psalm 70) by "Let them be turned back for a reward of their shame that say, Aha, aha." But now his mood, his outlook, and his vocabulary had undergone a radical change.[9] He twice quotes Romans 1:17 (the text of his revelation in the tower) and concludes *"Justitia dei . . . est fides Christi"* ("Christ's faith is God's righteousness"). This is followed by what Vogelsang calls a dithyrambic sequence of new and basically "Protestant" formulations, a selection of which we will review presently. These for-

---

6. Psalms 31:4.
7. *Ibid.,* 31:6.
8. Matthew 27:43.
9. Vogelsang, pp. 50–51.

mulations center in Luther's final acceptance of Christ's mediatorship, and a new concept of man's sonhood of God.

This was the breakthrough. In these lectures, and only in these,
Luther quotes St. Augustine's account of his own awakening four
times: in the very first lecture; in connection with the dramatic
disruption caused by Psalm 31; and twice in connection with
Psalm 71.

It seems entirely probable, then, that the revelation in the tower
occurred sometime during Luther's work on these lectures. Alter-
natively, instead of one revelation, there may have been a series
of crises, the first perhaps traceable in this manuscript on the
Psalms, the last fixed in Luther's memory at that finite event
which scholars have found so difficult to locate in time.

The finite event seems to be associated in Luther's mind with
a preceding period of deep depression, during which he again
foresaw an early death. The reported episode has been viewed
with prejudice because of its *place* of occurrence. Luther refers to
a *"Secretus locus monachorum," "hypocaustum,"* or *"cloaca,"* that
is, the monks' secret place, the sweat chamber, or the toilet. According to Scheel, this list originates from one transcript of a
Table Talk of 1532, when Luther is reported to have said *"Dise
Kunst hatt mir der Spiritus Sanctus auff diss Cl. eingeben"* ("The
holy spirit endowed me with this art on the Cl.").[10] Rörer, whom
the very critical Scheel considers the most reliable of the original
reporters, transcribes Cl. as cloaca. Nevertheless, Scheel dismisses
this interpretation; and indeed, no other reported statement of
Luther's has made mature men squirm more uncomfortably, or
made serious scholars turn their noses higher in contemptuous
disbelief. . . .

This whole geographic issue, however, deserves special mention
exactly because it *does* point up certain psychiatric relevances. First
of all, the locality mentioned serves a particular physical need
which hides its emotional relevance only as long as it happens to
function smoothly. Yet Luther suffered from lifelong constipa-
tion and urine retention. Leaving the possible physical causes or
consequences of this tendency aside, the functions themselves are

10. Otto Scheel, *Dokumente zu Luthers Entwicklung* (Tübingen, J. C. B.
Mohr, 1929), No. 238.

related to the organ modes of retention and elimination—i
fiant children most obviously, and in adults through all man
ambivalent behavior. There can be little doubt that at this particular time, when Martin's power of speech was freed from its
infantile and juvenile captivity, he changed from a highly restrained and retentive individual into an explosive person; he had
found an unexpected release of self-expression, and with it, of the
many-sided power of his personality.

Those who object to these possibly impure circumstances of
Martin's spiritual revelation forget St. Paul's epileptic attack, a
physical paroxysm often accompanied by a loss of sphincter control, and deny the total involvement of body and soul which
makes an emotional and spiritual experience genuine. Scholars
would prefer to have it happen as they achieve their own reflected
revelations—sitting at a desk. Luther's statement that he was, in
fact, sitting somewhere else, implies that in this creative moment
the tension of nights and days of meditation found release throughout his being—and nobody who has read Luther's private remarks
can doubt that his total being always included his bowels. Furthermore, people in those days expressed much more openly and
conceptualized more concretely than we do the emotional implications (and the implication in our emotions) of the primary
bodily functions. We permit ourselves to understand them in a
burlesque show, or in circumstances where we can laugh off our
discomfort; but we are embarrassed when we are asked to acknowledge them in earnest. Then we prefer to speak of them
haughtily, as though they were something we have long left behind. But here the suppressed meaning betrays itself in the irra-
tional defensiveness; for what we leave behind, with emotional
repudiation, is at least unconsciously associated with dirt and
feces. St. Paul openly counted all the glittering things which he
had abandoned for Christ "but dung."

A revelation, that is, a sudden inner flooding with light, is
always associated with a repudiation, a cleansing, a kicking away;
and it would be entirely in accord with Luther's great freedom
in such matters if he were to experience and to report this repudiation in frankly physical terms. The cloaca, at the "other end" of
the bodily self, remained for him sometimes wittily, sometimes

painfully, and sometimes delusionally alive, as if it were a "dirt ground" where one meets with the Devil, just as one meets with God in the *Seelengrund,* where pure being is created.

The psychiatric relevance of all this is heightened by the fact that in later years, when Luther's freedom of speech occasionally deteriorated into vulgar license, he went far beyond the customary gay crudity of his early days. In melancholy moods, he expressed his depressive self-repudiation also in anal terms: "I am like ripe shit," he said once at the dinner table during a fit of depression (and the boys eagerly wrote it down), "and the world is a gigantic ass-hole. We probably will let go of each other soon." [11] We have no right to overlook a fact which Luther was far from denying: that when he, who had once chosen silence in order to restrain his rebellious and destructive nature, finally learned to let himself go, he freed not only the greatest oratory of his time, but also the most towering temper and the greatest capacity for dirt-slinging wrath.

The problem is not how extraordinary or how pathological all this is, but whether or not we can have one Luther without the other. We will return to this question in conclusion. In the meantime, what we know of Martin's autocratic conscience, and what we begin to know of his tempestuous temperament, will stand us in good stead as we see the lecturer find his balance and his identity in the act of lecturing, and with them, some new formulations of man's relation to God and to himself.

In what follows, themes from Luther's first lectures are discussed side by side with psychoanalytic insights. Theological readers will wonder whether Luther saved theology from philosophy only to have it exploited by psychology; while psychoanalysts may suspect me of trying to make space for a Lutheran God in the structure of the psyche. My purposes, however, are more modest: I intend to demonstrate that Luther's redefinition of man's condition—while part and parcel of his theology—has striking configurational parallels with inner dynamic shifts like those which clinicians recognize in the recovery of individuals from psychic

11. Tr., V, No. 5537.

distress. In brief, I will try to indicate that Luther, in laying foundation for a "religiosity for the adult man," displayed the attributes of his own hard-won adulthood; his renaissance of faith portrays a vigorous recovery of his own ego-initiative. To indicate this I will focus on three ideas: the affirmation of voice and word as the instruments of faith; the new recognition of God's "face" in the passion of Christ; and the redefinition of a just life.

After 1505 Luther had made no bones about the pernicious influence that "rancid Aristotelianism" had had on theology. Scholasticism had made him lose faith, he said; through St. Paul he had recovered it. He put the problem in terms of organ modes, by describing Scholastic disputations as *"dentes"* and *"linguae"*: the teeth are hard and sinister, and form words in anger and fury; the tongue is soft and suavely persuasive. Using these modes, the Devil can evoke purely intellectual mirages (*mira potest suggere in intellectu*).[12] But the organ through which the word enters to replenish the heart is the ear (*natura enim verbi est audiri*),[13] for it is in the nature of the word that it should be heard. On the other hand, faith comes from listening, not from looking (*quia est auditu fides, non ex visu*).[14] Therefore, the greatest thing one can say about Christ, and about all Christians, is that they have *aures perfectas et perfossas:*[15] good and open ears. But only what is perceived at the same time as a matter *affectionalis* and *moralis* as well as intellectual can be a matter sacred and divine: one must, therefore, hear before one sees, believe before one understands, be captivated before one captures. *Fides est locus animae* (faith is the seat, the organ of the soul).[16] This had certainly been said before; but Luther's emphasis is not on Augustinian "infusion," or on a nominalist "obedience," but, in a truly Renaissance approach, on a self-verification through a God-given inner "apparatus." This *locus,* this apparatus, has its own way of seeking and searching—and it succeeds insofar as it develops its own *passivity.*

12. L.W.W.A., 3, 408.
13. *Ibid.*, 4, 9.18.
14. *Ibid.*, 3, 227.28.
15. *Ibid.*, 2, 28.13.
16. *Ibid.*, 3, 651.

Paradoxically, many a young man (and son of a stubborn one) becomes a great man in his own sphere only by learning that deep passivity which permits him to let the data of his competency speak to him. As Freud said in a letter to Fliess, "I must wait until it moves in me so that I can perceive it" (*"bis es sich in mir ruehrt und ich davon erfahre"*).[17] This may sound feminine, and, indeed, Luther bluntly spoke of an attitude of womanly conception—*"sicut mulier in conceptu."* [18] Yet it is clear that men call such attitudes and modes feminine only because the strain of paternalism has alienated us from them; for these modes are any organism's birthright, and all our partial as well as our total functioning is based on a metabolism of passivity and activity. Mannish man always wants to pretend that he made himself, or at any rate, that no simple woman bore him, and many puberty rites (consider the rebirth from a kiva in the American Southwest) dramatize a new birth from a spiritual mother of a kind that only men understand.

The theology as well as the psychology of Luther's passivity is that of man in the *state of prayer,* a state in which he fully means what he can say only to God: *Tibi soli peccavi,* I have sinned, not in relation to any person or institution, but in relation only to God, to *my* God.

In two ways, then, rebirth by prayer is passive: it means surrender to God the Father; but it also means to be reborn *ex matrice scripturae nati*[19] (out of the matrix of the scriptures). "Matrix" is as close as such a man's man will come to saying *"mater."* But he cannot remember and will not acknowledge that long before he had developed those willful modes that were specifically suppressed and paradoxically aggravated by a challenging father, a mother had taught him to touch the world with his searching mouth and his probing senses. What to a man's man, in the course of his development, seems like a passivity hard to acquire, is only a regained ability to be active with his oldest and most neglected modes. Is it coincidence that Luther, now that he

17. Sigmund Freud, *The Origins of Psychoanalysis* (London: Imago Publishing Co., 1954), p. 236.
18. Johannes Ficker, ed., *Luthers Vorlesung über den Römerbrief* (Leipzig: Die Scholien, 1930), p. 206.
19. L.W.W.A., 4, 234.

was explicitly teaching passivity, should come to the conclusion that a lecturer should feed his audience as a mother suckles her child? Intrinsic to the kind of passivity we speak of is not only the memory of having been given, but also the identification with the maternal giver: "the glory of a good thing is that it flows out to others."[20] I think that in the Bible Luther at last found a mother whom he could acknowledge: he could attribute to the Bible a generosity to which he could open himself, and which he could pass on to others, at last a mother's son.

Luther did use the words *"passiva"* and *"passivus"* when he spoke Latin, and the translation *passive* must be accepted as correct. But in German he often used the word *"passivisch,"* which is more actively passive, as passific would be. I think that the difference between the old modalities of *passive* and *active* is really that between *erleben* and *handeln,* of being in the state of *experiencing* or of *acting*. Meaningful implications are lost in the flat word *"passivity"*—among them the total attitude of living receptively and through the senses, of willingly "suffering" the voice of one's intuition and of living a *Passion:* that total passivity in which man regains, through considered self-sacrifice and self-transcendence, his active position in the face of nothingness, and thus is saved. Could this be one of the psychological riddles in the wisdom of the "foolishness of the cross"?

To Luther, the preaching and the praying man, the measure in depth of the perceived presence of the Word was the reaction with a total affect which leaves no doubt that one "means it." It may seem paradoxical to speak of an affect that one could not thus mean; yet it is obvious that rituals, observances, and performances do evoke transitory affects, which can be put on for the occasion and afterward hung in the closet with one's Sunday clothes. Man is able to ceremonialize, as he can "automatize" psychologically, the signs and behaviors that are born of the deepest reverence or despair. However, for an affect to have a deep and lasting effect, or, as Luther would say, be *affectionalis* and *moralis,* it must not only be experienced as nearly overwhelming, but it must also in some way be affirmed by the ego as valid, almost as chosen: one means the affect, it signifies something meaningful, it is signifi-

20. *Ibid.,* 5, 149.

cant. Such is the relative nature of our ego and of our conscience that when the ego regains its composure after the auditory condemnation of the absolutist voice of conscience we mean what we have learned to believe, and our affects become those of positive conscience: faith, conviction, authority, indignation—all subjective states that are attributes of a strong sense of identity and, incidentally, are indispensable tools for strengthening identity in others. Luther speaks of matters of faith as experiences from which one will profit to the degree to which they were intensive and expressive. . . . If they are more *frigidus,* however, they are not merely a profit missed, they are a terrible deficit confirmed: for man without intense convictions is a robot with destructive techniques.

It is easy to see that these formulations, once revolutionary, are the commonplaces of today's pulpits. They are the bases of that most inflated of all oratorical currency, credal protestation in church and lecture hall, in political propaganda, and in oral advertisement: the protestation, made to order for the occasion, that truth is only that which one means with one's whole being, and lives every moment. . . .

Meaning it . . . is not a matter of credal protestation; verbal explicitness is not a sign of faith. Meaning it, means to be at one with an ideology in the process of rejuvenation; it implies a successful sublimation of one's libidinal strivings; and it manifests itself in a liberated craftsmanship.

When Luther listened to the Scriptures he did not do so with an unprejudiced ear. His method of making an unprejudiced approach consisted of listening both ways—to the Word coming from the book and to the echo in himself. "Whatever is in your disposition," he said, "that the word of God will be unto you." [21] Disposition here means the inner configuration of your most meant meanings. He knew that he meant it when he could say it: the spoken Word was the activity appropriate for his kind of passivity. Here "faith and Word become one, an invincible whole." [22] . . .

Twenty-five times in the Lectures on the Psalms, against once

21. *Ibid.,* 4, 511.
22. *Ibid.,* 9, 639.

in the Lectures on the Romans, Luther quotes two corresponding passages from Paul's first Epistle to the Corinthians. The first passage:

> 22. For the Jews require a sign, and the Greeks seek after wisdom;
>
> 23. But we preach Christ crucified, unto the Jews a stumbling-block, and unto the Greeks foolishness;
>
> 25. Because the foolishness of God is wiser than men; and the weakness of God is stronger than men.[23]

This paradoxical foolishness and weakness of God became a theological absolute for Luther: there is not a word in the Bible, he exclaimed, which is *extra crucem,* which can be understood without reference to the cross; and this is all that shall and can be understood, as Paul had said in the other passage:

> 1. And I, brethren, when I came to you, came not with excellency of speech or of wisdom, declaring unto you the testimony of God.
>
> 2. For I determined not to know any thing among you, save Jesus Christ, and him crucified.
>
> 3. And I was with you in weakness, and in fear, and in much trembling.[24]

Thus Luther abandoned any theological quibbling about the cross. He did not share St. Augustine's opinion that when Christ on the cross exclaimed *"Deus meus, quare me derelequisti,"* He had not been really abandoned, for as God's son and as God's Word, He *was* God. Luther could not help feeling that St. Paul came closer to the truth when he assumed an existential paradox rather than a platonic fusion of essences; he insists on Christ's complete sense of abandonment and on his sincere and active pre-meditation in visiting hell. Luther spoke here in passionate terms very different from those of medieval adoration. He spoke of a man who was unique in all creation, yet lives in each man; and who is dying *in* everyone even as he died *for* everyone. It is clear that Luther rejected all arrangements by which an assortment of saints made it unnecessary for man to embrace the maximum of his own existential suffering. What he had tried, so desperately

23. I Cor. 1:22–25.
24. *Ibid.,* 2:1–3.

and for so long, to counteract and overcome he now accepted as his divine gift—the sense of utter abandonment, *sicut jam damnatus,*[25] as if already in hell. The worst temptation, he now says, is not to have any; one can be sure that God is most angry when He does not seem angry at all. Luther warns of all those well-meaning . . . religionists who encourage man "to do what he can": to forestall sinning by clever planning; to seek redemption by observing all occasions for rituals, not forgetting to bring cash along to the limit of their means; and to be secure in the feeling that they are as humble and as peaceful as "it is in them to be." Luther, instead, made a virtue out of what his superiors had considered a vice in him (and we, a symptom), namely, the determined search for the rock bottom of his sinfulness: only thus, he says, can man judge himself as God would: *conformis deo est et verax et justus.*[26] One could consider such conformity utter passivity in the face of God's judgment; but note that it really is an active self-observation, which scans the frontier of conscience for the genuine sense of guilt. Instead of accepting some impersonal and mechanical absolution, it insists on dealing with sincere guilt, perceiving as "God's judgment" what in fact is the individual's own truly meant self-judgment.

Is all this an aspect of personal adjustment to be interpreted as a set of unconscious tricks? Martin the son, who on a personal level had suffered deeply because he could not coerce his father into approving his religiosity as genuine, and who had borne with him the words of this father with an unduly prolonged filial obedience, assumes now on a religious level a volitional role toward filial suffering, perhaps making out of his protracted sonhood the victory of his Christlikeness. In his first mass, facing the altar—the Father in heaven—and at the same time waiting to face his angry earthly father, Martin had "overlooked" a passage concerning Christ's mediatorship. Yet now, in finding Christ in himself, he establishes an inner position which goes beyond that of a neurotic compromise identification. He finds the core of a praying man's identity, and advances Christian ideology by an important step. It is clear that Luther abandoned the appreci-

25. L.W.W.A., 3, 420.
26. *Ibid.,* 3, 289.

ation of Christ as a substitute who has died "for"—in the sense of
"instead of"—us; he also abandoned the concept of Christ as an
ideal figure to be imitated, or abjectly venerated, or ceremonially
remembered as an event in the past. Christ now becomes the core
of the Christian's identity: *"quotidianus Christi adventus"* [27]
("Christ is today here, in me"). The affirmed passivity of suffering becomes the daily Passion and the Passion is the substitution
of the primitive sacrifice of others with a most active, most
masterly, affirmation of man's nothingness—which, by his own
masterly choice, becomes his existential identity.

The men revered by mankind as saviors face and describe in
lasting words insights which the ordinary man must avoid with
all possible self-deception and exploitation of others. These men
prove their point by the magic of their voices, which radiate to
the farthest corner of their world and out into the millennia.
Their passion contains elements of choice, mastery, and victory,
and sooner or later earns them the name of King of Kings; their
crown of thorns later becomes their successor's tiara. For a little
while Luther, this first revolutionary individualist, saved the Savior
from the tiaras and the ceremonies, the hierarchies and the
thought-police, and put him back where he arose: in each man's
soul.

Is this not the counterpart, on the level of conscience, to Renaissance anthropocentrism? Luther left the heavens to science and
restricted himself to what he could know of his own suffering
and faith, that is, to what he could mean. He who had sought to
dispel the angry cloud that darkened the face of the fathers and of
The Father now said that Christ's life *is* God's face: *"Qui est
facies patris."* [28] The Passion is all that man can know of God;
his conflicts, duly faced, are all that he can know of himself. The
last judgment is the always present self-judgment. Christ did not
live and die in order to make man poorer in the fear of his future
judgment, but in order to make him abundant today: *"Nam
judicia sunt ipsae passiones Christi quae in nobis abundant."* [29]
Look, Luther said at one point in these lectures (IV, 87), how

27. *Ibid.,* 40 (part I), 537.
28. *Ibid.,* 4, 147.
29. *Ibid.,* 4, 330; cf. Vogelsang, p. 103, n.1, and p. 108, n.1.

everywhere painters depict Christ's passion as if they agreed with
St. Paul that we know nothing but Christ crucified.[30] The artist
closest to Luther in spirit was Dürer, who etched his own face
into Christ's countenance.

The characteristics of Luther's theological advance can be compared to certain steps in psychological maturation, which every
man must take: the internalization of the father-son relationship;
the concomitant crystallization of conscience; the safe establishment of an identity as a worker and a man; and the concomitant
reaffirmation of basic trust.

God, instead of lurking on the periphery of space and time,
became for Luther "what works in us." The way *to* Him is
not the effortful striving toward a goal by "doing what you can";
rather, His way is what moves from inside: *"Via dei est, qua nos
ambulare facit."* [31] God, now less of a person, becomes more
personal for the individual; and instead of constituting a threat
to be faced at the end of all things, He becomes that which
always begins—in us. His son is therefore always reborn: *"Ita et
nos semper oportet nasci, novari, generari"* ("It therefore behooves
us to be reborn, renovated, regenerated").[32] To "do enough"
means always to begin: *"Proficere est nihil aliud nisi semper
incipere."* [33] The intersection of all the paradoxes of the vertical
and the horizontal is thus to be found in man's own divided nature. The two *regna,* the realist sphere of divine grace and the
naturalist sphere of animality, exist in man's inner conflicts and
in his existential paradoxes: *"Die zwo Personen oder zweierlei
ampt,"* [34] the two personalities and the two callings which a Christian must maintain at the same time on this earth.

It does not matter what these two personalities "are." Theologians, philosophers, and psychologists slice man in different ways,
and there is no use trying to make the sections coincide. The main
point to be made here is Luther's new emphasis on man in *inner*

30. *Ibid.,* 4, 87.
31. *Ibid.,* 3, 529; cf. Vogelsang, p. 136, n.5.
32. *Ibid.,* 4, 365.
33. *Ibid.,* 4, 350.
34. *Ibid.,* 32, 390.

conflict and his salvation through introspective perfection. Luther's formulation of a God known to individual man only through the symbolism of the Son's Passion redefined the individual's existence in a direction later pursued in both Kierkegaard's existentialism and Freud's psychoanalysis—methods which lead the individual systematically to his own borders, including the border of his religious ecstasies.

Let us rephrase somewhat more psychologically what we have just put in theological terms. What we have referred to as the negative conscience corresponds in many ways to Freud's conceptualization of the pressure put by the superego on the ego. If this pressure is dominant in an individual or in a group, the whole quality of experience is overshadowed by a particular sense of existence, an intensification of certain aspects of subjective space and time. Any fleeting moment of really bad conscience can teach us this, as can also, and more impressively, a spell of melancholy. We are then strangely constricted and paralyzed, victims of an inner voice whispering sharply that we are far from that perfection which alone will do when the closely impending, but vague and unpredictable, doom arrives; in spite of that immediacy, we are as yet sinners, not quite good enough, and probably too far gone. Any temporary relief from this melancholy state (into which Luther, at the height of his worldly success, sank more deeply than ever before) is only to be had at the price of making a painful deal with the voice, a deal which offers the hope that maybe soon we will find the platform for a new start; or maybe at the hour of trial we will find that according to some unknown scale we will prove barely but sufficiently acceptable, and so may pass— pass into heaven, as some proud minds have asked, by just *getting by*? In the meantime, our obsessive scrupulosity will chew its teeth out and exercise its guts on the maybe-soons, the already-almosts, the just-a-bit-mores, the not-yet-quites, the probably-next-times. Not all minds, of course, naturally exercise themselves in this way; but everybody does it to some degree, and almost anybody can be prevailed upon to participate by an ideological system which blocks all exits except one, that one adorned with exactly matching symbols of hope and despair, and guarded by the system's showmen, craftsmen, and torturers. . . .

A predominant state of mind in which the ego keeps the super-ego in victorious check can reconcile certain opposites which the negative conscience rigidly keeps separate; ego-dominance tends to be holistic, to blend opposites without blunting them. In his state of personal recovery, Luther (like any individual recovering from an oppressive mental state) had recourse to massive totalisms from which he derived the foundation stones for a new wholeness. The whole person includes certain total states in his balances: we are, Luther proclaimed, totally sinners . . . and totally just . . . always both damned and blessed, both alive and dead. We thus cannot strive, by hook or by crook, to get from one absolute stage into another; we can only use our God-given organs of awareness in the here and now to encompass the paradoxes of the human condition. Psychologically speaking, this means that at any given moment, and in any given act or thought, we are codetermined to a degree which can never become quite conscious by our drives *and* by our conscience. Our ego is most powerful when it is not burdened with an excessive denial of our drives, but lets us enjoy what we can, refute what we must, and sublimate according to our creativity—always making due allowance for the absolutism of our conscience, which can never be appeased by small sacrifices and atonements, but must always remain part of the whole performance. Luther thus said in his terms what Freud formulated psychologically, namely, that only on the surface are we ever entirely driven *or* completely just; in our depths we are vain when we are most just, and bad conscience can always be shown to be at work exactly when we are most driven by lust or avarice. But this same inner psychological condition saves God (theologically speaking) from that impossible characteristic for which Martin had not been able to forgive Him, namely, that of being. The Father only in certain especially meritorious moments, rather than for all eternity, as He should be. To the ego, eternity is always now.

Luther's strong emphasis on the here and now of the spiritual advent, and on the necessity of always standing at the beginning . . . is not only a platform of faith, it is akin to a time-space quality dominating the inner state which psychoanalysts call "ego-strength." To the ego the past is not an inexorable process, experienced only as preparation for an impending doom; rather, the past is part of a present mastery which employs a convenient mixture of forgetting, falsifying, and idealizing to fit the past to the present, but usually to an extent which is neither unknowingly delusional nor knowingly dishonest. The ego can resign itself to past losses and forfeitings and learn not to demand the impossible of the future. It enjoys the illusion of a present, and defends this most precarious of all assumptions against doubts and apprehensions by remembering most easily chains of experiences which were alike in their unblemished presentness. To the healthy ego, the flux of time sponsors the process of identity. It thus is not afraid of death (as Freud has pointed out vigorously); it has no concept of death. But it *is* afraid of losing mastery over the negative conscience, over the drives, and over reality. To lose any of these battles is, for the ego, living death; to win them again and again means to the ego something akin to an assumption that it is causing its own life. In theological terms, *"creaturae procedunt ex deo libere et voluntarie et non naturaliter"* [35] ("what lives, proceeds from God freely and voluntarily, not naturally, that is, not by way of what can be explained biologically").

Luther's restatements about the total sinfulness and the total salvation which are in man at any given time can easily be shown to be alogical. With sufficient ill will they can be construed as contrived to save Martin's particular skin, which held together upswings of spiritual elations and cursing gloominess, not to speak of lusts for power and revenge, women, food, and beer. But the coexistence of all these contradictions has its psychologic —as has also the fury of their incompatibility. Martin's theological reformulations imply a psychological fact, namely, that the ego gains strength *in practice,* and *in affectu,* to the degree to which it can accept at the same time the total power of the drives and the total power of conscience—*provided* that it can nourish what Luther called *"opera manum dei,"* [36] that particular combination of work and love which alone verifies our identity and confirms it. Under these conditions, apparent submission becomes mastery, apparent passivity the release of new energy for active pursuits.

35. *Ibid.,* 9, 45.
36. *Ibid.,* 3, 289.

We can make negative conscience work for the aims of the ego only by facing it without evasion; and we are able to manage and creatively utilize our drives only to the extent to which we can acknowledge their power by enjoyment, by awareness, and through the activity of work.

If the ego is not able to accomplish these reconciliations, we may fall prey to that third inner space-time characterized by the dominance of what Freud called the *"id."* The danger of this state comes from what Freud considered biological instincts which the ego experiences as beneath and outside itself while at the same time it is intoxicated by them. Dominance by the id means that time and space are arranged in one way—toward wish fulfillment. We know only that our tension rises when time and circumstances delay release and satisfaction, and that our drivenness is accelerated when opportunities arise. The self-propelled will tends to ignore all that has been learned in the past and is perceived in the present, except to the extent to which past and present add fuel to the goal-directedness of the wish. This id-intoxication, as Luther formulated so knowingly, can become total poisoning, especially when it is haughtily denied.

Some monastic methods systematically descend to the frontiers where all ego dangers must be faced in the raw—where an overweening conscience is appeased through prayer, drives tamed by asceticism, and the pressure of reality is itself defeated by the self's systematic abandonment of its identity. But true monasticism is a late development and is possible only to a mature ego. Luther knew why he later said that nobody under thirty years of age should definitely commit himself to it.

GORDON RUPP

Luther and Government

> "Yes, heroic Swan. I love thee even when thou gabblest
> like a goose: for thy geese helped to save the Capitol."
> S. T. Coleridge on Luther's *Table Talk*.

AMONG THE LESSER FIGURES surrounding the giant Luther in the famous memorial at Worms are the figures of
the Elector Frederick the Wise of Saxony and of the Landgrave
Philip of Hesse. They are salutary reminders that there is no
merely ecclesiastical reading of the Reformation.

Luther did not forget that, humanly speaking, he owed the
safety of his person and of the good cause to the Elector Frederick
(not to forget Mr. Secretary Spalatin who deserves a chapter in

---

From Gordon Rupp, *The Righteousness of God* (London: Hodder &
Stoughton Ltd., 1953), pages 286–309. Reprinted with permission of the
publisher.

the unwritten history of the influence of Court Chaplains and Private Secretaries).[1] He owed it to his prince and his advisers that in the critical months (1517–1521) he did not go the way of John Huss, and that Wittenberg remained the strange, calm center of the destructive cyclonic whirlwind. When the first Protestant martyrs died in Brussels, Luther wrote a fine hymn in their honor, and when his English friend (almost the only Englishman we might call his disciple) Robert Barnes was burned in London, he wrote him a splendid obituary notice; but in his own case what was literally a "war of nerves" was never consummated in his flesh. It was a strange turn which made Frederick, the extravagantly devoted collector of relics, into the first patron of the Reformation, and more is needed to account for it than the pride of an ambitious ruler in the pet theologian of his pet university.

It was that practical, commonsense astuteness (which Luther so much admired, akin as it was to his own wisdom) and a certain obstinate integrity which enabled Frederick the Wise to turn the bribes, threats, entreaties, the twists and turns of papal diplomacy to his own and to Luther's advantage, even though there were moments, as immediately after Luther's interviews with Cajetan in 1518 and in Cologne in November, 1520, when it was touch and go. Philip of Hesse, a tragic and less noble figure, and of a younger generation, is a different kettle of fish. Luther generally left Melanchthon, with Martin Bucer, to deal with him, and he represented all the ominous political pressures and interests which Luther distrusted on his own side, and which, in the last decade of his life, he watched mounting in power and influence.

But if Luther had good cause to be grateful to his princes, the gibe of undue subservience comes a little oddly from the lips of Erasmus. It must always be remembered that one of Luther's key texts was "Put not your trust in princes," and he frightened his friends and disgusted his enemies by addressing potentates in church and state with the same measure that they meted out to him, and in the case of Henry VIII epithets in full measure, pressed down and running over. And this, it would be easy to

1. A useful sketch has been provided by I. Hoess. "Georg Spalatins Bedeutung für die Reformation und die Organisation der lutherischen Landeskirche." *Archiv für Reformationsgeschichte,* 42 (1951), 101–136.

prove, is a constant element in his career, as marked after the Peasants' War of 1525 as before it.

It takes us deep into his theology and its application (for the practical application of biblical exegesis to the affairs of the contemporary world always seemed to Luther a solemn part of the calling of a theological professor) that the last mission of his life was concerned with his rulers, the attempt to mediate in the territory of which he was a *Landeskind* in an ugly affair of brotherly enmity, which stimulated the worst vices of the German gentry. The last sermons of his life are therefore concerned to speak plainly of the vices of governors and their need to obey the laws of God.[2]

No teaching of Luther has been more misrepresented than his teaching about the nature, extent, and limits of temporal power.

Partly this has been due to an attempt to by-pass Luther's theology. Thus Professor Pascal tells us that the real key to Luther lies not in his theology and his ideas, but in the "consistency of class interests," and proceeds to tie Luther up into knots, which in the end are of his own contriving, since while the sociological element is really present in the story of the Reformation, it does not account for nearly half the story of sixteenth-century Europe, let alone Martin Luther.[3]

Nor can we explain Luther in terms of the classical problems of political philosophy. Luther was no political philosopher; he was, in P. Congar's phrase, "a man of the Word," a preacher and a professor of biblical theology, with strict views about the need for parsons to mind their own business. If his dwelling place in the middle of sixteenth-century Saxony was indeed a watchtower from which a man might survey the heavens, it did not permit him to overlook the corners of the earth. Though, as we shall see, he had a theology of politics, he was at all points removed from the systematic, doctrinaire theoretician. His political judgments were those of a keen, commonsense empiricism, and he had a distrust of the high-sounding slogans of contemporary idealism, whether of so-called wars for righteousness—of Pope Julius II against Venice,

2. W.A.Br., 11, 273 ff.; W.A., 51, 186.189.
3. R. Pascal, *The Social Basis of the German Reformation* (London, 1933).

or Duke George's Friesland campaign, or the "Christian" mani-
festos of the Peasants' War.

He stands midway between the long, intricate, medieval disputation between the spiritual and the temporal powers in Christendom
and the modern dilemma of church and state. He will not easily
fit into either group of problems. . . .

We may mention at the outset the most common criticism of
Luther's teaching, that he sets up a baneful dualism between
private and public morality, which paved the way for the divorce
between religious and political morality in modern Germany, and
indeed made possible the terrible infamies of the modern secular
state. We shall concentrate on a positive exposition of Luther,
which may deal with this criticism on the way.[4] We may and
must admit that the distinction between two kingdoms, and two
kinds of rule, is fundamental to Luther's view of God's government of the world.

THE TWO KINGDOMS: SPIRITUAL AND TEMPORAL

As in the case of the biblical word *Basileia* in the phrase "Kingdom of God," so Luther's thought is better expressed in terms of
the "rule" than the "realm" of government.

Gustav Törnvall has clarified the issue by insisting that we look
at this doctrine from the aspect of God's own rule. It is when we
look from below, in terms of the spheres of the operation of that
rule, that misconception arises and we misinterpret Luther either
in terms of one *Corpus Christianum* . . . or in terms of a too
spiritualized conception of the church. . . . But like so many other
of Luther's teachings, it is clarified only when we think *coram
Deo*. Luther has a profound doctrine of Providence and of creation. He insists that God is always active in all His works, mani-
festing His bounty and goodness through all His creatures, and
that in fact all creatures are His "veils" or "masks" (larvae)

4. Among writings especially concerned with *Obrigkeit* are: *Address to the
Christian Nobility of the German Nation* (1520); "Of Earthly Authority"
(*Von Weltlicher Obrigkeit*) (1523). The writings against the "fanatics" and
concerning the Peasants' War: "Can Soldiers Be Christians?" (1526); "On
Keeping Children at School" (1530); the Eighty-second Psalm (1530); Psalm
101 (1534); the Genesis Commentary (1535–1545).

through which He disguises His own unbearable Majesty and yet deals with His world and with His children. The two kinds of rule are ways by which God Himself runs His world, without ever abdicating His own present authority, and His own laws. The idea that there are areas of life where God has no control, and where men can rule by their own will, and make up the rules as they go along—the whole notion of the modern omnicompetent and secular state—is not only foreign to Luther's thought but would have appeared to him as a deadly blasphemy.

Törnvall is equally, and justifiably, insistent that this rich doctrine of God's creation, and continuously creative Providence, cannot be cut off from His doctrine of redemption in Christ. Luther knows what Isaac Watts has told us in his hymns, but what English Protestants have often forgotten, that the kingdoms of nature and of grace are one in Christ.

> There is not a God of general Providence who stands behind secular government, and who as such is separated from the revelation in Christ. He is not a certain, more abstract aspect of the Divine Being, who finds His expression in Creation, nor can this be understood as a preparatory disposition for the side of God seen in relation to Redemption, but He is the same God who comes to us in spiritual government who is Creator and Lord of all the orders of human society.[5]

And because this is a doctrine *coram Deo,* it is an apperception of God's rule given by revelation and embraced by faith.

The distinction between the kingdom of Christ and the kingdom of this world is classical in Christian history, and goes back to the New Testament. Luther says:

> We must divide the children of Adam into two classes: the first belong to the kingdom of God, the second to the kingdom of the world. Those belonging to the kingdom of God are all true believers in Christ, and are subject to Christ. For Christ is the King and Lord in the kingdom of God [Psalm 2] . . . all who are not Christians belong to the kingdom of the world and are under the Law. Since few believe and fewer live a Christian life . . . God has provided for non-Christians a different government out-

5. A. Törnvall, *Andligt och världslight regemente Los Luther* (Stockholm, 1940), p. 79.

side the Christian estate and God's kingdom and has subjected them to the sword, so that even though they would do so, they cannot practice their wickedness, and that if they do, they may not do it without fear nor in peace and prosperity . . . for this reason the two kingdoms must be sharply distinguished and both be permitted to remain: the one to produce piety, the other to bring about external peace and to prevent evil deeds: neither is sufficient in the world without the other.[6]

God separates his spiritual kingdom sharply from his temporal. . . . St. Peter and St. Paul had not a foot-breadth nor a straw to call their own or by which they might keep themselves, let alone be rulers or lords. Yet at that time there were both kingdoms at Rome: one ruled by Emperor Nero against Christ: the other Christ ruling through his apostles Peter and Paul against the Devil.[7]

The second quotation reminds us of a fact which blurs all theorizing and prevents a smooth and rounded doctrine in this matter, the conflict and dynamism in history, the ferment of evil, to which Luther's doctrine of the Devil bears witness.

God's spiritual government is that of the "Kingdom of God," the "Kingdom of Christ," and is exercised through the gospel, as a "Kingdom of Hearing" (through faith). If all men were truly Christian that would be sufficient, and there would be no need of the secular government.

If all the world were composed of real Christians, that is, true believers, no prince, king, lord, sword, or law would be needed. For what were the use of them, since Christians have in their hearts the Holy Spirit who instructs them and causes them to wrong no one, to love everyone, willingly and cheerfully to suffer injustice and even death from everyone. Where every wrong is suffered and every right is done, no quarrel, strife, trial, judge, penalty, law, or sword is needed.[8] . . .

But Christians are rare birds—"among thousands there is scarcely one true Christian"[9]—hence "Christ's rule does not extend over all but Christians are always[10] in a minority and are in

6. W.M.L., 3, 234–237.
7. W.A., 51, 238.35.
8. W.M.L., 3, 234.
9. *Ibid.,* 3, 236.
10. *Ibid.,* 3, 237.

the midst of non-Christians." It was one of the grave counts which Luther had against the peasants that they attached the name "Christian" to their own banner, and thought in terms of a "Christian" movement. "But, dear friends, Christians are not so common that they can get together in a mob." [11] "You ask, Who are the Christians and where does one find them? I answer, They are not many, but they are everywhere, though they are spread out thin and live far apart, under good and bad rulers." [12]

> It is true that Christians so far as they are concerned are subject to neither law nor sword and need neither: but first take heed and fill the world with real Christians before ruling it in a Christian and evangelical manner. This you will never accomplish: for the world and the masses are and always will be unchristian, although they are all baptized and are nominally Christian. . . . Therefore it is out of the question that there should be a common Christian government over the whole world, nay, even over one land or company of people since the wicked always outnumber the good. Hence a man who would venture to govern an entire country or world with the gospel would be like a shepherd who should place in one fold, wolves, lions, eagles, and sheep together and say "Help yourselves, and be good and peaceful among yourselves; the fold is open: there is plenty of food: have no fear of dogs and clubs." The sheep indeed would keep the peace and would allow themselves to be fed and governed in peace—but they would not live long! Nor would any beast keep from molesting another.[13]

God rules the two spheres of his world by two instruments.

"God has established two kinds of government among men: the one is spiritual: it has no sword but it has the Word by which men . . . may attain everlasting life. The other is worldly government through the sword which aims to keep peace among men and this He rewards with temporal blessing." [14]

This earthly government is a kind of parable of the spiritual kingdom.

"For God wills that the temporal rule [*Weltregiment*] should

11. *Ibid.,* 4, 231.
12. *Ibid.,* 5, 89.
13. *Ibid.,* 3, 237.
14. *Ibid.,* 5, 39.

be an image of the true blessedness and of the kingdom of heaven, like a conjurer's mirror or mask." [15]

God rules the temporal "regiment" through the law, of which the symbol is the sword.

"The law is given for the sake of the unrighteous that those who are not Christian may through the law be externally restrained from evil deeds . . . since however nobody is by nature Christian or pious, God places the restraints of the law upon them all so that they may not dare give rein to their desires and commit outwardly wicked deeds." [16]

Luther believed the confusion of the two kingdoms to be pernicious. He believed that the papacy had entangled the spiritual vocation of the church in political and economic and juridical pressures to the detriment and destruction of the souls of men. He believed the religious idealists who were the ideological leaders of the Peasants' War were equally pernicious. Zwingli (and Oliver Cromwell!) holding sword in one hand and Bible in the other is as much a contradiction of the gospel as Boniface VIII claiming to be the fountain of both kinds of jurisdiction.

> For the Devil is always trying to cook and brew the two kingdoms into one another. The temporal ruler tries to teach and rule Christ in the Devil's name and tell him how he ought to run the church and the spiritual power. The false papists and the fanatics are always trying to teach and run the temporal order: so the Devil gets busy on both sides and has quite a lot to do. But God'll teach him! [17]
>
> God's kingdom is a kingdom of grace and mercy, not wrath and severity, but the kingdom of the world is a kingdom of wrath and of severity . . . now he who would confuse these two kingdoms . . . as our fanatics do, would put wrath into God's kingdom and mercy into the world's kingdom.[18]

GOVERNMENT "REGIMENT"

Our world, which has moved nearer the edge of things than the late Victorian age could understand, is better fitted to understand

15. W.A., 51, 241.39.
16. W.M.L., 3, 235.
17. W.A., 51, 239.24.
18. W.M.L., 4, 265.

Luther's insistence on the fact that ordered government and stable peace are God's good gifts and blessings to be reverently accepted and solemnly guarded. These are gifts that God as creator has bestowed on his children.

> Earthly government is a glorious ordinance of God and a splendid gift of God, who has established and instituted it and will have it maintained as something that men cannot do without. If there were no worldly government no man could live because of other men: one would devour the other, as the brute beasts do . . . so it is the function and honor of earthly government to make men out of wild beasts and to prevent men from becoming wild beasts. . . . Do you not think that if birds and beasts could speak they would say "O ye men, you are not men but Gods compared with us. How safe you live and hold your property, while among us no one is sure for an hour . . . because of the others. Out upon your unthankfulness." [19]
>
> So we see that God scatters rule and kingdoms among the heathen . . . just as he does the dear sun and rain. So he calls such earthly rule among the heathen his own ordinance and creation.[20] . . .

The gifts of God are more than gifts, for they are the instruments of the Providential activity of God: "For what is all our work in field, garden, house, war, ruling, toward God but child's play, through which God gives his gifts to field and house and all the rest? They are the masks [larvae] of our Lord God through which he will remain hidden and yet do all. . . . God bestows all good things but you must take the bull by the horns, you must do the work and so provide God with an opportunity and a disguise." [21]

In his great *Social History,* Ernst Troeltsch has shown that two principles, world renunciation and world acceptance, live side by side in constant tension throughout Christian history. On the one hand, there are those who have heard the divine command to come out and be separate, and to keep unspotted from the world. Often they have obeyed by abandoning civilized society as evil and contaminating, and have sought to solve their ethical problems

19. *Ibid.,* 4, 159.
20. W.A., 51, 238.19.
21. *Ibid.,* 31 (part I), 436.7.

by contracting out of those offices and responsibilities of political and economic life where the ethical conflict between the Sermon on the Mount and natural law is most acute. This was the way of many of the sects of the Middle Ages, of the Reformation, as it is still the attitude of sects and parties in the modern church. The religious orders of the medieval church were a series of valiant attempts, among other things, to prevent the spiritual life from becoming entangled in things, in great and small possessions. Their distinction between the precepts and counsels of the gospel softened something of the sharpness between the "religious" and the "secular" life, for at least in theory it did not acquiesce in a double standard of morality. On the other hand, there was the attempt to bring the Christian gospel into direct and permeating influence upon the vast areas of political and economic and cultural life, the attempt, impressive and even magnificent, at a Christian civilization.

The working out of this in medieval society, with the delicate and always changing balance of spiritual and temporal powers at every level of the intricate pyramids, from pope and emperor at the top to priest and squire or municipality and monastery at the bottom, was reflected in a whole theological literature concerning the relation, under God's Providence, of the two powers. The later medieval prospect in which the growing ferment of nationality and the bursting energies of separate kingdoms threatened to burst the medieval unity, and where the spiritual power presented a shocking parody of spiritual leadership by becoming entangled and immersed in legal, financial, and political affairs, showed something of the peril of the principle of world acceptance, once the spiritual vocation was neglected. That was Luther's charge. He did not foolishly imagine that politics and economics and law were bad things, or that the world could get on without them, or that a church across the world could escape complicated practical problems. But his charge was that the two powers had become confused, and that the church as a spiritual entity had forsaken its prime vocation. . . .

Luther sought to reject three false solutions of the problem of Christian existence in the world. First, he denied the medieval distinction between the precepts and the counsels of the gospels and insisted that the Sermon on the Mount has meaning for the wayfaring Christian in the world. Second, he rejected the fanatical and sectarian repudiation of law, which contracted out of the obligations and responsibilities of government. At the same time he sought to avoid the disaster which had overtaken the institutional church by returning to the distinction between the things pertaining to Caesar and those belonging to God (though in another sense Caesar also belongs to God). Thus he explained his object in the Preface to his *Von Weltlicher Obrigkeit* (1523).

"I hope to instruct the . . . secular authorities in such a way that they shall remain Christians and that Christ shall remain Lord, yet so that Christ's commandments need not for their sake be changed into 'counsels.' " [22]

The problem of the relation between public and private morality belongs to all ages. Can a Christian be a magistrate, executioner, policeman, soldier? The sectarian, modern and medieval, says "No," and by taking refuge in personal or group piety, he contracts out of the obligations of society and erects the very dualism of which Luther himself is sometimes charged.

On the other hand, as human life shows, problems continually arise. A Christian man may have several official capacities: he may be a Christian man, a father of a family, a master of a business, a local magistrate, a town councilor, and may well be confronted during the week with differing ethical decisions, which he is tempted to solve in terms of the reflex of the social pattern in which he is engaged. This tension runs through all civilized life, and it is acute for the Christian who is concerned with the loftiest of all ethics, the Christian doctrine of love. But what Luther has to say is not, in the first place, concerned to grapple with this ethical tension, though something so fundamental is bound to be reflected in his exposition. Luther, we have seen, is thinking primarily of the Rule of God through his creation, and through that ordered government which in his bounty and kindness he has provided for his children.

Luther distinguished between a man's "person" and his "office": "person" is what a man is *"coram Deo."* As persons we are all equal before God, since in Jesus Christ there is neither male nor

22. W.M.L., 3, 229.

female, cleric nor layman. In his sight and in this relation, all human righteousness is condemned and we can stand before God on the ground only of God's own Righteousness in Christ. But God has provided "offices" in the world, through which the orderly use of creation is carried on. These are not abstract entities, to be considered apart from the people who are called to occupy them. But in them a man may fulfill his vocation as father, husband, magistrate, teacher, farmer, and the like. When a man serves God and his neighbor in such an office, it is not to be evaluated in terms of accident, self-interest, or opportunism, but it is a "calling."

A man's calling, his vocation, is the place where he fulfills the concrete, particular reference of the will of God. By faith, hope, and love, the Christian man lives in the kingdom of Christ and he serves God and his neighbor with the glad and creative obedience of a Christian man. But God has not left the majority of men, who are not Christians, to their own devices. They, too, are under God's provident care, and the ordered life of home, society, and state are part of his provision for them, and his rich, good gifts. Nor is the kind of righteousness they own a mere sham righteousness, nor God's oversight of them a kind of lower level of justice. . . .

A Christian man is called to endure and suffer wrong, without reprisal. But as a magistrate or policeman he may be called on to enforce drastic (and in the sixteenth century that often meant savage) sanctions on evildoers. These are not two sets of moralities, for love is the meaning and vindication of both sets of righteousness, for the end of both is the service of our neighbor and the glory of God.

"Christians among themselves," says Luther, "need no law or sword . . . but since a true Christian lives not for himself but for his neighbor and . . . the sword is a very great benefit and necessary to the whole world to preserve peace . . . to punish sin and to prevent evil . . . he serves, helps, and does all he can to further the government . . . he considers what is for the profit of others." [23]

> Therefore should you see that there is a lack of hangmen,
> police, judges, lords, or princes and find that you are qualified,

23. *Ibid.*, 3, 239.

you should offer your services and seek the job, so that necessary government may by no means be despised and become inefficient or perish.[24]

But you ask, whether the policemen, hangmen, lawyers, counsel, and the like can also be Christians and in a state of salvation. . . . I answer: if the state and its sword are a Divine service as was proved above, then that which the state needs to wield the sword must also be a Divine service . . . when such duties are performed not with the intention of seeking one's own ends but only of helping to maintain the laws there is no peril in them. . . .[25]

Worldly government through the sword aims to keep peace among men and this God rewards with temporal blessing . . . thus God himself is the founder, lord, protector, and rewarder of both kinds of righteousness. There is no merely human ordinance in either but each is altogether a Divine thing.[26]

So far from leaving politics to itself and free to make its own laws, Luther would have regarded the attempt to establish a secular state apart from the laws of God as the summit of human folly and pride. Here is an extract which we might call "The Planners":

For such godless people are so sure and secure in their own wisdom as if our Lord God must sit idle and not come into their clever councils. And so he has to chat for a while with his angel Gabriel and says, "Friend, what are the clever ones planning in that council chamber that they won't take us into their counsel? Perhaps they're planning to build another Tower of Babel. . . . Dear Gabriel, go down, and take Isaiah with you and give them a little reading in through the window and say 'with seeing eyes shall ye not see, with hearing ears shall ye not hear, with understanding hearts shall ye not understand. Make your Plan and nothing will come . . . for mine is not only the Plan but the deed.' " [27]

Thus we are not to think that God is interested only in Christians and has left the world to its own devices. God has given all men the light of reason and the law of nature. Luther accepts the fact that natural law is reflected in the legal systems of mankind, in the accumulated wisdom of the past, and in the common pro-

24. *Ibid.*, 3, 241.
25. *Ibid.*, 3, 249.
26. *Ibid.*, 5, 39.
27. W.A., 51, 203.26.

verbial wisdom of the people. In a passage that will surprise many people, he says:

> Let whoever wants to be wise and clever about earthly govern-
> ment read the pagan books and writings . . . out of which our
> own Imperial law has come. . . . And it is my conviction that
> God has given and preserved such pagan books as the poets and
> histories, as Homer, Virgil, Demosthenes, Cicero, Livy, and also
> that fine old lawyer Ulpian . . . so that the pagan and godless
> should have their prophets, apostles, theologians, or preachers for
> their earthly governance . . . so they had Homer, Plato, Aristotle,
> Cicero, Ulpian as God's people had Moses, Elijah, Isaiah, and
> their kings, and princes Alexander and Augustus as their David
> and Solomon . . . and where could anybody make a finer book
> of heathen wisdom than the common, simple children's book of
> Aesop's fables? Yes, because the children learn it and it is so
> common it counts for nothing, and yet it is worth four doctors
> who have never been able to grasp one of the fables in it.[28]

Yet Luther distrusts lawyers (he had some reason to in the context of his time and he puts in a plea for equity and natural wisdom).

> So the heathen Plato writes that there are two kinds of Law:
> *Justum Natura* and *Justum Lege*. I will call the one sound law and
> the other sick law, for that which flows out of the power of nature
> flows freshly without need of law, although it runs also through
> the law. But where nature is absent and all things have to be done
> by written law, then all is poverty and patchwork.[29]

Luther's stress on equity and his reference to Aristotle's *Epieikia* is his own adaptation of a frequent late medieval reference. He regards much of the work of government as a kind of "make do and mend." "Civil law and righteousness is a real beggar's cloak." [30]

In this connection Luther can even use the nominalist formula, which in connection with *iustitia christiana* he had fiercely repudi- ated. Here, in the matter of "civil righteousness" a man must "do what in him lies" (*"facienti quod in se est"*).[31]

28. *Ibid.*, 51, 242.36.
29. *Ibid.*, 51, 214.15.
30. *Ibid.*, 40, 2.526.
31. Marsiglius or Marsiglio of Padua (1270–1342), author of the *Defensor pacis* in which he argued that law and government derived from the people.

The following passage shows how differently Luther conceives of this "Law of Nature" from the medieval philosophers, and the democratic rationalism of Marsiglius in the fourteenth and Priestley in the eighteenth centuries.[32]

> For if natural law and reason were in all heads and all human heads alike, then idiots, children, and women could rule and make war as well as David, Augustus, Hannibal . . . yes, all men would be alike and none would rule over another. And what an uproar and wild state of affairs would be the upshot of that? But now has God so created them that men are unlike one another, and that one should rule and another obey. Two can sing together (that is, praise God alike) but they cannot speak together (that is, rule), for one must speak and another listen. So you'll find among those who brag and boast about their natural reason and law there are a good many thorough and big natural idiots. For that noble jewel which is called natural law and reason is a rare thing among the children of men.[33]

In his later writings Luther speaks often of the "Three Hierarchies": "The first is the household, the second the state, the third the church."[34]

In his last great commentary on Genesis, Luther drew the lesson from the stories of the Patriarchs, who served God in the world in their vocations as parents and as husbands and as economic men, and he pointed the contrast with an over-clericalized contemporary society where these humbler callings were often disparaged. What he has to say about home and government is not to be dissociated from his teaching about the church. Taken as a whole, his teaching about the "Earthly Rule" and "Spiritual Rule" makes an impressive unity, showing how presently and actively God carries out His provident care of His creation, in and through Jesus Christ. Luther did not try, as we sometimes do, to fob off laymen's problems with parsons' solutions. "Why should I teach a tailor how to make a suit?" says Luther. "He knows it

---

Joseph Priestley (1733–1804), English chemist and nonconformist minister, who spent the last ten years of his life in America. [ed.]

32. *Ibid.*, 40, 1.292.
33. *Ibid.*, 51, 212.14.
34. *Of Councils and Churches* (1539); W.A., 50, 652; 39, 2.34.

himself. The same is true of the prince. I shall only tell him that
he should act like a Christian." [35]

The last actions of his life illuminate his teaching. His loyalty
and reverence for lawfully constituted authority made him accept
the call to make a terrible and costly journey in midwinter to
advise and mediate in a quarrel between two nobles. He did not
meddle with the lawyers and the politicians, though he gave his
advice when asked. At the same time he preached plain and outspoken expositions of Scripture, which went to the root of the
high matter of the Christian duties of the parties to the quarrel.
Thus the spiritual "office" of the preacher was by no means confined to purely "spiritual" matters, but gave the practical, outspoken application of Holy Scripture to the condition of a place
and time.

Luther's doctrine of the two forms of rule, taken as a whole,
bears impressive testimony to the unity of all life, of creation and
redemption. . . .

The created orders, the callings of human society, the *iustitia
civilis,* and the law, are themselves the instruments of God's own
personal action. We are not to think of them as abstract entities
or impersonal instruments. God does not conceive these "offices"
as like the holes in a solitaire board into which in due season he
puts persons, like marbles. Nor may we drive a wedge between
creation and redemption as though in the one case God were
concerned with making things, and in the other with bringing
men into fellowship with himself. "God is the author of both
kinds of righteousness." And the end of all righteousness is to
bring God's creation home where it belongs. The law is the
"strange work" of God—and this means that all the orders of
creation are part of God's active, personal, moving, redeeming
action. All God's Birnam Woods come at last to Dunsinane. The
splendid pageant of creation, all nature, all history, groaning and
in travail until now, belong to the grand theme of the universe,
the righteousness of God.

AUTHORITY (*"Obrigkeit"*)

Luther's doctrine of obedience to authority is rooted for him in
the biblical doctrine of Christian obedience, and Romans 13:1 is

35. W.A., 10 (part III), 380.10.

its *locus classicus:* "Let every soul be subject to the higher powers, for the powers that be are ordained by God." But it is to be balanced by Acts 5:29: "We must obey God rather than men." That is why Bishop Berggrav could write, "In the fight against Nazism, Luther was a magnificent arsenal of weapons for our church."

We have already noted how strongly Luther was impressed as a monk with the duty of holy obedience, and how vehemently he opposed those who sought to evade its responsibilities in the supposed or pretended interests of the Observants. He believed that God willed and intended law and order, and it was not the least part of his spiritual agonies during the period 1517–1521 that his own conscience charged him with going against accredited authority and bringing disorder and chaos into Christendom. Luther expected citizens to obey their magistrates for the same reason that he expected university students to obey their proctors. In Erfurt in 1510 he had experienced the effect of a minor revolution in which the town council had been violently expelled, and the *Volksjustiz* hanged. Some days later some mercenary soldiers were involved in a brawl which developed into an ugly riot between town and gown, in which the arts buildings of the university, the library, and two student hostels were looted and burned. Luther had firsthand experience of the inability of a people's government to handle its own extremists, and only inadequate and tardy measures were taken. We have no direct comment of Luther on the business, but when a similar town and gown affair blew up in Wittenberg in 1520 he took drastic and unpopular action with regard to his students. Amid threats to his person and life, Luther went into the university pulpit and spoke "against the tumult as though I were partial to neither side: I simply spoke of the evil of sedition in the abstract whether supported by the citizens or students and I commended the power of the magistrates as one instituted by God. Good heavens, how much hatred I won for myself! They shouted out I was taking the part of the town." Here, in 1520, was Luther making the same unpopular stand that he made in 1525 against the peasants.

Thus he thought of "obedience" as the "crown and honor of all virtue," and he thought that the ideal situation for any land was where all classes served one another in love. But he was only too aware—though, like most of his contemporaries, the causes and

extent of the disturbances were unknown to him—that existing
society was straining under great new social pressures, that there
was a dynamism of unrest, and that a new and, it seemed, cynical
resentment was filtering into Germany through the cities of Italy
and their warrior bands, through returning mercenaries, and from
the preaching of the "fanatics" in Bohemia and Switzerland.

Luther believed that it was the Christian duty not to resist evil
but to endure it. We have seen how integral a part it was of his
"theology of the Cross" that the Christian is called upon to suffer
with Christ all the shame and agony of injustice and wrong. His
saying to the peasants *"Leiden! Leiden! Kreuz! Kreuz!"* . . . was
written precisely because the rebels claimed that theirs was a Christian movement and a Christian revolution.

In 1520 Luther made his *Address to the Christian Nobility,*
which included the knights and the free cities of the empire, as
well as the princes. He appealed to the secular arm on precise
theological grounds, in a state of emergency in which the spiritual
arm, refusing a free, Christian council, had repeatedly failed to
amend. He appealed to the authorities on the ground of the common priesthood of all believers, and because the office of the
magistrates, to bear the sword, fitted them to intervene on behalf
of the community. He has been criticized for not recanting at
Worms and putting himself at the head of national resistance to
Rome, on the basis of the Gravamina of the German nation. That
shows little understanding of Luther. He refused that temptation,
though he was aware of it—"Had I desired to foment trouble, I
could have brought great bloodshed upon Germany. Yea, I could
have started such a little game at Worms that the emperor would
not have been safe. But what would it have been? A mug's game.
I left it to the Word." [36] Luther evaded the almost desperate
wooing of the knights under Hutten and Sickingen. He can
hardly be blamed for fearing that the even more dubious political
revolt of the peasants, led by his deadly foes against whom he had
written for several years, would ruin all his work and drown the
Reformation in a welter of bloodshed, destruction, and anarchy.

Luther was convinced that revolution and rebellion were contrary to natural as well as to Divine law and that revolution could

36. W.M.L., 2, 399.

not only endanger the whole fabric of society but must result in worse evils than those it tried to remedy. So he says, and it is a timely thought for us all to meditate: "Changing a government is one thing. Improving a government is another."

And again: "I take and always will take his part who suffers from rebellion, however unjust his cause may be: and will set myself against him who rebels, let his cause be ever so just, because rebellion cannot take place without injury and shedding of blood." [37]

At any rate, had Luther's teaching been followed, the frightful events of the next century and a half of European history might have been greatly mitigated. Certainly Luther did not have to face the cruel dilemma of tyrannicide as it had to be faced later in the century. But perhaps we think too academically, and I do not think we ought too easily to assume that there is a Christian right or duty to participate in revolution, especially when that involves the bloody overthrow of organized government. And certainly the heroic modern German Lutheran, Dietrich Bonhoeffer, knew real agony of mind before actively joining in the resistance to Hitler through which he lost his life.

Luther did not approve of the examples of tyrannicide in the history of Greece and Rome. But he insists that the Christian duty of nonresistance is not a counsel of despair. In the first place, "tyrants cannot injure the soul," but are only injuring their own: "do you not think that you are already sufficiently revenged upon them?" And perhaps we can agree with Luther, even after the Nuremberg trials, that the most dire retribution for wicked men is that they should be "wicked men" given up, as St. Paul says, to "reprobate minds." In the second place, there can be worse things than tyranny: "a wicked tyrant is more tolerable than a bad war." In the third place, God is at hand and he is able to deal with tyrants. "God is there," says Luther. In the fourth place, since most men were not Christians, there was the probability that other subjects would rise in revolt. And last, God could raise up other rulers to make war on the tyrant.[38]

37. 1522! Admonition to all Christians to beware of insurrection and rebellion.
38. "Can Soldiers Be Christians?" W.M.L., 5, 49.

Nevertheless there is a point when, at all costs, the Christian must disobey. Luther's treatise *Of Earthly Authority* was written to meet just this situation in which the Catholic rulers were forbidding men to read Luther's Bible and demanding that such Bibles be surrendered. Luther tells Christians: "You should say, 'It does not become Lucifer to sit by the side of God . . . if you command me to believe and to put away books I will not obey: for in this case you are a tyrant and overreach yourself and command where you have neither the right nor the power.'" [39]

Again: "Never remain silent and assent to injustice, whatever the cost," for he who remains silent makes himself an accomplice. [40]

Luther tells a soldier impressed into an unjust war: "You should not fight or serve. 'Nay,' you say, 'my lord compels me, takes my fief, does not give me any money, pay, or wages, and besides I am despised, put to shame as a coward, nay as a faith-breaker in the eyes of the world, as one who has deserted his lord in need.' I answer, 'You must take that risk.'" [41]

If need be, the Christian preacher must allow himself to be deposed rather than be silent: "It is not rebellious to let oneself be deposed, but it would be rebellious if one who preaches the gospel did not chastise the vices of the authorities. For such is the behavior of lazy and useless preachers." [42]

Luther had no room for doctrinaire democracy, and for him Herr Omnes was no abstract "common man," but a peasantry that he saw with the shrewd eyes of a Pieter Brueghel, partly because he had sprung from among them. He had only scorn for Karlstadt, that model of a left-wing intellectual, who, dressed as a peasant, "Brother Andrew," tilled his plot of land while continuing to draw his professorial stipend. Luther himself undertook a dangerous trip at the height of the Peasants' War into Thuringia, where he was threatened with physical violence from the peasantry.

The emphasis upon the godly prince and the power of the magistrate in Western Europe was the inevitable counterpoise to the clericalized church-state. But you will find in Luther none of the subservience discoverable in the Henrician bishops in England.

39. W.M.L., 3, 257.
40. W.A., 28, 286.359.
41. W.M.L., 5, 68.
42. W.A., 31 (part I), 196.

When all is said and done, the passages in which Luther criticizes the crowd are far outnumbered by those in which he delineates the vices and temptations of the princes. Nearly four centuries before Lord Acton, Luther speaks of the corrupting effect of power:

> For power, honor, riches, authority . . . to have these and not to be conscious of it, and not to be proud against one's subjects is no achievement of common reason or simple human nature, but it needs the virtue of a Hercules or a David inspired by God.[43]
>
> The heart of man . . . is itself prone to presumption: and when beside this power, riches and honor fall to his lot, these form so strong an incentive to presumption and overconfident security as to move him to forget God and despise his subjects. Being able to do wrong with impunity he lets himself go and becomes a beast, does whatever he pleases and is a ruler in name, but a monster in deed.[44]
>
> But if a prince . . . lets himself think that he is a prince, not for his subjects' sake, but because of his beautiful blond hair, as though God had made him a prince so that he may rejoice in his power and wealth and honor, take pleasure in these things and rely upon them, he belongs among the heathen, nay, he is a fool. That kind of prince would start a war over an empty nut and think of nothing but satisfying his own will.[45]

And in a memorable saying: "He who wants to be a ruler, must have the Devil for his godfather." [46]

As in 1523 he had said that "a prince is a rare bird in heaven" and that "princes are usually the greatest fools or the worst knaves on earth, therefore one must constantly expect the worst from them, and look for little good," [47] so in 1534 he extends the judgment, "For if a prince is a rare bird in heaven, then councilors and men about court are still rarer birds in heaven." [48] If we feel sometimes that Luther's heaven must be as full of space as Sir James Jeans's "Mysterious Universe," we might remember his poignant

43. *Ibid.,* 51, 252.7.
44. W.M.L., 3, 124.
45. *Ibid.,* 5, 60.
46. W.A., 51, 264.6.
47. W.M.L., 3, 258.
48. W.A., 51, 254.12.

comment on infant mortality in the sixteenth century, that he thought heaven must be full of little children!

Moreover, Luther was as certain as the Thirty-nine Articles, and a good deal more certain than some of the Caroline divines, that rulers must not interfere in spiritual things. This was his reason, in 1522, for disobeying the plain and express command of the Elector Frederick that he should remain in hiding on the Wartburg, and for his famous letter of Ash Wednesday 1522, in which he told the elector: "I come to Wittenberg under a far mightier protection than that of an elector. Far be it from me to desire protection from your Grace . . . in this cause no sword can or shall afford counsel or succor." [49]

In 1534 he states clearly the dangers of secular interference: "When temporal princes or lords in a high-handed manner try to change and be masters of the Word of God and decide themselves what shall be taught and preached—a thing which is as forbidden to them as to the meanest beggar: that is seeking to be God themselves . . . like Lucifer." [50] Or, as he said five years later, like Henry VIII!

But Luther does not think only of the temporal ruler under natural law, but of the Christian ruler: "I say this not because I would teach that worldly rulers ought not to be Christians or that a Christian cannot bear the sword and serve God in a temporal government . . . would God they were all Christians or that no one could be a temporal prince unless he were a Christian." [51] . . .

The ruler "should picture Christ to himself and say, 'Behold, Christ the chief ruler came and served me . . . I will do the same, not seek my advantage in my subjects, but their advantage' . . . thus a prince should empty himself in the heart of his power and authority and interest himself in the need of his subjects, dealing with them as though it were his own need. Thus did Christ with us: and these are the proper works of love." [52]

A whole section of Luther's tract of 1523, *Von Weltlicher Obrigkeit,* is devoted to the theme of the Christian ruler, and Luther gives him four guiding principles:

49. March 5, 1522.
50. W.A., 51, 240.30.
51. W.M.L., 5, 84.
52. *Ibid.,* 3, 265.

1. He must seek his inspiration from God.
2. He must seek the good of his subjects before his own.
3. He must not allow his sense of equity to be obliterated by the lawyers.
4. He must punish evildoers with measured severity (Luther says elsewhere that in case of doubt, mercy must always take precedence of justice).

Thus Luther left a good deal of room for Christian influence to be brought to bear upon the political order, and not only in his teaching about the office of the ruler, but in his doctrine of the calling of all Christians to serve God in the common life, not only in their vocation, but through their vocation.

One of Luther's most remarkable political writings is his exposition of Psalm 101, which he wrote in 1534 for the new Elector John Frederick. He lacked the wisdom of the Elector Frederick the Wise and the piety of the Elector John, was known to be self-opinionated and to have surrounded himself with friends and flatterers who whispered to him the same Italianate notions which Henry VIII had greedily imbibed. Rumors of the great changes at court reached Wittenberg and gossip told of a ruler susceptible to the pleasures of the table. Luther's tract is as outspoken as any tract he ever wrote. It gave great offense to the court at Torgau. If John Frederick had been wondering what his predecessors had that he hadn't, Luther left him in no probable, possible shadow of doubt. But the tract is more than a tract for the times, more than the devotional exposition of a Psalm (Luther thinks of David as the best type of Christian ruler): it contains material for an interpretation of history. Luther was very interested in history and had read a good deal, besides being saturated in the biblical history. In accordance with his conception of temporal government as under God's general providence for all men, Luther's illustrations in this writing are drawn almost equally from Scripture and from secular history (classical and medieval), and in accordance with his high rating of common wisdom it is notable that in these few pages there are some 170 proverbial sayings quoted.

Luther believed that the great operative changes in history and ameliorations of human law were the work of great men, men

called and moved by God, what he calls the *"Wundermann"* or
the *"Vir Heroicus."* That this doctrine is opposed entirely to the
doctrine of the *Führerprinzip* was wistfully admitted in a Ger-
man-Christian essay by Otto Scheel in 1934, who said rather rue-
fully that Luther's doctrine could not be fitted to the modern
thought of the Führer. Nor is there much affinity with Carlyle's
Heroes and Hero Worship. If Luther had some regard for heroes,
he had none at all for hero worship, and believed the man who
takes action on the basis of his own will and pride is not a hero,
but a fool.

Says Luther:

> God has made two kinds of people on earth, in all estates: some
> have a special fortune before God which he teaches and awakens
> as he wills to have it. They have, as we say, a fair wind upon
> earth, luck and victory. What they start comes to a good end,
> and even if all the world withstand them yet the work goes
> through without hindrance. For God who put it into their hearts
> moves their mind and courage and gives them hands so that it
> must come out well . . . so it was with Samson, David, Jehoiada,
> and the like . . . and not only those, but also among the heathen,
> and not only princes but among townsfolk, peasants, and crafts-
> men. As in Persia King Cyrus, in Greece the princes Themistocles
> and Alexander the Great, Augustus and Vespasian among the
> Romans . . . such men I do not call trained or educated but cre-
> ated and moved by God to be princes or rulers.[53]

Such *viri heroici* do not need books or instructions to tell them
what is just, for in them natural law and reason work out of their
very nature. Such a prince, in point of wisdom, Luther considered
Frederick the Wise to have been, but he makes it clear that he
takes no such view of John Frederick. Luther calls those who imitate real greatness fools and apes put up by the Devil. They can
only achieve folly and had better confine themselves to written
precepts and the advice of good councilors. At the time the imitation hero may seem to carry all before him in his pride, but when
his "hour comes" (Luther's eschatological word *"Stündlein"*), the
imitator of true greatness falls in utter shame and disaster. The
real hero, or better, the great man, for the word is not used in

53. W.A., 51, 207.21.

the romantic sense, is like the exception in grammar, like the word *poeta,* which is not to be explained in terms of the common rules. Luther realizes that for most of the time such great men are not available. What goes on then is a kind of gradual patchwork improvement. "For the world is a sick thing . . . like a hospital [54] . . . or it is like a fur pelt or skin, the hair and skin of which is in poor condition." If the ruler is not a hero who can make a new skin, he must patch the old and make do and mend until the time comes when God will raise up a great man under whose hand everything goes better and who either changes the laws, or so administers them that "all is green and blooming in the land with peace, virtue, protection, and sanctions so that it can be called a healthy government." [55] When one considers the historical writing at Luther's disposal I do not find this theory fanciful or eccentric.

Finally, Luther's thought about temporal rule is bounded by eschatology, like all the classical Christian interpretations of history. Like many of his contemporaries, like the first Christians and a notable succession of Christian leaders down the centuries, Luther believed himself to be living on the edge of history. He had no notion of our modern themes of progress, organic development, and automatic self-contained historicism. He had no Utopianism. He had no thought of a gradual moral and physical improvement of one particular culture as a primary objective of Christian attention. We cannot even claim for him that he conceived of a political machinery for social change, though he hit hard at specific social and economic evils. We might find in this that medieval pessimism so vividly exemplified in Otto of Freising and his Tale of Two Cities, if we did not remember all that Luther has to say of faith and of the Word of God. And at least Luther's is not the pessimism of our modern secular eschatology, without faith, without hope, and without love. Luther finds this a sick world, but not without a remedy, not without a Good Physician. "The Plan of Our Lord God is better, who intends to bring heaven and earth into one heap—and make a new world." [56]

54. *Ibid.,* 51, 214.29.
55. *Ibid.,* 51, 215.3.
56. *Ibid.,* 51, 261.20.

BENGT HÄGGLUND

The Doctrine of Justification

M OST IMPORTANT FOR LUTHER'S DOCTRINE of
justification is his own study of the Holy Scriptures. In his
own well-known testimony concerning his discovery of the true
meaning of Romans 1:17 he tells how through long meditation on
St. Paul's texts he attained to the right understanding of the concept of righteousness, of *iustitia,* as opposed to *omnes doctores.* In
his interpretation of the *iustificatio impii,* that which was decisive
he undoubtedly learned from Paul and the Psalter. In view of this
it is at first surprising to note how little he took from contemporary theology, in which he was so thoroughly versed. Every attempt to derive his new discovery—even as his theology in general
—in some way from the theological sources used by him is vain

From Bengt Hägglund, "The Background of Luther's Doctrine of Justification in Late Medieval Theology," *Lutheran World* VIII (1961), pages 24–
46. Reprinted with permission of the author and the publisher.

if we overlook the decisive thing—namely, Luther's independent occupation with another source, with the Holy Scriptures, and his striving for the right understanding of the Bible. Only with due consideration of this can Luther's relation to medieval theology be rightly appraised.

A study concerning the theological background of Luther's doctrine of justification may have as its starting point his own assertions, proceeding thence to the sources mentioned or actually employed; or it may seek to understand the sources chosen for their representative character in their own contexts. It is the latter method which we are choosing for this study. It is not our task at all to make a direct study of Luther but only—while keeping Luther's doctrine of justification in mind—to examine the relevant lines of thought in the late medieval sources.

There is a danger lest the negative or the positive bearing of these sources on Luther be established too hastily. If the bearing is to be rightly characterized, the medieval sources must first be understood in their own connections—with no ulterior purpose but to understand them. . . .

Another danger to be guarded against here is that of too hastily construed typical views. Often, on the part of Protestants, the desire prevails to draw the boundaries between Luther's theology and all earlier traditions rather sharply. As a result the various theologies are often oversimplified and reduced to types. One must observe that this is but *one* method and perhaps not always the right one. Moreover, Luther, in spite of all his polemics and critical opinions, viewed his predecessors in an altogether different manner. He did not only wish to distinguish his views from theirs. He was also able to tie in with certain lines of thought in earlier theology and did so wherever he could. Within one and the same typical view we can discover both positive and negative bearings on Luther's theology.

German Mysticism

The relation between medieval mysticism and the theology of the Reformation has not yet been clarified in present-day research. The decided rejection of mystical theology, which we find first in liberal theology and then also—starting from other premises—in dialectical theology, has caused many scholars to draw the line of distinction between Luther and mysticism very sharply. This tendency still prevails very widely today and may often have made it difficult to see a real relationship between Luther and mysticism.

Any discussion of this subject must first of all clearly distinguish the various kinds and tendencies of medieval mysticism, a thing which is often overlooked. In an essay on "Luther and Mysticism" (*Lutherjahrbuch,* 1935, pp. 32–54), E. Vogelsang develops this point in detail. He shows that while Luther sharply criticizes Areopagitical mysticism, he rated Romance mysticism (Bernard, Hugo von Victor, Bonaventure) very highly. Yet he also criticized some views of these theologians and rejected certain of their ideas. But so-called German mysticism (Tauler, *Theologia deutsch*) he mentioned only with praise and approval. . . .

The question as to the actual significance of medieval mysticism for the development of Luther's theology is therefore as yet not at all unequivocally settled. If one is to judge it rightly, one must proceed not from isolated assertions of Luther but must begin with mysticism itself insofar as it is still a matter of question. For there is more divergence of opinion concerning the theology of mysticism itself than there is about the purely historical question as to Luther's relation to mysticism.

In the following we shall sketch a few of the principal features of German mysticism which are important for Luther's doctrine of justification:

The ideal of mysticism—as we find it in Tauler and *Theologia deutsch*[1]—is the *homo deificatus,* literally, "the deified man." The

---

1. Tauler's sermons are here quoted according to Schlosser's edition, *Johann Taulers Predigten,* I–III (Frankfurt am Main, 1826). This edition reproduces the best printed editions in modern transcription.

Theologia deutsch (germanica) is quoted according to the edition of W. Uhl, *Der Franckforter, Kleine Texte für Vorlesungen und Übungen* 96 (Bonn, 1912) [cited as "Fr."]. With this is compared the printed edition of 1518, which was republished by Mandel: *Quellenschriften zur Geschichte des Protestantismus,* H. 7 (Leipzig, 1908) [cited as "Th.d"].

[A modern English translation of *Theologia deutsch* is *Theologia Germanica: The Way to a Sinless Life,* edited by Thomas S. Kepler (Cleveland and New York, 1952). [ed.]

idea of justification—which, by the way, is seldom referred to by the use of this term—must be clarified in view of this fundamental idea.

Man's goal and his true life consist in this, that God is born in his soul, and becomes the one who wills and works in man. Through this "birth of God" God becomes one with man, a thing which is made possible through the fact that he once united himself with human nature in Christ. "Thus a true inner life begins, ✓ and proceeding from thence, God himself becomes the man, with the result that there is nothing anymore that is not God or of God, and also that there is not anything that arrogates anything to itself" (Fr., Chap. 53; Th. d., Chap. 55). . . .

This unity with God comes about through the Son's having become man. Only through the fact that God became man can man become God. Only through this deification can that be restored which Adam lost. This means that also in me God must become man. "Thus God must also become man in me, so that God takes to himself all that is in me within and without, that there may be nothing in me that resists God or hinders his work" (Fr., Chap. 3; Th. d., Chap. 3).

> In a sermon, which, however, probably does not come from Tauler himself, this "becoming man" is explained in such a way that the individual Christian identifies himself with the human nature that is united with God in Christ, through which his own individuality is abolished. God has taken on human *nature,* and so man, when united with God, must also get out of himself and "accept himself in the free, undivided human nature" (Sermons, I, 56). "Note, therefore, that you neither are nor are called this or that human being" (*ibid.,* p. 57). As all diversity is done away with in God, so man, in whom unity with God has become reality, must separate himself both from the things of the world *Cf. Eckhart* and from himself. This is the "departure" of which the mystics speak so often. Man must depart from the diversity of the world and also from himself, in order that he may seek only God's praise and glory.

This "out of oneself" (cf. Luther's "extra nos") can therefore at times be put alongside the philosophical idea of a common human nature beyond individuality. But it is not a purely meta-

physical idea, since the process is always at the same time conceived of as a union with Christ.

Only through a complete denial of himself, through the renunciation of all that is called "self," "selfhood," etc., can man love
that which is good for its own sake. He is to love that which is
good, righteous, and true not as an "attribute" (i.e., what he can
ascribe to himself), but only as God himself is that which is good
and perfect. The most important criterion of such selfless love of
that which is good is the so-called *resignatio in infernum* (being
resigned to hell). The deified man is satisfied even if damned,
for he is interested only that God's will is done, and he loves the
good and the perfect not only when he possesses it himself but
also when he must forgo it. "He does not regret his condemnation
and suffering when it is fair and right and is not against God but
is God's will" (Fr., Chap. 11; Th. d., Chap. 11). "One who truly
loves will love God or the eternal good equally whether he has
it or lacks it, whether sweet or bitter be his lot, in love or in sor-
row and the like" (Fr., Chap. 10). . . .

What is the way to deification, that is, to the realization of unity
with God?

Doubtless Tauler has in mind some preparation for the reception
of grace. He can even say that man must first do his part. "When
therefore the Holy Ghost finds that man has done his part, He
then comes with His light and illuminates the natural light, pouring in supernatural virtue; that is faith, hope, and Divine love and
His grace" (*Sermons*, II, p. 127). But this "preparation" is so described that it presents a sharp contrast to the traditional pattern
of *facere quod in se est* (doing what one can).

The only demand made is that man turn from himself and also
from everything that is not God. Through "resignation" and "separation" the soul becomes free for the reception of grace. In a
sermon on the gospel of Pentecost, emphasis is laid on the fact that
the disciples, when they received the Holy Spirit, were sitting still
and "enclosed," "gathered in themselves." "This Holy Spirit is
given to every man as often and in such measure as man turns
with all his might away from all creatures and to God" (*Sermons*,
II, p. 139).

If man is to know God, he must be equally distant from all things, even as the vault of heaven is equally distant from all parts of the earth. He must also forget himself and lose himself. This recognition occurs beyond all diversity, above time and space (*Sermons,* I, pp. 60 ff.).

The way to obtain righteousness is therefore "resignation," to die to self. Man must become nothing in himself in order to submerge in the divine "now" (Sermons, I, pp. 82 ff.). There should take place "a departure, yea a transition, out of oneself and beyond oneself, we should deny all that we have, all willing, desiring and doing" (Sermons, I, p. 92; cf. also p. 200). Sin consists in the fact that man ascribes to himself that which is good; self-will and pride constitute the fundamental sin. The movement away from sin therefore consists in the renunciation of self-will and of the desire to consider oneself as good or worthy of that which is good.

This "resignation" or this "departure" from oneself can also be designated as humility and obedience. Disobedience is seeking in all things what is one's own. True obedience is therefore defined as follows: "Man should be utterly free from himself and that which is his, that is, selfhood, self, I, me, mine, etc., so that he little seeks himself and what is his, and in all things is of the opinion as if he did not exist, and should also think so little of himself as if he did not exist and as if another had done all his works" (Fr. Chap. 15; Th. d. Chap. 13).

On the one hand, Tauler says that man should strive with all his might for this "resignation of himself and all things" (Sermons, I, p. 98); on the other hand, he strongly emphasizes that man himself is not capable of this preparation. "The first and the highest preparation to receive him, he himself must prepare in man" (Sermons, II, p. 132). "You would fain be prepared, partly by yourself and partly by him; but this cannot be; you can neither think of nor desire this preparation, but God is already there before you to prepare you" (*Sermons,* I, p. 156). "Therefore, where the Holy Spirit is to be received, he must himself prepare the place, he must himself create that receptivity for himself" (*Sermons,* II, p. 138).

For mysticism as represented by Tauler and *Theologia deutsch* it is quite clear that the salvation of man can be achieved only through the work of God. "Moreover, salvation, to speak briefly, does not depend on any creature or on the creature's work, but it depends only on God and on his working" (Fr., Chap. 9; Th. d., Chap. 9). The strict Augustinian line is followed here, and the conceptions of the preparation for grace are developed in clear contrast to the *facere quod in se est* espoused by the Scholastics. . . .

What we have thus far discussed corresponds to what is otherwise called justification, although the word justification is rarely used in this connection. Mysticism made the discovery that there is something higher than all virtues, a "righteousness" that surpasses all human works and all that can be achieved in the realm of the creature, a supernatural, a perfect righteousness. It consists in man's becoming nothing and God's becoming all in man. This "humility," amounting to a radical renunciation of self, a "being small in the presence of God," "surpasses all righteousness and all obedience" (*Sermons,* II, p. 117). Only then does man become righteous when that which is perfect, which is uncreated, incomprehensible to all creatures, comes to dwell in the soul. If this is to be, the soul must be free from all creatures, receptive to the things of God in true humility (Fr., Chap. 1; Th. d., Chap. 1). Thus the terminology of justification is in mysticism interchanged with the terminology of unity with God. However, the exact parallelism and the close relation between "justification" and "deification" must not be overlooked. The idea of a righteousness that is superior to all human virtue has its assigned place in the theology of mysticism and takes on a special flavor.

In the doctrine of sin, Tauler and *Theologia deutsch* embrace the strictest Augustinism. . . . Original sin affects the whole man. He is utterly depraved. He turns away from the immutable to the mutable good (Fr., Chap. 2; Th. d., Chap. 2). Thus the inner direction of human striving has been perverted. Sinful man in all things seeks himself and not God. This can also be designated as a sickness of nature, concupiscence, "frailty," "defects." Everything that proceeds from us is thereby polluted. This lust cannot be overcome and is bound up with guilt in the sight of God. Nor does it cease to exist in the "justified man," and therefore man must always look to forgiving grace for deliverance. His own works and his own righteousness dare never be considered meritorious before God.

> The idea, found in *Theologia deutsch,* is characteristic: sin really consists in the fact that man ascribes some good to himself. Not the eating of the apple was in itself the sin of Adam but the "appropriation of the creature," ascribing to himself what only belongs to God. All that is good is God's alone. If man thinks that he himself has, does, or can do something good, he is turning away from God. This is the Fall—with respect to the Devil as well as to man.

On this fundamental idea rests the conception of the self, selfhood, etc., as the epitome of evil, and the demand of a radical, selfless humility, a renunciation of oneself, in order that God alone may work and rule. When the truth is recognized, "appropriating will fall away of itself. So man then says, Behold, poor fool that I am, I thought it was I; now it is and was truly God" (Fr., Chap. 5; Th. d., Chap. 5). The way to deliverance consists in man's own "subjectivity" being changed through the union with God into God's own becoming the active subject in man. The doctrine of sin corresponds exactly to the ideal of the *homo deificatus,* sin really consisting in man's appropriating to himself what belongs to God alone.

The passivity of man at the reception of grace is emphasized in a radical manner in two respects: (1) man's striving to be free from himself and to turn toward grace is a work of the Spirit, just as we have seen above that also the active preparation for grace is a work of God in man. (2) The principal way to the reception of grace really is rather a suffering, a dying, a "resignation" than a deed. Self-will, all activity that proceeds from man himself, is to be extinguished, in order that God alone may become the one who wills and works in man. "One must also know that eternal salvation depends solely on one thing and on nothing else. And if indeed man or his soul is to be or to become blessed, then this one thing alone shall and must be in the soul" (Fr., Chap. 9; Th. d., Chap. 9).

All that belongs to salvation, to redemption, is exclusively a work of God. Salvation is something supernatural, inasmuch as it cannot be wrought at all by that which is created. Already on this account man is incapable of cooperating in redemption. It is all the work of God; through the coming of God the deification of man comes to pass. . . .

We have now arrived at the point where we can say exactly what Tauler means by "justification." It comes to pass only when God comes to be present in man's inmost being. He pours in his grace and makes man a partaker of the supernatural virtues. But all this belongs to the "third man," i.e., it is not a process which can be experienced psychologically but something absolutely supernatural. The word of Paul, "that Christ may dwell in your hearts," becomes, for Tauler, an expression of this grace. That which is given to the inner man is nothing less than Jesus Christ Himself, who dwells in our hearts by faith, transforming the inmost essence of the soul and shaping it according to His own image. In this mystical conception faith and the new obedience, faith and the infusion of grace merge into one thing. From the inmost ultimate essence of the soul (the third man) the renovation "spreads" to all "higher and lower powers." The distinction between justification as declaring man just and justification as making him just is unknown in this connection.

In Tauler's mysticism, faith and love are, so to speak, fused into a higher unity. The renunciation of all his own works on the part of man and stress on man's inability to prepare himself for the reception of grace stand in clear contrast to the *facere quod in se est* of Scholasticism. God's sole operation in the work of redemption is given decided prominence in Tauler's work. The fact that resignation or humility is viewed as a necessary preparation does not contradict this. For it is not only that this humility can be brought about solely by the Spirit, but also that the "virtue" of resignation or passivity—to put it paradoxically—does not pertain to the outer man and therefore cannot be considered a human activity in the usual sense. "The third man," the *"Seelengrund,"* [2] which participates in this, is the transcendent man, belonging to the realm of the supernatural and the divine. All working is here

2. The ultimate essence of the soul. [ed.]

divine working, whose reverse side is a complete and radical self-abnegation.

The doctrine of redemption in Tauler's mysticism, from this point, can with perfect right be characterized by the formula *sola gratia*. . . .

The fundamental view of God here excludes in fact the idea of merit. . . . God is not considered as a being standing over against man, so that he could be influenced by merit of any kind on man's part. God is not the object of man's actions but the active subject; he is the one who works in man. Ascribing to myself something as something good, something that would be my own, or something meritorious—this is considered as the fundamental sin. . . .

A few words concerning the Christology of mysticism: Is redemption really considered as depending on Christ? From the course our discussion has taken thus far it might seem that we were dealing with a general mystical scheme of deification. However, the fundamental importance of the incarnation and the reconciliation of Christ is frequently emphasized. Christ is the only way to the Father. Only through the life of Christ does a man attain to unity with God. "And whoever goes another way or imagines he would or could come to the Father or to everlasting salvation otherwise than through Christ deceives himself, when he does not go on the right way and does not enter in by the right door" (Fr., Chap. 52; cf. Chap. 53; Th. d., Chap. 53 and 54).

> Both the incarnation and the crucifixion are stressed as the basis of redemption. Because God in Christ has assumed human nature, we, who belong to the same nature, can be united with God. . . . Because Christ suffered the punishment for our disobedience, he has reconciled us with the Father and restored to us the gift of the Spirit which we lost in Paradise. . . .

It is therefore not true when it is said that mysticism knows Christ only as an example and emphasizes in this connection only the imitation of Christ. . . .

In spite of the importance which Tauler and *Theologia deutsch* attribute to the cross of Christ, justification is ultimately not presented as an imputation of Christ's righteousness, as it is by Luther. Attention is directed to that which takes place in man's inmost

being. Only through the birth of God in the ultimate essence of
the soul is man justified. "All the deeds and miracles which God
has done and still may do in or through all creatures or which
God himself may do in all his goodness, so far as it is and is done
outside of me, it will never save me, but [only] so far as it is in
me and takes place in me, is loved, confessed, tasted, and felt"
(Fr., Chap. 9; Th. d., Chap. 9). This emphasis on the birth of God
in the soul as the true place in which justification is realized means
that the idea of an *aliena iustitia* (another's righteousness) or a
forensically conceived imputation lies outside the doctrinal system
of mysticism as it is treated in this essay.

NOMINALISM

The question as to Luther's relation to the theological school
to which he once belonged has been closely connected with the
whole question as to just what the "new approach" of the Reformation was. Ever since Denifle's extensive investigation on *The
Occidental Expositors Up to Luther on "Justitia Dei"* (Romans
1:17) *and "Justificatio"* (supplement to Denifle's *Luther und
Luthertum,* Vol. I, Mainz: Quellenbelege, 1905) scholarship has
concentrated on the question concerning Luther's so-called tower
experience. . . .

It is not the entire problem of the development of Luther's doctrine of justification with which we shall be engaged. Our assign-
ment deals only with the preliminary question concerning the
background of this doctrine in late medieval theology. And in this
we are concerned first of all with the studies that deal directly
with the doctrine of justification in nominalism. . . .

In the following we shall deal with the nominalist doctrine of
justification in the form which Gabriel Biel gave to it. . . . In
Gabriel Biel we meet nominalist theology in the form in which it
was most thoroughly studied by Luther. We shall therefore limit
ourselves to a study of the doctrine of justification as it is developed in Biel's "Collectorium." The 1514 Lyons edition (*Collectorium super quattuor libros sententiarum,* i.e., a collection of theses
from the nominalist school) is used in this study; the quotations
are however given according to the heads *liber, distinctio,* and

quaestio (book, distinction or chapter, and question or section) so that they can also readily be found in other editions.

The justification of the sinner, according to Gabriel Biel, consists essentially in the infusion of grace and love, resulting in the forgiveness of sins. This justification is the second work of God (the first is creation, the third is salvation), the restoration of fallen creation. It is attached to the third article of the creed as the basis, the center, and the goal of the work of the church. "Three things concur in the justification of the sinner—namely, the infusion of grace and love through which the sinner is forgiven his sins. And he himself becomes pleasing to God and is incorporated into the church as a living member" (Lib. III, dist. 25, qu. 1).

> Righteousness is closely related to love, which does not seek its own. "Love . . . which seeks not its own, makes all things common" (*ibid.*). That is to say, love, as one of the cardinal virtues, is defined from the very beginning as the right conduct toward others, which consists in one's sharing oneself and one's possessions with others. The love involved in friendship, *amicitia,* is therefore the highest form of righteousness and indeed the perfection of all virtue.
>
> "Now there are different aspects of righteousness, since righteousness is a virtue governing the desires, that one may conduct oneself properly toward another. For one may behave toward another in a twofold manner. Firstly by sharing oneself with another as much as one can. Secondly by sharing with him something else than oneself, as by sharing one's possessions. The virtue of being inclined to the former act is called friendship, by which one gives oneself to one's neighbor as much as one can and as much as the neighbor can receive one; and this is the most perfect ethical virtue . . ." (Lib. III, dist. 34, qu. 1).

As man becomes righteous through right conduct toward his neighbor, so he becomes righteous in the theological sense through right conduct toward God, that is, through love to God. Because he does not possess this love in himself, an infusion of love must take place, which therefore can be identified with justification. This fundamental pattern is essential for the definition of justification in Biel's thought. This involves, however, many difficulties,

which he discusses thoroughly in the well-known Chapter 17 of
the first book.

The supposition is that the sending of the Holy Spirit makes
man righteous in his will and therefore makes him acceptable and
dear to God. "And the gifts of the will, by which the affections
are corrected, are appropriated through the Holy Spirit who proceeds through the manner of love; therefore the Holy Spirit is said
to abide in them according to the well-known word in Romans 5,
'The love of God is poured out in our hearts by the Holy Spirit
which is given to us'" (Lib. I, dist. 14, qu. 1, nota 3). . . .

> Actually, two things are required if man is to be "dear and ac-
> ceptable to God": firstly, that he be in such a condition that God
> is willing to reward him with eternal life, that is, he must be
> baptized and must not have rendered the state of grace null and
> void by voluntary sins; secondly, that he actually deserve, by rea-
> son of an *actum meritorium* (that is, by a morally good deed), to
> be rewarded with eternal life.

We observe here that justification is, as it were, built on two
columns: on the presence of the grace that shapes the soul in a
supernatural way and upon the *actus meritorius,* which ultimately
consists in love to God.

These two basic considerations Biel would by no means give
up. His earnest contention is only that they be considered as necessary requirements for salvation in such a way that when they, or
one of them, are present, God must necessarily grant eternal reward. He argues here on the basis of God's omnipotence, per se,
for which all things are possible, so that no logical contradiction
is involved (*potentia absoluta*).

Viewing the Divine power in itself, or in the abstract, one can
maintain that God can accept a man and grant him salvation without any inherent "form." "Considering the absolute power of God,
a man can be acceptable and dear to God without any form in-
hering in himself, inasmuch as we are speaking of an acceptation
especially by grace" (that is, mercy, "by virtue of which he desires
to grant to the rational creature who does not place any obstacle
in the way of the greatest accidental [that is, non-inherent] perfection, such as blessedness and eternal life") (Lib. I, dist. 17, qu. 1,

art. 2; cf. art. 1). An *actum meritorium* can conceivably be present without supernatural grace and God could accept any good moral deed as a condition for granting eternal life. For the meritorious deed (as such) is the same whether the supernatural grace is behind it or not. Thus God could save man as he is in his purely natural state, that is, without the infusion of grace.

The idea of *habitus,* that is, the idea of a "habit" or "quality," is here rendered relative by means of the conception of a *potentia absoluta.* This conception is, however, combined with the idea of merit. But is it possible that the idea of merit could be rendered relative as well? In other words, could one also imagine that God could justify a sinner without merits or despite his merits? In the passage considered here this possibility is not mentioned. A natural love to God, a shunning of mortal sin, is basic for divine acceptation. Elsewhere, however, Biel did at least touch upon this question.

When grace and sin (*culpa* or guilt) as attributes of man are considered in the absolute it is not logically necessary to hold that they exclude each other. By virtue of his absolute power, God could absolve a sinner from eternal punishment and infuse him with grace, and condemn to punishment someone who possesses grace. Only by virtue of Divine "ordination," or God's ordering of things (*ex sola ordinatione divina*), can sin and grace not be together in the soul. It is, however, different when the terms sin and grace are used connotatively, that is, so that sin includes reprobation and grace includes acceptation. Then it is logically necessary to hold that one who has sin, that is, is excluded from eternal life, cannot at the same time possess grace, that is, be accepted for eternal life. . . .

Biel himself thinks that viewing his subject according to God's absolute power has a function to perform as the strongest possible rejection of Pelagianism. According to Pelagius, God is necessarily obligated to reward with eternal life that which is morally good. Biel not only opposes this line of thought but also the conception of Peter Aureoli that God must also reward the infusion of the supernatural gift with eternal life. God's free mercy is always the ultimate basis of salvation; the established order for this is also contingent, since it is established solely through God's free gracious will. Because God, "when he saves someone, does so in a purely contingent manner, freely, and through his mercy, not for the sake of any form or any gift offered, except that God has mercifully ordained that, having such a gift, he may merit eternal life." Thus, "disregarding all form, he grants eternal life so freely and mercifully by his grace, and always (without any injustice on his part) it is possible that he may not grant it, for he is the one to whom none can say, 'Why do you do thus?' and whatever things he can do are just because he does them, and thus he does them justly" (I, dist. 17, art. 2, concl. 3).

> In this point Biel holds to the strictest voluntarism: "The divine will itself is the rule of all things that happen. Therefore, it is not because a thing is right or just that God does it, but, because God wills it, it is just and right. He could therefore destroy him who loves him; and if he should do so, he would not do it unjustly, for none can say to him, 'Why do you do thus?'" (*ibid.* corol. 1).

We have quoted these sentences in order to show in what radical form the idea of the *potentia absoluta* was entertained by a positive churchman and theologian like Biel. At the same time he insists that in fact none is saved without the infusion of grace. The assertions with respect to the *potentia ordinata* (the "ordained power" of God) are not annulled by the reflections on that which belongs to the *potentia absoluta*. "No one can be dear and accepted in the sight of God for eternal life according to the law as it has been ordained if he does not have some quality infused into him, which is love and grace." Here the important sentence is added, "This conclusion cannot be proved by natural reason, because one cannot infer by natural reason what some infused attitude or character [*habitus*] is. It can, however, be shown by abundant authority of Scripture and of the saints" (Lib. I, dist. 17, qu. 1, art. 2, concl. 2).

If this is so, why did Biel place alongside it the view according to the *potentia absoluta*. The immediate answer is: in order to show what is logically necessary and what is not necessary in the strict sense, but is only of a contingent order. We are dealing with a type of dialectic arising from the urge to prove everything according to the strict rules of logic. The reflections on the *potentia absoluta* do not mean that a second, a higher order of salvation has been established; it is only a discussion of possible ways of thinking. It is a discussion on what can be said of God's dealings when the matter is reduced to that which is strictly necessary according to logic. This must be especially emphasized in considering Luther's relation to nominalism. One would often expect Luther to tie in with this idea of the *potentia absoluta*. In fact, he did not do so, but he criticized also this side of the doctrine of justification in nominalism. He was sufficiently versed in this theology to know that the reflections on the *potentia absoluta* were not introduced on biblical or really religious grounds. . . .

Therefore it is hardly correct to say that nominalism has *two* solutions of the question of justification, one according to the *potentia absoluta,* or God's absolute power, and one according to the *lex ordinata,* or God's ordinances. Fundamentally, it has but *one* solution—namely, the identification of justification with the infusion of love, with the reception of grace through the sacraments. Nominalism, however, discovered the conceptual difficulties of the traditional doctrinal pattern and discussed all the questions arising from it, so that the presentation at times appears to be a dissolution of the pattern. But this dissolution is only a dialectical way to the only solution in harmony with the church's doctrine. Here and elsewhere the nominalists operate dialectically, ultimately in order to establish more securely the conclusion that it draws in harmony with the church's doctrine.

For the comparison with Luther this is important. For it is not the case that Luther, so to speak, took over the one half of nominalist argumentation and further developed its natural implications. On the contrary, by taking a position decidedly opposed to the final result of the nominalist doctrine of justification, he forsakes the dialectical way by which the nominalists arrived at this result. In fact, he criticizes not only the idea of a meritorious deed and an infused quality of grace but also the idea of pure "acceptation" as developed in nominalism. His doctrine of imputation, despite certain formal resemblances to the line of thought here dealt with, stands in decided contrast to the nominalist dialectic. This contrast can be briefly stated: (1) Luther's doctrine of imputation resulted from intensive study of the Bible. (2) It is tied to the history of salvation. (3) Imputation is to be interpreted not only as a logical possibility, but it is the order of the justification of the sinner actually established by God (it therefore belongs, so to speak, in the highest degree to the *potentia ordinata*), since it is based on the work of Christ. (4) It is the expression of the deepest concern of the Reformation, not of some abstract reflection on the logical implications of the church's doctrine.

With his doctrine of the *potentia absoluta*, Biel does not want to dissolve the usual pattern of the process of justification. Nominalism, for example, criticizes the proofs concerning God. That does not mean that it wants to change the church's doctrine of God. In like manner the doctrine of an infused quality espoused by theology was shown to be rationally undemonstrable, by reference to the *potentia absoluta*. This does not mean that this doctrine, i.e., the doctrine of infusion, was disputed as a necessary theological supposition.

As Iserloh's thorough study on Ockham has shown,[3] the theology of the *potentia dei absoluta* in Ockham amounts to an actual dissolution of the ordinary pattern of the way of salvation. In all cases the necessity of the acts of grace is removed by the idea of the absolute power. The reflections on the ultimate possibility of the *potentia absoluta* and the principle of the law of contradiction occupy the center of interest, so that the way of salvation of the Bible and of the church no longer receive due consideration. . . .

This judgment does not hold to the same degree for the theology of Gabriel Biel. He modified the doctrine of the *venerabilis inceptor* (as he was called because of his enterprising spirit) to a marked degree and assigned a much more important and independent position to the *potentia dei ordinata* in favor of the traditional doctrine of the church. As has already been said, he does not permit the reflections concerning the *potentia absoluta* to annul the actual importance of the divinely established way of salvation. The way in which he at times combines the two lines of thought is shown by the question "whether of necessity God grants the grace of doing what is in one."

3. E. Iserloh, *Grace and Eucharist in the Philosophical Theology of William of Ockham* (Wiesbaden, 1958).

Biel answers this question in the affirmative, in doing which he is compelled to distinguish between the *necessitas coactionis* (or *absoluta*), that is, the absolute necessity, and the *necessitas immutabilitatis* (or *necessitas ex suppositione*), that is, the necessity arising from God's immutable nature. A compulsion or an absolute necessity does not obtain. Nevertheless, one can say that God must necessarily grant his grace to one who does his part. This, to be sure, is a contingent order, yet it is one that God established. Because God is immutable, he cannot change this order. The question referred to above must therefore be answered in the affirmative insofar as it pertains to the *necessitas immutabilitatis* (Lib. II, dist. 27, qu. 1, dub. 4), in exactly the same manner as one can say: "If someone is predestined, then he must also be redeemed." In this case, as in the one referred to above, both parts of the conclusion indicate something contingent. Nevertheless, the inference is necessary—by virtue of the established order. The question is unequivocally settled in favor of the "ordinary" or "ordained" power of God.

With this question we have already touched upon the first stage of the way of salvation as Biel develops it—namely, the *facere quod in se est* (doing one's part), which here, and often at other times, is designated as a prerequisite of justification.

> The *facere quod in se est,* according to Biel, means that a person removes whatever is a hindrance to grace. The obstacle (*obex gratie*) is any mortal sin. But then a person wonders how a man of himself—in his purely natural state—can remove mortal sin. The answer is that he cannot indeed remove the guilt of sin committed. He can, however, by his natural powers, refrain from assent to sin and from the sinful act. Indeed, he can even hate sin and desire not to sin. The *facere quod in se est* thus far coincides with the contribution that belongs to penance, but at the same time it also has a positive side; it embraces also "choosing a good attitude to God" (Cf. Lib. II, dist. 27, qu. 1, dub. 4; *ibid.* concl. 4 and Lib. IV, dist. 9, qu. 2, art. 1). Biel thus thinks that man can prepare himself for the reception of grace to such an extent that he can turn his will in a new direction, turn away from sin to the will of God. In so doing he has already taken a stand regarding the difficult question of free will. . . .

Biel, in this connection, first offers a number of definitions, which are important for our problem:

1. What does the term *"bonum morale"* or "moral good" mean? A distinction is made concerning the terms *"bonum meritorium," "bonum morale,"* and *"bonum ex genere,"* that is, deeds that are meritoriously good, morally good, or that are good by their very nature. Biel thinks that an act may be morally good even without reference to God. Only a *bonum meritorium* demands that an act be ultimately related to eternal life.

2. When we speak of the purely natural state (*de puris naturalibus*), it does not mean that the general cooperation of God is excluded; "the general influence of God is not excluded, which as the first cause concurs with the secondary agent." The definition of the term "natural state" reads: "But with the purely natural state is meant the nature or substance of the soul with the qualities and actions belonging to nature, exclusive of qualities and gifts supernaturally infused by God alone."

3. The expression *"implere precepta"* (to fulfill the command-ments) can be understood in a twofold way: either fulfillment ac-cording to substance (*quantum ad substantiam*) or fulfillment according to the intention of the one giving the commandment (*quantum ad intentionem precipientis*). The "intention" means that an act has merit as its aim and eternal life as its reward, according to the principle: "God, who gives the command, intends by every command that by observing it we merit entrance into life eternal" (Lib. II, dist. 28, qu. 1, art. 1).

According to these definitions Biel comes to the conclusion, in the first place, that "man's free will can produce an act that is morally good by virtue of his natural condition and without grace," a thing which is based on the fact that the will is able to act ac-cording to reason and therefore can choose an act which reason will pronounce right and good.

A second conclusion is that free will, by its natural powers and without the gift of grace, is able to shun mortal sin. For if the will can in every case act according to right reason, it must also be the case that in every choice the act that is not sinful can be chosen. The various difficulties that are encountered in choosing the good (the affections, the blindness of reason, etc.) do not annul that essential freedom, which belongs essentially to the will and is actually present when a choice is made. . . .

The conception that the human will by its natural powers is able to love God above all things is founded on the supposition that the will is able to follow the dictates of right reason. If it is possible for a man—in the case of false love—to love a created object above all things, how much more must it be possible for the will to heed reason when it judges that the *summum bonum* (the highest good), or God himself, should be loved above all things (Lib. III, dist. 27, qu. 1, propos. 1). . . .

In spite of all the acumen that Biel displayed in the discussion of all the implications of the doctrine of grace, he failed to see that the term *diligere deum super omnia* (loving God above all things) is ambiguous as long as it is applied both to the philosophical *summum bonum* and to the first commandment of the Divine law. Ultimately, he simply identifies "love" in the sense of the intention of the will to that which is good with *charitas* or the love implied when we speak of love to God (cf. Lib. III, dist. 27, qu. 1, dub. 2, propos. 1–5). No wonder that the criticism of the reformers is directed, above all, against the principles involved in the *facere quod in se est* and the *diligere deum super omnia.*

That the nominalist doctrine of grace is to be regarded principally as a negative basis of the Reformation doctrine of justification is shown also when we consider the fundamental conception of a *meritum de congruo* and of a *meritum de condigno.*

By *meritum* Biel means a deed, freely chosen, which is accepted as worthy of a certain reward. "For the consideration of merit in an act, two things are required. Firstly, its free choice; secondly, its acceptation for reward. A meritorious act is an act freely chosen by the will and accepted for the granting of a reward" (Lib. II, dist. 27, art. 1, nota 2). . . .

The words in Acts 15:11, "we believe that through the grace of the Lord Jesus Christ we shall be saved," are interpreted to mean that nature is accepted through Divine mercy and adorned with love or created grace as a supernatural gift, through which such meritorious acts are produced. In this way eternal life can be merited *de condigno,* or worthily. "In reality God accepts no one for eternal life unless he has poured into him the quality [*habitus*] of love" (Lib. I, dist. 17, qu. 3, art. 2).

When the Holy Scriptures speak of the reward for works (and thereby a heavenly reward is meant), grace is always presupposed, because without grace no work is worthy of such reward. The gift, moreover, is twofold: the *"uncreated* grace," which is identical with the Holy Spirit or with the gracious will of God, and the *"created* grace," which is a *habitus inclinans ad diligendum,* that is, a character inclined toward loving, namely, the infused love (Lib. II, dist. 17, qu. 2). Not until our works are considered according to this twofold grace can they count as merits with respect to the heavenly reward. "If they are considered as proceeding from the Holy Spirit dwelling in man, and from cooperating grace, as well as from the will of God which accepts them as worthy, they *are* worthy of such a generous . . . reward. . . . There is also found something in proportion to these in the meritorious act, for the Holy Spirit is there dwelling in man, by grace as it were, as the first cause, who corresponds to the ultimate goal, the triune God, who is objective blessedness itself. There is grace, which makes man pleasing and is supernaturally infused, as it were, the seed of glory. And as the seed of the tree by its virtue contains the entire tree, so grace by its virtue contains the rewards" (Lib. II, dist. 27, qu. 1, art. 2, concl. 1).

What Biel says concerning the *meritum de condigno,* on the whole, corresponds to Augustine's words, "When God crowns our merits, he crowns nothing else than his own works." But we get a different picture of his fundamental view when we take into consideration the doctrine of *meritum de congruo.*

A *meritum de congruo* exists when a freely chosen act is accepted for a particular reward not on the principle of justice but on that of generosity. "A *meritum de congruo* is an act voluntarily chosen and accepted for a reward, not because it is justly due to the recipient but solely because of the generosity of the one accepting it" (Lib. II, dist. 27, qu. 1, art. 1, nota 3). . . .

The *meritum de congruo,* which God rewards with the first infusion of grace, consists in the fact that the will, guided by right reason, chooses the right attitude toward God, thereby removing the obstacle to grace and avoiding the act of sin. "By the removal of the hindrance of the soul and the right attitude toward God chosen with free will a man can merit the first grace *de congruo* [in fairness]" (Lib. II, dist. 27, qu. 1, concl. 4).

Justification according to Biel consists in participation in justifying grace, growth in grace, and finally eternal salvation. Christ by his suffering and death has opened the gate of the kingdom of heaven for all the elect. But what he has done is not complete. "It is never the only and the entire cause of merit." In addition the works of man as *meritum de congruo* and *meritum de condigno* are required. . . .

The verdict of the reformers concerning this doctrine of justification, charging that it excludes Christ Himself as our righteousness, and faith in Him as the condition of justification, can readily be understood. . . . This verdict can hardly be called polemical exaggeration but corresponds fairly exactly to what the sources say. Criticism must also agree with the chief impression which Luther and the other reformers got—after many years of study —of the nominalist doctrine of justification.

Finally, the point in which Luther's doctrine of justification differs most decidedly from that of nominalism can perhaps be intimated by a quotation, in order that the peculiarity of the nominalist way of thinking may be illuminated still more sharply by comparison with Luther's position.

In a sermon which Luther preached in 1528 on John 16:3 he says: "But to know the Father means to know His Divine will and counsel concerning us—namely, that Christ should be born and die for us, in order that we might be saved by an alien righteousness. He wants to receive no one into his heavenly kingdom on the basis of his own righteousness, but whoever gets into heaven must get into it through an alien righteousness, which he has not earned. . . . As Adam brought damnation upon us by an alien sin, so Christ has saved us by an alien righteousness. This they do not want to believe; for the sake of this proclamation they call us damned heretics. Our testimony and confession is: Not through yourself but through Christ will you be saved. These two you must distinguish from one another, yourself and Christ. *You* did not come down from heaven, *you* were not born of Mary, but you were made out of dirt. Therefore Christ's doing is different from yours. Therefore the Gospel says: No one obtains the forgiveness of sins through himself and what is his, but through the work of Christ. That is an alien work, alien righteousness. That they cannot endure" (W.A., 27, 146 seq.).

The result of our study may be summarized as follows:

1. Nominalism knows righteousness (also as righteousness before God) only as a virtue, viewed theologically as love toward God and one's fellow men. Mysticism, on the other hand, knows righteousness also as something absolutely supernatural, as participation in God himself.

2. According to nominalism, justification is the reward of virtue, conditioned by that which man is capable of doing and has to accomplish in order to receive grace.

3. In contrast to nominalism, the Reformation is concerned about "grace alone" and about God's ascribing to men the "alien" righteousness of Christ.

4. With respect to the relationship to mysticism, that which is characteristic of the Reformation lies in the idea of the "alien righteousness of Christ," as well as in the emphasis on the Word as the mediator of the righteousness of God. "Grace alone" and in a certain respect the basic understanding of righteousness and the denial of the idea of merit are nothing new when compared with mysticism, although the reformers at these points expressed themselves with far greater and more decisive clarity.

GERHARD EBELING

Luther's Words

LUTHER'S WORKS WERE WORTHY OF HIS WORDS. To be concerned with words alone, whether as a teacher or a writer, a lawyer or a preacher, may appear a comfortable activity, while "to ride in armor, to suffer heat, frost, dust, thirst, and other discomforts, would be real work." "It is true," says Luther, "it would be difficult for me to ride in armor. All the same, I would like to see the horseman that could sit still for a whole day looking at a book, even if he did not have to compose, think, or read or worry about anything else. Ask a clerk, a preacher, or a speaker what kind of work writing and speaking is; ask a school-

From Gerhard Ebeling, *Luther: An Introduction to His Thought,* translated by R. A. Wilson (Philadelphia: Fortress Press, 1970). Copyright © in the English translation, William Collins Sons & Co. Ltd., London, and Fortress Press, Philadelphia, 1970, pages 43–58. Reprinted with permission of Fortress Press.

master what kind of work the teaching and education of boys is.
A pen is light, certainly . . . but at the same time the best part
(the head), the noblest member (the tongue), and the loftiest
activity (speech) of the human body have to bear the brunt and
do the most work, while with others it is the hand, the foot, and
the back or some similar limb which does all the work, while at
the same time they can sing merrily and joke as they please, which
a writer cannot do. Three fingers do everything (so they say of
writers), but the whole body and soul take part in the work." [1]
Thus speech, the word, is the highest activity of man, and also the
work that demands most of him: "The body and soul take part in
the work"; this is more accurate than our expression "brainwork."

In Luther's case, this work grew to an unimaginable extent.
As early as 1516—a year before the violent struggle broke out—
we hear in a letter to a fellow member of his order, who was a
friend of his, the complaint that he was utterly overburdened:
"I almost need to have two secretaries or clerks. The whole day
long I do virtually nothing but write letters . . . I preach in the
monastery and at table; every day I am also asked to preach in
the parish church, I am Director of Studies and Vicar-General
of the Order, that is, prior eleven times over, administrator of
the fisheries in Leitzkau, and steward of the Herzberg affairs in
Torgau; I lecture on Paul, and am gathering material for lectures
on the Psalms; besides this there is correspondence, which as I
have said claims the major part of my time. It is very rarely that
no inroads are made on my time for the breviary and for cele-
brating mass; not to speak of my personal struggle against the
temptations of the flesh, the world, and the Devil. See what an
idler I am!" [2] But we do not have to rely on these personal testimonies. Our knowledge of the work Luther in fact achieved confirms them in full. Two individual examples we happen to possess
illustrate this. From Palm Sunday to the Wednesday in Easter
Week of 1529, that is, in eleven days, Luther preached eighteen
sermons in Wittenberg, in addition to everything else. Or consider the extent, and most of all the profundity and significance,

1. W.A., 30 (part II), 573.7f., 10–16, and 18; 574.6 (1530); Bonn Ed., 4,
171.22 f., 25–32, and 34–40.
2. W.A. Br., 1, 72 (No. 28), 4–13 (26 October 1516).

of the literary production of a year such as 1520, which shows an unparalleled intensity of intellectual creation. Several printing presses were occupied simultaneously to keep pace with him.

At the same time, he was not concerned with *his own* word. The certainty that he was dealing with the Word of God, and that this was his duty to the world, gave him courage to make the boldest utterances, but also brought him moments of bitter disappointment, such as in 1530, when for a time he refused to preach to the ungrateful congregation of Wittenberg.[3] This feeling can be perceived in his *Exhortation to All Clergy Assembled at Augsburg,* written in the same year: "Not that we have any great pleasure in preaching. For speaking for myself, there is no message I would rather receive than that which would relieve me of the duty of preaching. I am so weary of it because of the intolerable burden the Devil and the world place upon me. But the poor souls will not have it. There is also a man, who is called Jesus Christ, who says no. I am ready to follow Him, since I am even more beholden to Him."[4] "We who preach the gospel," say the startling words of one sermon, "are a highway over which Satan rides."[5]

This task was carried out by means of, and for the sake of, the Word, which did not spring from his own mind and heart, but was drawn from the text of Holy Scripture and came to utterance as a result of constant attention and strenuous study. It was also a liberation from his own literary works. This is expressed at the conclusion of the Christmas sermon of 1522: "O that God should desire that my interpretation and that of all teachers should disappear, and each Christian should come straight to the Scripture alone and to the pure Word of God! You see from this babbling of mine the immeasurable difference between the Word of God and all human words, and how no man can adequately reach and explain a single Word of God with all his words. It is an eternal Word, and must be understood and contemplated with a quiet mind, as the eighty-third Psalm says: 'I will hear what God himself speaks in me' (Vulgate, Psalm 84:9: R.S.V., Psalm 85:8).

3. W.A., 32, 4.16 ff. (1530).
4. W.A., 30 (part II), 340.13; 341.3 (1530); Bonn Ed., 4, 135.18–24.
5. W.A., 27, 251.16 (1528).

No one else can understand except a mind that contemplates in silence. For anyone who could achieve this without commentary or interpretation, my commentaries and those of everyone else would not only be of no use, but merely a hindrance. Go to the Bible itself, dear Christians, and let my expositions and those of all scholars be no more than a tool with which to build aright, so that we can understand, taste, and abide in the simple and pure Word of God; for God dwells alone in Zion." [6] After resisting for a long time the project of a complete edition of his works, he finally consented, but in 1539 and 1545, in the prefaces to the first volumes of the German and Latin writings respectively, he emphasizes that he would gladly have seen all his books destroyed and buried in oblivion.[7] Moreover, he expected this: "I comfort myself with the thought that with time my books will remain covered in dust, except where I have written something good [through God's grace]." [8]

To obtain a concrete conception of Luther's word, we must glance briefly at his extant writings and classify them according to their nature and origin. To undertake the study of his writings is to set sail upon an ocean. More than eighty years have already been spent upon what is at the present time the standard edition of his works, the Weimar edition. Although almost all his writings are available in this edition, the end is scarcely in sight, since, besides additions, its deficient quality in some parts makes a revision in the form of supplements and corrections necessary, while the preparation of an index in particular presents great difficulties. The Weimar edition consists at the present time of a hundred folio volumes of approximately seven hundred pages each.

In spite of its evident deficiencies, this edition is of great importance for our knowledge of Luther by comparison with earlier editions, not merely with regard to the text, dating, and commentary, but also because it includes extensive material that literally "lay forgotten in the dust." There are two great complexes of such material. The first consists of transcriptions from the period of Luther's maturity. The many volumes of tran-

6. W.A., 10 (part I, sec. 1), 728.9–21 (1522).
7. W.A., 50, 657.2 f. (1539); 54, 179.13 f. (1545); Bonn Ed., 4, 421.15 f.
8. W.A., 50, 658.2–4 (1539).

scriptions of sermons, which cover much previously unknown material, are of particular importance. The transcriptions of disputations and lectures from this later period in the main enlarge what we already possess, and to some extent bring us nearer to the original wording. Of incomparably greater importance, however, is the material from Luther's early period, about which previous centuries had no authentic knowledge apart from a handful of dates. When one considers that the first work that Luther himself had printed [9] takes us back only to the spring of 1517, and that up to the second half of the nineteenth century this formed for practical purposes the limit before which no insight into his intellectual activity was possible, it can be seen how much the situation in research on Luther has changed. For beginning with the year 1509, though to a limited extent at first, Luther's marginal notes in numerous textbooks [10] give us the first direct evidence of his thinking, while from 1513 we suddenly have a stream of works, some of them in an excellent manuscript tradition. There is the virgin forest, filling twelve hundred pages of the Weimar edition, of his preparatory work for the first course of lectures, that on the Psalms from the years 1513 to 1515. [11] Then there are his lectures on the Epistles to the Romans, [12] Galatians, and Hebrews. [13] Thus, from the beginning of his professorship to the struggle over indulgences, we possess an unbroken documentary record of his theological development, texts that were never intended for publication and were not even known in their entirety to those who heard his lectures at that time. They are merely preparatory notes, serving to clarify his own mind, and consequently to be dated at the very moment of his spiritual and intellectual struggle. It is only by means of this material, which is far

9. W.A., I, 154–220. "The Seven Penitential Psalms with a Commentary in German."

10. W.A., 9, 1–115 (on Augustine, Peter Lombard, Tauler, etc.). Other material has so far appeared only in a separate edition: *Luthers Randbemerkungen zu Gabriel Biels Collectorium in quattuor libros sententiarum und zu dessen Sacri canonis missae expositio,* edited by H. Degering, 1933.

11. W.A., 3 and 4, 1–526. Fascicules of a new edition of the lectures on the Psalms began to appear in 1963, provided with an exhaustive apparatus: W.A., 55, 1 (Glosses) and W.A., 55, 2 (Scholia).

12. W.A., 56.

13. W.A., 57.

from being exhausted, that we have been able to study in detail Luther's conversion from Scholasticism to Reformation theology in constant comparison with the tradition from which he came and the literature on which he was working—a laborious but stimulating subject for research. I know of no parallel in the whole of history in which a spiritual upheaval of such proportions can be studied with anything approaching the same fullness of original sources.

Three general observations must be made on what we possess of Luther's words.

First, it is already obvious that the state of the tradition varies greatly. In some cases we still possess his original manuscripts, and in others only the earliest printed version. Sometimes we must make do with the transcriptions made by his hearers, or even with mere copies of transcriptions, and sometimes again with printed versions prepared by others with or without Luther's authority. Thus in handling the texts one must obviously be aware of this, in order not to be misled by a watering down of the language or a shift of theological emphasis on the part of an unsympathetic student. On the whole, however, a first-class tradition exists for the bulk of his work, which serves as a guide for the profitable use of the secondary material.

Secondly, when considering the importance of Luther for the German language, it is easy to forget that a large part of his work is in Latin. This is naturally true of all his lectures, in which only an occasional, usually emotional, German expression occurs. Thus for example in 1515, in a controversial anti-Scholastic discussion of Romans 4:7, he exclaims *"O Sautheologen"* ("pigs of theologians")![14] Similarly, it is Latin which is predominant in all works that are meant for those with a theological education, though again there are occasional German interjections such as *"Das ist zu viel!"* ("That is too much!") in *De servo arbitrio;*[15] and Latin is also used in the vast majority of the letters. The church usage, Scholasticism, and humanism combined to give Latin this unique position, and one cannot overestimate its impor-

14. W.A., 56, 274.14 (1515); Bonn Ed. (2nd ed.), 5, 242.11.
15. W.A., 18, 610.5 (1525); Bonn Ed., 3, 103.40 f.

tance for Luther's thought. On the whole, it is his Latin writings that provide our real access to his theological thought.

Finally, for reasons we have still to consider, Luther's work was influenced to an extraordinary degree by the situation for which it was written. In order to be aware of any changes that may have occurred in his thought, and above all to understand his every utterance in the concrete circumstances of its origin and purpose, the situation that gave rise to it and the aim it was intended to achieve, the circumstances that surrounded it, and the persons to whom it was addressed, its necessity, and the specific issues that placed a limitation on it or liberated its ideas—that is, to understand it as words spoken to others—one must always take into account the time at which it was written. That is why the first concern of an adequate edition and interpretation of Luther's works must necessarily be that of chronology. A summary view of the mass of available material is naturally best obtained by classifying it according to the basic situations in which Luther spoke, and the literary forms that corresponded to them.

The first of these categories includes everything that belongs directly to his academic work, that is, his lectures and disputations. The lectures extend, with brief interruptions occasioned by external circumstances, from 1513 to 1546. They are exclusively concerned with biblical exegesis. This, of course, was an obligatory task from the end of 1512, as a result of his appointment to the *lectura in Bibliam,* as successor to Johannes von Staupitz. But it was unusual for a Scholastic theologian to rest content with the exposition of Scripture and not to pass on to dogmatic teaching, normally in the form of a commentary on the *Sententiae* of Peter Lombard. Luther made a decision here which was closely associated with his conversion to Reformation principles, though it is not possible to give an accurate date, since there was no longer any possibility of Luther's transferring from biblical exegesis. His exclusive concern with the Scriptures should also be contrasted not merely with Scholasticism, but also with the humanist form of instruction adopted by Melanchthon, based on *loci theologici* and a continuous exegesis. Luther mainly dealt with Old Testament books, especially—I list them in the order of the canon— Genesis, Deuteronomy, the Psalms, Ecclesiastes, the Song of Solomon, Isaiah, and the minor prophets. The only New Testament writings on which he lectured were epistles: Romans, Galatians, I Timothy, Titus, Philemon, I John, and Hebrews. This choice was partly due to outward circumstances. The exposition of the Gospels was the responsibility of other professors; Luther handed over that of the Epistle to the Romans to Melanchthon, who in the course of the years lectured five times on it, while Luther did so only once, during his early period. It is of great practical significance that Luther began his teaching with the exposition of the Psalms (1513–1515), the book of the Bible with which he was most familiar through his monastic office, and which spoke to him most directly, pregnant as it is with religious emotion; and that he then proceeded methodically to the study of St. Paul, lecturing on Romans (1515–1516), Galatians (1516–1517), and Hebrews (1517–1518), which was also traditionally regarded as Pauline, and finally returning, a proof as it were of his theological progress, to the Psalter (1518–1519). In 1519 the first commentary on Galatians[16] was printed, and between 1519 and 1521 the *Operationes in Psalmos*.[17] He later lectured again on these texts. It is also characteristic that the emphasis is on the Old Testament. Among other reasons for this was the fact that Luther felt himself more of an expert in Hebrew than in Greek, by comparison with the Greek scholar Melanchthon. The form of exegesis he used is also important. In the early lectures, up to and including the lectures on Hebrews, he still held to the Scholastic division into interlinear and marginal glosses (that is, brief explanations, which were written between the lines and on the edges of a text of the Bible printed with wide spacing for the purpose of lecturing) and *scholia* (that is, longer explanations of chosen passages, written on a separate sheet). When he returned to the beginning of his course, and at the same time began the publication of printed works with his commentaries on the Psalms and Galatians, his theological maturity had also brought a liberation from Scholastic forms, and he turned to continuous exegesis of the whole context.

In addition to lectures, an important part was played in the

16. W.A., 2, 436–618.
17. W.A., 5, 1–673.

university teaching of that time by disputations—something similar to the modern seminar, although following a quite different method. In the precise formulation of theses, which was the professor's task even in the disputations on which the awarding of degrees depended, and in those that were held merely for the sake of practice, Luther was an expert. He showed great patience in correcting the mistakes of his students, and in the contributions that he made himself he argued with telling force. The Scholastic form of disputation disappeared with the beginning of the university reforms in Wittenberg, but was readopted in a modified form in 1535. It became an essential instrument in inculcating Reformation theology in the university and in resisting false developments within the Reformation; the great disputations with the antinomians[18] are a notable example of this.

The translations of the Bible must also be regarded as part of his academic work. In the case of the Old Testament it was a task carried out in partnership with others, while the revision of the whole of the Scripture was placed in the hands of a commission, whose minutes are still extant.[19] One can see in practice what Luther describes in his "On Translation: An Open Letter": "And it often happened that for a fortnight, or three or four weeks, we sought and inquired for a single word, and yet sometimes did not find it. We worked in this way on the book of Job, Master Philip, Aurogallus, and myself, so that sometimes we scarcely succeeded in finishing three lines in four days." [20]

Luther constantly moved between the lecture room and the pulpit. In both he was concerned with the same issues, although he was carrying out different tasks, in part, though not solely, because he was addressing what was to some extent a different audience. But because the issues were the same, the two forms of the word, theological teaching and preaching, were very close to each other. *Doctrina,* in Reformation usage, can refer to both, without prejudice to either aspect. Another similarity is that he saw both entirely as the spoken word, temporal in the strictest sense, uttered here and now; and he did not concern himself a

18. W.A., 39 (part I), 334–584 (1537–1540).
19. In W.A. D.B., 3 and 4.
20. W.A., 30 (part II), 636.16–20 (1530); Bonn Ed., 4, 183.24–28.

great deal about the preservation of the spoken word in writing. He completed in literary form only the first part of the Commentary on the Psalms (Psalms 1–22) and an early version of the Commentary on Galatians.[21] Similarly, Luther himself prepared for publication only a small number of the *Postillen* (homilies) and of the sermons, insofar as they appeared in print at all. This was partly due to a shortage of time and partly to the cooperation of willing helpers. The greatest service was rendered by Georg Rörer, who from 1522 up to the time of Luther's death transcribed both his lectures and his sermons. These are also of the utmost importance from the linguistic point of view, for they are the earliest direct transcriptions of spoken German. Of course we possess them only in a cryptic form, as a mixed German and Latin text in a telegraphic style; for the transcription was carried out using a system of abbreviation developed for Latin, and consequently involved a partial translation into Latin, with the inclusion of directly recorded German words. Thus a kind of paraphrase and retranslation is necessary in order to bring us back to the original. But this procedure has the advantage that it gives us a more accurate indication of the impression made by his words, whereas Luther's own German, which sounds old-fashioned to us, can produce, as a direct result of this patina of historical authenticity, the false impression that its original effect was similar. More than two thousand sermons are still extant. Since for the most part they are on the traditional epistles and gospels of the church, and therefore often comment on the same text year after year, they make it possible to study changes in his exegesis. And the series of sermons largely devoted to successive chapters from the gospels, which were delivered on weekdays, are a welcome supplement to the exegetical lectures, which are deficient with respect to the gospels.

Of course our view of Luther as a writer has been formed principally by his controversial works, in which he developed an uncanny talent for forceful polemic, sometimes going beyond tolerable limits. His much discussed coarseness must be regarded as a reflection of his times. But it cannot be denied that as Luther

21. Cf. notes 16 and 17.

grew older he went far beyond what was normal in this respect, especially as his outbursts of empty insults are always associated with a deadly serious struggle about matters of ultimate importance, and at the same time with a sparkling wit that sprang from his vast ascendancy over his opponents. To give a fair picture, it is necessary to give a gross example of this, not exactly fit for the drawing room. In a work written in 1541 against Duke Heinrich von Braunschweig-Wolfenbüttel, entitled *Wider Hans Worst (Against the Clown)*, Luther intervened in an exchange of polemics that was already in progress, and that was full of violent abuse, between the duke of Brunswick on the one hand, and the elector of Saxony and the landgrave of Hesse on the other. The already poisoned atmosphere was certainly not cleared by observations such as the following: "You shouldn't have written a book unless you had heard a fart from an old sow, when you should have opened your mouth wide to it and said, 'Thank you very much, beautiful nightingale, that will make good text for me'!" [22] This sort of thing ought naturally not to be treated in isolation from the enormous inner strain under which he wrote, and we must also bear in mind its association with a cheerful calm on a much higher level, which is expressed, for example, in the introductory words of the same work with a triumphant freedom:

> Speaking for myself, I am very happy that books of this sort should be written against me; for it warms not only my heart, but my knees and my heels, when I see that through me, poor wretched man that I am, the Lord God so embitters and maddens both the princes of hell and princes of this world, so that they virtually explode and burst asunder from madness, while I sit in the shade of faith and the Our Father and laugh at the Devil and his hangers-on, bawling and writhing in their great anger. With all this they achieve nothing, except to make their own case worse every day, and advance and make better mine [that is, God's] . . . for by this they make me young and fresh, strong and happy. [23]

22. W.A., 51, 561.9–12 ,1541); Bonn Ed., 4, 373.10–13.
23. W.A., 51, 469.17–26 and 29 f. (1541); Bonn Ed., 4, 322.14; 323.2 and 5 f.

I have begun by commenting on this side of Luther's writings, in order to make clear by contrast that the real impulse that drove him to write lay elsewhere than in such extreme manifestations. Why was Luther not satisfied with lecturing and preaching? Why did he take up the pen? The primary reason was not the urge of the scholar nor the controversial zeal of a reformer, but the responsibility of a pastor for a pure, clear, comprehensible, convincing, and liberating proclamation of the gospel. He had himself struggled to understand the righteousness of God, which, as the gospel reveals, means that the righteous live by faith. This struggle had to be proclaimed publicly to the people in the language which they spoke, that is, in German. In view of the fact that Luther was soon to become a controversialist, and was at the time a Scholastic theologian, it is an astonishing fact that his first publication was a devotional work in German, an exposition of the seven Penitential Psalms, which appeared in the spring of 1517.[24] This provides a key to his entire theology, and so to his literary work as a whole. Then, in spite of the dispute over indulgences, which began shortly afterward and developed with extreme rapidity into the great struggle with the Catholic Church, and in addition to the controversial writings and theological treatises which this demanded, there followed a constant and frequent succession of German devotional works, entirely non-polemical, and exclusively concerned with what makes a man a Christian: expositions of the Ten Commandments or the Lord's Prayer,[25] and brief, profound, and yet universally comprehensible sermons on the contemplation of the passion of Christ,[26] on preparation for death,[27] on individual sacraments: the Eucharist,[28] baptism,[29] penance,[30] and also the "Treatise Concerning the Ban." [31] There were also others on ethical subjects: on the mar-

24. Cf. note 9.
25. W.A., 1, 247–256 (1518); 2, 57–65 (1519); 2, 74–130 (1519); 6, 11–19 (1519); 6, 20–22 (1519); 7, 194–229 (1520); Bonn Ed., 2, 38–59.
26. W.A., 2, 131–142 (1519); Bonn Ed., 1, 154–160.
27. W.A., 2, 680–697 (1519); Bonn Ed., 1, 161–173.
28. W.A., 2, 738–758 (1519); Bonn Ed., 1, 196–212; 6, 349–378 (1520); Bonn Ed., 1, 299–322.
29. W.A., 2, 724–737 (1519); Bonn Ed., 1, 185–195.
30. W.A., 2, 709–723 (1519); Bonn Ed., 1, 174–184.
31. W.A., 6, 61–75 (1520); Bonn Ed., 1, 213–226.

ried state[32] and usury,[33] and, the crown of this whole literature, the "Treatise on Good Works" [34] and the treatise "On the Freedom of a Christian." [35] A large amount of devotional literature had already appeared previously in German. But Luther's word represented such an astonishing innovation, both in the fundamental understanding that inspired it, and also from the linguistic point of view, that it would inevitably have come to be regarded as epoch-making, even if it had never been associated with the mighty external upheaval of the Reformation. But precisely this upheaval of the Reformation cannot be dissociated from this quiet and unassuming literary work, any more than the Reformation can be dissociated from the results which Luther attained, *orans et laborans* in the isolation of his monastic cell, from his reading of the Scriptures—results, the inevitable consequences of which he was willing to face.

The impulse that was at work in these early instructions in the Christian faith, written for general reading, was maintained in similar later works, including the catechisms[36] and the hymns.[37] These are the most impressive of their kind in the language, and through them the Word of God became the nourishment and refuge of whole generations. The same basic impulse is also present both in numerous controversial writings, and also in strictly theological works (for which Luther in fact made time only because of the necessities of the struggle in which he was involved, and which were not the products of the leisure of a scholar with literary leanings).

The final group of the extant works of Luther consists of a complex of writings in which his word found its most personal form. This group includes in particular his letters, of which we possess about 2,800. They cover the whole range from everyday affairs to matters of national importance, from the most private utterances to letters written on the highest official level. Apart from the strictly theological statements they contain, they form

32. W.A., 2, 162–171 (1519).
33. W.A., 6, 1–8 (1519); 6, 33–60 (1520).
34. W.A., 6, 196–276 (1520); Bonn Ed., 1, 227–298.
35. W.A., 7, 12–38 (1520); Bonn Ed., 2, 1–27.
36. W.A., 30, 1.
37. W.A., 35.

as it were a compendium of theology, which had been drawn from his immediate experience and which provided one and the same person with the proper language for addressing princes and prelates, brothers and sisters in temptation, and not least, his own wife, Käthe, and his young son, Hänschen. A distinctive mixture of intimacy and wide-ranging practicality marks the tradition of what is known as his *Table Talk,* which consists of notes that Luther's companions made during or after meals, from the beginning of the 1530s, on the numerous conversations which were conducted at table. They preserve for us, in fascinating variety and concrete detail, Luther's thought and judgments, appearing as it were in their everyday dress.

We shall be concerned from now on with the context and purpose of Luther's word, having given only a very sketchy outline here of the numerous forms in which it has been handed down. To conclude this brief summary, we shall anticipate the rest of our work by mentioning a few characteristics of his word.

To begin with its outward effect, his word, once it had been uttered, found a unique response. The wide public appeal that Luther achieved overnight was without question very complex in nature. All the religious longing and unrest, ecclesiastical problems and abuses, political tensions and upheavals, social discontent and ferment, changes in education and in the understanding of reality, which manifested themselves in a confused form at the end of the Middle Ages, were suddenly voiced and transformed into a unified movement (unified at least apparently and at first) by Luther's word. A new historical phenomenon appeared: there was suddenly something resembling a public opinion, more intensive and far-reaching than at almost any previous time. An objective symptom of this unique response is the wide circulation of Luther's writings, and especially of his devotional and religious works. One study on this subject has reached the following conclusion: "Of about thirty works of this nature that Luther published between March, 1517 and the summer of 1520, we know of 370 impressions by 1520." "Luther needed only to publish a new work in Wittenberg, for printers in Leipzig, Nuremberg, Augsburg, Strasbourg, Basel, and other cities to fall upon it and reprint it, and this was usually done by two, three, or four presses in the same city." "There is evidence extant that every popular devotional work that Luther published up to the summer of 1520, that is, until the appearance of the *Address to the Christian Nobility,* was reprinted on the average twelve times, sometimes less, sometimes more, and in some cases as often as twenty-four times." [38]

As we have said, many factors combined to produce this effect. However cautious we are, we must not forget that these are the words of one who spoke to his own time what it needed to hear, words uttered with the compelling force of what can be uttered in the light of the day, with the liberty of one who is completely absorbed by what he has to say, and with the practicality of one who is hitting the nail right on the head. His word is drawn from the Holy Scripture and inspired by it alone. It is equal to the overwhelming task demanded by the Scriptures of translating them into the language of his own age in accordance with the principle that he himself laid down for the interpretation and exegesis of the Scripture: "You must ask the mother at home, the children in the street, and the common man in the marketplace, and see on their own lips how they speak, and translate accordingly, so that they understand it and realize that you are speaking German to them." [39] The Holy Scriptures and the present day intersect as it were at a single point, in the conscience that hears the Word. It was Luther's concern that the Word of God should be heard in this way.

38. H. Dannenbauer, *Luther als religiöser Volksschriftsteller* (Tübingen, 1930), 30.
39. W.A., 30 (part II), 637: 19–22 (1530); Bonn Ed., 4, 184. 25–28.

LENNART PINOMAA

The Doctrine of Predestination

THE CONTRAST BETWEEN THE TRUE LUTHER and the traditional Luther is sharpest at the point of the understanding of free will. The issue has to do with the matter of preparation for grace (*dispositio ad gratiam*). Is there anything man can do to prepare himself to receive God's grace? In answering this question negatively Luther wrote in *Assertio omnium articulorum* (1520), referring to the pope: "You argue that free will can prepare for the reception of grace, but Christ says contrariwise that such a thing is rejected, increasing the distance between man's possibilities and grace." [1] This same thought is

From Lennart Pinomaa, *Faith Victorious: An Introduction to Luther's Theology,* translated by Walter J. Kukkonen (Philadelphia: Fortress Press, 1963). Copyright © 1963 by Fortress Press, pages 27–34. Reprinted with permission of the publisher.

1. W.A., 7, 143 (1520).

expressed repeatedly in *The Bondage of the Will.* The very opening statement of purpose itself is significant. In the first part of
the book Luther quotes Erasmus's definition of free will: "I conceive of 'free will' in this context as a power of the human will
by which a man may apply himself to those things that lead to
eternal salvation, or turn away from the same." [2] Concerning this
definition Luther says:

> Erasmus informs us, that "free will" is a power of the human
> will which can of itself will and not will the Word and work of
> God, by which it is to be led to those things that exceed its
> grasp and comprehension. If it can will and not will, it can also
> love and hate; and if it can love and hate, it can in a measure
> keep the law and believe the gospel. For, if you can will and not
> will, it cannot be that you are not able by that will of yours to do
> some part of a work, even though another should prevent your
> being able to complete it. Now, since death, the cross, and all
> the evils of the world are numbered among the works of God
> that lead to salvation, the human will will thus be able to will its
> own death and perdition. Yes, it can will all things when it can
> will the contents of the Word and work of God! What can
> be anywhere below, above, within or without the Word and
> work of God, except God himself? But what is here left to grace
> and the Holy Ghost? This is plainly to ascribe divinity to "free
> will!" For to will the law and the gospel, not to will sin, and to
> will death, is possible to divine power alone, as Paul says in more
> places than one [cf. I Corinthians 2:14; II Corinthians 3:5].[3]

Luther could not agree with Erasmus that free will could make
us children of God. Free will limited the all-embracing activity of
God and made sinful and enslaved man a being equal and similar
to God. Free will was to Luther a reflection of man's most brazen
pride, his desire to be "like God." The combination of the words
"free" and "will" was to him a horrible thing, representing Satan's
kingdom in all mankind.[4] At its best free will is at its worst,
because it resists the righteousness of faith.[5] Luther understood
the biblical antithesis between flesh and spirit to mean that in the

2. *The Bondage of the Will,* p. 137 (W.A., 18, 661).
3. *Ibid.,* p. 140 (W.A., 18, 664).
4. *Ibid.,* p. 201 (W.A., 18, 707).
5. *Ibid.,* p. 278 (W.A., 18, 760).

state of false righteousness man is "flesh," that is, confident in his own resources. This righteousness rests upon man's own works, efforts, and strivings. In the very act of trying by the utmost spiritual activity to make himself acceptable to God, man is "flesh." He seeks his own glory as he proffers to God his piety and perfection.

Erasmus too placed free will within the framework of flesh and spirit. For him free will meant freedom of spirit, and any imperfection was due to resistance afforded by the flesh. The English humanist Colet had introduced Italian humanism to Erasmus. In the academy of Florence, Paul was interpreted along the lines of ancient philosophy. Erasmus too began to think of spirit as Divine and of body as animal. The spirit aspires upward, but the body hinders its progress. Already Augustine had taught that before the Fall the spirit ruled the body but subsequently the body gained the upper hand and began to dominate the spirit. This domination of the flesh explains the tragic conflict within man. In Erasmus's view reason represents the Divine aspect of the soul.

In Luther's view reason is the most characteristically human element in man and therefore reflects most clearly the self-centered state of man. It reveals the "mind of the flesh." Reason signifies man's natural religion in conflict with God's righteousness.[6] Luther writes in *The Bondage of the Will*:

> "By the law is the knowledge of sin," says Paul (Romans 3:20). Here he shows how much and how far the law profits, teaching that "free will" is of itself so blind that it does not even know what sin is, but needs the law to teach it! And what can a man essay to do in order to take away sin, when he does not know what sin is? Surely this: mistake what is sin for what is not sin, and what is not sin for what is sin! Experience informs us clearly enough how the world, in the persons of those whom it accounts its best and most zealous devotees of righteousness and godliness, hates and hounds down the righteousness of God preached in the gospel, and brands it heresy, error, and other opprobrious names, while flaunting and hawking its own works and devices (which are really sin and error) as righteousness and wisdom. By these words, therefore, Paul stops the mouth of "free will," teaching that by the law it is shown sin, as being ignorant of its sin; so

6. Cf. L. Pinomaa, "Järjen Jumala-kuva ja uskon Jumala-kuva," *Luthertutkielmia* (Helsinki, 1939), p. 120.

far is he from allowing it any power to make endeavors toward good. . . .[7]

The commandment of God does not imply that man is able to keep it. Luther writes: "So when Ecclesiasticus says, 'If thou art willing to keep the commandments, and to keep the faith that pleaseth me, they shall preserve thee,' I fail to see how 'free will' can be proved from his words."[8] No more does the admonition, "Choose!" imply that man is able to choose. Luther continues: "Wherefore, my good Erasmus, as often as you confront me with the words of the law, so often shall I confront you with the words of Paul: 'By the law is the knowledge of sin,' not power of will."[9] The alternatives are: Christ or man's free will. If man can do what is required of him, Christ is unnecessary. As Luther sees it, the position of the Bible is clear: "The Scripture sets before us a man who is not only bound, wretched, captive, sick and dead, but who, through the operation of Satan his lord, adds to his other miseries that of blindness, so that he believes himself to be free, happy, possessed of liberty and ability, whole and alive."[10] Luther considered as stupor or daze the notion that the words "turn ye" and "if thou wilt turn" establish the power of free will.[11] He writes:

Therefore, all that is said against concluding in favor of "free will" from this word "love God," must also be said against concluding in favor of "free will" from any other words of command or requirement. If we suppose that the command to love shows us the tenor of the law and our duty only, but not our power of will or ability (inability, rather), then the same is shown by all other words of demand. . . . The words of the law do not prove the power of "free will," but show us the extent of our duty and our inability.[12]

Luther was well acquainted with the pattern of Erasmus's thought. He quotes Erasmus: "If man does nothing, there is no room for merit, and where there is no room for merit there will

7. *The Bondage of the Will,* pp. 286 f. (W.A., 18, 766).
8. *Ibid.,* p. 151 (W.A., 18, 672).
9. *Ibid.,* p. 159 (W.A., 18, 677).
10. *Ibid.,* p. 162 (W.A., 18, 679).
11. *Ibid.,* p. 164 (W.A., 18, 681).
12. *Ibid.,* p. 165 (W.A., 18, 681).

be no room for punishment or rewards." [13] But free will cannot be proved on the basis of merit—at least not with the Bible.[14] The whole Bible proclaims that we are saved by grace.

The following quotation represents a key point in Luther's train of thought:

> Now, since reason praises God when he saves the unworthy but finds fault with him when he damns the undeserving, it stands convicted of not praising God as God but as One who serves its own convenience—that is, what it looks for and praises in God is self, and the things of self, and not God and the things of God. But if a God who crowns the undeserving pleases you, you ought not be displeased when he damns the undeserving! If he is just in the one case, he cannot but be just in the other.[15]

This key passage is a graphic demonstration of what justification of the ungodly looks like within the framework of Scholastic Aristotelianism. When philosophy and theology are asked the same questions, it becomes manifest that human reason wants to make even God its servant. This is the intent and purpose of rationalism and idealism: God must behave as we think he ought to behave. Theology must make sense in the same manner as other things make sense. Luther is fully aware of the problem involved:

> Doubtless it gives the greatest possible offense to common sense or natural reason, that God, who is proclaimed as being full of mercy and goodness, and so on, should of His own mere will abandon, harden, and damn men, as though He delighted in the sins and great eternal torments of such poor wretches. It seems an iniquitous, cruel, intolerable thought to think of God; and it is this that has been a stumbling block to so many great men down the ages. And who would not stumble at it? I have stumbled at it myself more than once, down to the deepest pit of despair, so that I wished I had never been made a man. (That was before I knew how health-giving that despair was, and how close to grace.) This is why so much toil and trouble has been devoted to clearing the goodness of God, and throwing the blame on man's will.[16]

13. *Ibid.*, p. 237 (W.A., 18, 733).
14. *Ibid.*, p. 184 (W.A., 18, 695).
15. *Ibid.*, p. 234 (W.A., 18, 731).
16. *Ibid.*, p. 217 (W.A., 18, 719).

Luther was very familiar with the rocks on which reason stumbled. He writes:

> We are nowhere more recklessly irreverent than when we trespass upon and argue about these inscrutable mysteries of judgments. We pretend all the while that we are showing incredible reverence, in that we are searching the Holy Scriptures, which God told us to search (John 5:39). But them we do not search; whereas, in the place where He forbade us to search, there we do nothing but search, with endless audacity, not to say blasphemy! [17]

By the words "we do not search" Luther is referring to the fact that men do not want to search the clear passages of Scripture which speak of Christ, but only to investigate and meditate upon God's unsearchable mysteries which are beyond human comprehension.

Luther expresses his personal attitude toward predestination with the words: it is not for our investigation! We must pay attention to the infinite grace of the gospel right up to the very brink of the precipice where predestination begins, but there we must stop. We must not try to force our way into the mysteries of the Divine Majesty. If we look into the sun with our naked eyes, it will blind us. We must trust God's inscrutable justice and thank Him if we are preserved from doubts and despair (*Anfechtung*) associated with predestination. Above all we must cling to the revealed saving will of God.

Luther starts with God's omnipotence, to which the Bible bears witness from beginning to end, and with the Holy Spirit's work, without which no man can believe or be saved. He who proposes to be saved by a faith of his own creation makes himself his own savior, and makes Christ unnecessary.[18] Luther saw the whole problem in the form of the alternative: either self-made faith or Christ. If predestination is simple in meaning—that is, if the term "predestination" always has the same connotation in philosophy and theology—then presumably faith also is simple. We confuse the psychological and theological viewpoints and make repentance and faith into works of man—all in order not to diminish the sense of responsibility! Luther asks:

17. *Ibid.*, p. 216 (W.A., 18, 718).
18. *Ibid.*, p. 258 (W.A., 18, 747).

Can the endeavors of "free will" lay hold of eternal salvation, when it cannot keep hold of a farthing, or a hair of the head? When we have no power to hold down the creature, can we have power to hold down the Creator? Why are we so crazy? [19]

Reason, flesh, and free will are set over against faith, Spirit, and enslaved will. The former represent man's self-styled divinity and saving activity, the latter represent Christ and the salvation God has prepared in Him.

Through the years there have been those who have sought to extricate themselves from the difficulty involved here by explaining that *The Bondage of the Will* is a departure from Luther's real line of thought. However, if this book is rejected, Luther's main concern is ignored. He himself says that all the rest of his books might be destroyed if only the *Catechism* and *The Bondage of the Will* are preserved, for these are the only worthwhile books he has written.[20]

Luther's dualistic framework is entirely different from that of Erasmus. Erasmus sees everything in the light of the antithesis between God and man. Luther, on the other hand, views life in the light of the antithesis between God and Satan. In Luther's view man is not an independent power alongside God. Man may imagine that his will is free and his reason independent, but in reality he is a captive and slave of Satan. It does not follow, however, that because man's will is enslaved in the matter of his relationship to God, man is helpless in matters of this world. Luther's explanations of the commandments in the *Small Catechism* contain no reference whatsoever to man's impotence or helplessness.

Rejection of reason at this point is not to be interpreted as denial of logic. Luther knew and acknowledged the meaning of logical reasoning. Even though it is inadequate with respect to salvation and knowledge of God, in matters of social ethics it has decisive significance.

Luther's purpose in writing *The Bondage of the Will* was not to stress predestination but to set forth the way of salvation. His concern was to indicate how misinterpretation of passages dealing

19. *Ibid.*, p. 256 (W.A., 18, 746).
20. W.A.Br., 8, 99 (1537).

with predestination can be avoided. Predestination or no predestination, the gospel must be preached! Faced with most serious anxiety in regard to predestination he wanted to cling to saving faith.

We might summarize Luther's thoughts under the following points: (1) These questions are not for investigation or deliberation, since they are beyond human reason. (2) We must cling to faith in the God who has revealed Himself in Jesus Christ; we must find refuge in grace and the gospel, that is, in the revealed will of God. (3) While acknowledging that we cannot understand everything, we must yet be assured that God makes no mistakes, regardless of how things may appear to us. (4) Finally, the whole problem is to be viewed in the light of reason, the light of grace, and the light of glory. Since the light of nature or reason and the light of grace fail to illumine all the aspects of the question of God's justice, the light of glory supplies the final answers. Luther puts it this way:

> But the light of glory insists otherwise, and will one day reveal God, to whom alone belongs a judgment whose justice is incomprehensible, as a God whose justice is most righteous and evident —provided only that in the meanwhile we *believe* it, as we are instructed and encouraged to do by the example of the light of grace explaining what was a puzzle of the same order to the light of nature.[21]

Luther sees predestination as the extension or continuation of incomprehensible, infinite grace, and as an acknowledgment of God's majesty and man's impotence. But this extension of the revelation of Divine grace, God's judgment upon all human effort, must not be made into a philosophical doctrine. Reason must not plod ahead after faith has called a halt. In matters of faith, reason is blind. Luther knew no philosophical predestination. To realize this fact is to have a key to Luther's thought.

21. *The Bondage of the Will*, p. 317 (W.A., 18, 785).

B. A. GERRISH

Luther's Belief in Reason

THE ESSENTIALS OF LUTHER'S ATTITUDE toward reason and philosophy are not difficult to piece together, in spite of the lack of any systematic treatise on the subject from his own pen. All that is required is a careful examination and organization of some of the allusions (both the briefer, and the more extended, ones) scattered throughout his writings. The only insurmountable hindrance would be a hopeless inconsistency, if Luther were really as muddled as some of his opponents have alleged. But such proves not to be the truth: in actual fact, Luther's thinking in this area, as in so many others, falls into certain constantly recurring patterns, which can readily be discerned by a careful and sympathetic reader.

From B. A. Gerrish, *Grace and Reason: A Study in the Theology of Luther* (Oxford: Clarendon Press, 1962). Copyright © Oxford University Press, 1962, pages 10–27. Reprinted with permission of the publisher.

Many of the most important allusions to reason are to be found in the *Church Postils* of 1522.[1] The *Table Talk* also seems frequently to have centered around problems of reason and philosophy.[2] The so-called *Larger Commentary on Galatians* contains the most important passages. . . . Two other works are worthy of special mention in connection with Luther's attitude toward reason. Oddly, perhaps, the *Lectures on Genesis* (published in four parts, 1544–1554) have several crucial passages.[3] More important, no doubt, are the references in the Weimar edition of the *Disputations* (W.A., Vol. 39, two parts), a collection covering the years 1535–1545. . . .

In a single extremely informative passage Luther both states and answers the problem with which we are concerned, namely: What does he mean by slighting reason?[4] He has been saying, in his explanation of Isaiah 60:1–6, that the prophet rejects the natural light of reason, showing it to be mere darkness: for, if we had light within ourselves, the gospel need never have shone upon us. "Light illumines, not light, but darkness." There is no intermediate light (the light of reason) between Christ and darkness, as the Schoolmen wrongly suppose. Indeed, the more "reasonable" men are, the further they generally are from the True Light. But suppose somebody objects:

> How can everything that natural reason teaches be darkness? Isn't it clear enough that two and three make five? Again, isn't a man who wants to make a coat wise if he takes cloth for it, foolish if he takes paper? Isn't he a wise man who marries a godly wife, and isn't he a fool who marries an ungodly wife? And there are countless other examples in all of mankind's life.

1. W.A., 10 (part I, sec. 1). Many of the postils may be found translated in J. N. Lenker, *Luther's Church Postil* (*Gospels* in 5 vols., *Epistles* in 3 vols.).

2. W.A. Tr., 6 vols. For translations see Smith and Gallinger, *Conversations with Luther*. The old translations of Hazlitt and Henry Bell are not without interest. In his book, *Luther's Table Talk: A Critical Study*, Preserved Smith evaluates the *Tischreden* as historical documents.

3. W.A., 42–44. The early chapters will be found in Lenker's translation. The new American edition of Luther's works has recently commenced a fresh translation of the *Genesisvorlesung*.

4. Postil for Epiphany, on Isaiah 60:1–6; see esp. the passage beginning W.A., 10 (part I, sec. 1), 527.11 ff.

As the objector is made to point out: Christ himself commends
the wisdom of the man who builds upon rock. Luther's reply to
the imaginary objector sums up in a single sentence the crux of
his standpoint on the place of reason: "That is all true; but you
must here distinguish God and men, things eternal and things
temporal." He proceeds to explain his meaning as follows:

> In temporal affairs and those which have to do with men, the
> rational man is self-sufficient . . . : here he needs no other light
> than reason's. Therefore, God does not teach us in the Scriptures
> how to build houses, make clothing, marry, wage war, navigate,
> and the like. For here the light of nature is sufficient. But in godly
> affairs, that is, in those which have to do with God, where man
> must do what is acceptable with God and be saved thereby—
> *here,* however, nature is absolutely stone-blind, so that it cannot
> even catch a glimpse . . . of what those things are. It is pre-
> sumptuous enough to bluster and plunge into them, like a blind
> horse; but all its conclusions are utterly false, as surely as God
> lives.

Underlying this statement of his position is Luther's fundamental
dualism of an earthly and a heavenly kingdom. It remains now
to enlarge a little on the main features of this dualism, so far as
they affect our main theme.

Reason's sphere of competence, the area within which it may
legitimately be exercised, is the "Kingdom of Earth" (*das irdische
Reich*). Now and again, Luther offers lists of the kinds of activities which reason supervises within this specified area, and the
lists do not greatly vary. Reason is able to do many things: it can
judge in human and worldly matters, it can build cities and
houses, it can govern well.[5] The world[6] knows how to build, how
to keep house, how to manage estate and servants, how to be outwardly pious and to lead a decent, honest life.[7] In the main, Luther
seems to be thinking precisely of those human activities which
we, too, would describe as "mundane," that is, such activities as

5. Postil for fourth Sunday after Easter, on John 16:5-16; W.A., 12,
548.14 ff.
6. For Luther "world" and "reason" are in many passages interchange-
able, and he switches from one to the other without any difference of
meaning. So, for example, in the postil for Epiphany Sunday, cited above.
7. W.A., 21, 389.21 ff. (Ascension, on Mark 16:14-20).

we need to perform in order to exist at all. But he does extend the list far enough to include "government" (in the political sense). Reason is able to found kingdoms and commonwealths, to fence them in and make them firm with useful laws, to direct and govern them with good counsel and sound precepts, to prescribe many things indispensable for the preservation of commonwealths and of human society (*societatis humanae*—virtually, "civilization"). Reason, in fact, is the "soul of law and mistress of all laws." The philosophy of government rests upon the principle that reason (in a sufficiently liberal amount) is the possession of the few, while laws prescribed by reason must serve for the many.[8]

Beyond these "mundane" affairs, Luther will even allow reason some insight into moral and religious issues, though here, obviously, we are near the border line of the "heavenly kingdom." Reason has some respect for the Second Table of the Law, and those who transgress it are sometimes punished; and yet the world scarcely regards as sin at all that which the last two precepts forbid.[9] Reason does, to be sure, see clearly that good is to be promoted, evil avoided, but it cannot tell *what is* good or *what is* evil. Natural reason is like a man who wants to go to Rome, knows that there is a right road to get him there, but cannot decide which it is. In other words, reason is only aware of a purely formal sense of moral obligation: it cannot attach it to specific duties or concrete policies of conduct.[10] More particularly, reason cannot decide what is right or wrong *before God*.[11] It is not hard to see how, in Luther's thinking, moral issues lie close to the border of the heavenly kingdom: our conduct is directed toward our fellow men (*coram hominibus*), yet always under the eye of God (*coram Deo*). In the last analysis, what reason does not know is the road *to God*; and this is the conclusion to Luther's illustration of the "road to Rome," although he seemed at the outset to be discussing a purely ethical issue.

The severe limitations upon reason's grasp of more strictly theo-

---

8. W.A., 40 (part III), 612.35 ff. (on Isaiah 9:1).

9. Tr. 1, no. 200. Luther followed the Roman practice of reckoning the prohibition of covetousness as containing two separate commandments.

10. W.A., 10 (part I, sec. 1), 203.10 ff. (Christmas, on John 1:1–14).

11. W.A., 12, 548.23 (fourth Sunday after Easter, on John 16:5–16).

logical issues are closely parallel. If reason stumbles at the doctrine of the Incarnation, that is not because reason refuses to believe in God, but rather that it does not understand who God is; consequently, it invents a God after its own fancy. Reason agrees that God's Word is to be honored, but arrogantly sets itself up as judge deciding what is and what is not God's Word.[12] Luther even goes so far as to say in one place: "Let us here learn also from nature and reason what to think of God." Reason knows that God wants to save from all evil, therefore, that He is the source of all good. "The natural light of reason reaches so far that it regards God as kind, gracious, merciful, tenderhearted." But reason falls short at two points: first, although it believes that God *can* aid, it does not believe that God *will* do so *for it*; second, though it knows *that* God is, it does not know *who* or *what* God is. The meaning of the second charge is, presumably, that reason attaches its notions of Deity to the wrong object, that is, not to the God who reveals Himself in Christ.[13] . . . In general, Luther is clearly drawing the familiar Scholastic distinction between the knowledge "that God is" (*quod sit Deus*), which is within the reach of natural reason, and the knowledge "what God is" (*quid sit Deus*), which is beyond natural reason. . . .

Reason does, then, have a legitimate sphere of competence, within which it is autonomous; it begins to be called in question only when it approaches the boundary line of the heavenly kingdom. In its own strictly demarcated area man's native intelligence needs no special word from God—though, of course, it is itself a gift from God, an endowment bestowed upon man at his birth. Not all a believer's doings call for some special prompting of the Spirit. Even the biblical saints and heroes generally acted as reason guided: when Abraham received no certain word from heaven, he did as reason dictated. The "saints" are like other men in busying themselves in the common routine tasks—and yet, Luther adds in a significant remark, though they do the same things as the ungodly, their works are made acceptable to God by their faith. Genuine saints do nothing out of the ordinary, save when specially commanded by a definite word and the Spirit's prompt-

12. W.A., 10 (part I, sec. 1), 240.7 (Christmas, on John 1:1–14).
13. W.A., 19, 206.7 ff. (on Jonah 1:5).

ings. Man was created for domestic and civic (or "political") occupations. What Luther terms the *"communia"* (the institutions of social life) were ordained of God: it is here that man finds his calling—be it even in milking the cows and plowing the fields—not in the monasteries. With admirable common sense Luther advises his flock to imitate the biblical heroes in their ordinary occupations, not in the special things that they did; for the human mind is affected by a foolish tendency to admire only what is uncommon, strange, extraordinary. The Christian should be dutifully engaged in what the papists superciliously call "lay works," though Luther prefers to speak of "civil works," since, by faith and the Word, the works a man does in the social order may be made genuinely "spiritual." For the proper performance of these works God has given us "natural reason." [14]

As long as reason is exercised within these limits, Luther has nothing but praise to heap upon it. Reason is the "head and substance of all things." It is the best thing in this life—indeed, it is something divine. Reason is personified as the "inventress and mistress of all the arts, of medicine and law, of whatever wisdom, power, virtue, and glory men possess in this life." Reason is what marks off mankind from the brute beasts, and the Holy Scriptures themselves have appointed her queen of the earth (Genesis 1:28). Nor has her rule been taken from her by the Fall: she remains a kind of "divine sun" . . . , in whose light the affairs of this life are to be administered.[15] Reason is the greatest, the inestimable, gift of God.[16] In another place, Luther concedes that the light of nature (reason) is a part of the True Light—though here the rider is added, "when it recognizes and honors him by whom it has been ignited." [17]

Of course, reason is not infallible even within its own proper domain, neither is it omniscient. Sometimes its judgments are erroneous—for example, in matters of public government and administration.[18] It is unable to meet the demands laid upon it even in

14. W.A., 43, 104. 37 ff. (*Genesisvorlesung*, on Genesis 20:2).
15. *Disputatio de homine*, theses 4–9, W.A., 39 (part I), 175. The Disputation will now be found in English, American edition, Vol. xxxiv.
16. W.A., 40 (part III), 612. 31; on Isaiah 9:1.
17. W.A., 10 (part I, sec. 1), 203:8; on John 1:1–14; Christmas postil.
18. See again the exposition of Isaiah 9:1, W.A., 40 (part III), 613.3 ff.

this present world. For to "live soberly, righteously, and godly in this present world" (Titus 2:12) is like keeping sober in the ale house, chaste in a brothel, godly in a dance hall, guiltless in the midst of murderers. Here nature and reason are lost.[19] Again, reason often displays its ignorance even in the earthly kingdom. The world is full of daily miracles, and it is only their frequency that dulls our sensitiveness to their wonder. Luther is particularly fond of illustrating this point (made more than once in his works) by reference to the "miracle of birth." [20] But reason's fallibility and evident lack of omniscience do not alter Luther's basic judgment; in the worldly kingdom, it is God's most precious gift.

In the heavenly kingdom, on the other hand, reason is nothing but darkness. The words of Christ could never be grasped or fathomed by reason, but only as the Holy Spirit reveals them to simple believers. The apostles themselves were of this sort: ignorant fishermen, for the most part, who learned to understand the Scriptures not in the "schools," but through revelation.[21] The world knows nothing of Christ's doctrine. The message of salvation has to be preached: had it been known before Christ, he would never have needed to descend from heaven or to send his servants into all the world. Of such things as concern God's kingdom and how to escape sin and death, the world knows nothing.[22] Christ's conversation with Nicodemus shows clearly "what reason can do." Reason belongs to the flesh: it is so blind that it can neither see nor know the things of God.[23] While it may properly be called "light" of a sort, it knows nothing of "spiritual wisdom." Even if it knows of God's existence, it still does not know "His will toward us." [24] The Scriptures must be our guide in the kingdom of heaven, not reason. It would be a monstrous piece of frivolity to cast aside the authority of Scripture and follow reason.[25] Human reason has experience only of temporal things, therefore it is ridiculous to introduce it into a controversy on a spiritual issue, such as

19. W.A., 10 (part I, sec. 1), 41.5 ff. (Christmas, on Titus 2:11–15).

20. Tr., 4, no. 5015; W.A., 43, 374.11.

21. W.A., 21, 234.30; 235.5 (Easter Monday, on Luke 24:13–25).

22. W.A., 21, 389.21 ff. (Ascension, on Mark 16:14–20).

23. W.A., 10 (part I, sec. 2), 298.5, 12; and 301.27 (Trinity, on John 3:1–15).

24. W.A., 40 (part III), 613.14; from the exposition of Isaiah 9:1.

25. W.A., 42, 92.33.

the supremacy of the pope. Here it must not be placed on the same level with the Divine Law. "For the directions of worldly order and reason are far below the Divine Law." It is futile to defend the divine order by human reason (unless first it be illuminated by faith): this would be like illuminating the sun with a feeble lantern or resting a rock upon a reed. Human reason can only stumble along, like a man on stilts.[26] In short, if we want to find Christ, we must not seek Him, as Mary did, "amongst His kinsfolk," but in His Father's House—that is, in the Word. Mary did not know how to find Christ, and so she sought Him in the wrong place; we also seek Him in the wrong place if we look to reason or to the Fathers and the councils of the church. All these things belong to the world.[27]

The blindness of reason in matters which properly belong to the heavenly kingdom is exhibited in its erroneous judgments concerning God. It concludes either that there is no God, or that He is disinterested in human affairs. It is only the Holy Scriptures that give us a true understanding of the efficient and final causes of creation; reason can go no further than the material and formal causes.[28] As John the Baptist did not come of himself, but was "a man sent from God," so neither the gospel nor any sermon on the True Light can come of itself or from human reason: they must be sent from God. The doctrines of men will never show Christ.[29] We must not measure the Word by reason: this is the error of the fanatics. Human nature always objects to the way God does things. Luther confesses that he has often tried to suggest to God some possible improvements in the government of the world—sound, well-intentioned advice which would certainly tend toward God's greater glory! No doubt, God laughed at this "wisdom": "I am no passive God, but an active God, whose wont it is to command, to rule, to direct." [30] "Frau Hulda" (Luther's nickname for reason) blames God for the evil done by men: for why did He make them the way they are? [31] Reason, in the last analysis, is arrogance; therefore, God deliberately finds ways of humbling

26. *Against the Papacy* (1520), W.A., 6, 290.27 ff.
27. W.A., 17 (part II), 29.7 ff. (first after Epiphany, on Luke 2:41–52).
28. W.A., 42, 93.11 (on Genesis 2:21).
29. W.A., 10 (part I, sec. 1), 216.20 (on John 1:6; Christmas Day).
30. W.A., 44, 373 ff., esp. 376.30 and 377.7 (on Genesis 39:21–22).
31. W.A. Tr., 6, no. 6889.

it. Sometimes He turns away His face, seeming to be the very Devil himself. Sometimes He deprives even His saints of Christ, just as He took Jesus away from Mary for three days. And sometimes He prescribes rites with the intent of humiliating and causing offense.[32] The last of these devices is especially interesting. Luther mentions circumcision as a kind of test case for judging the arrogance of reason, "that smart woman, Madam Jezebel." For natural reason could not imagine anything more utterly foolish than the command to circumcise. If Abraham had listened to reason, he would never have believed that the command came from God at all. Circumcision made the Jews a laughingstock, so utterly pointless did the practice seem. Luther replies that the point of circumcision is precisely to offend reason, to force it to surrender its vanity. If God had given a token that reason could approve, then man's arrogance would have remained. "And so God is not interested in circumcision itself, but in the humbling of haughty nature and reason." Such, at least, is the "temporal cause" for circumcision; there is also a "spiritual cause," and of this Luther proceeds to give the meaning. But the main point for our purposes is his view of the "temporal cause." He gives further examples of "articles of faith" which reason finds silly. "All this is immeasurably above and against reason." "All God's works and words are against reason." "In this God is seeking only that man may have the humility to bring his reason into captivity and be subject to Divine truth." [33]

Reason, then, is not the appropriate organ of knowledge in the spiritual kingdom. The only source of spiritual knowledge is the Word. Hence reason, in refusing to hearken to the Word, takes on the character of disobedience and pride.[34] It is faith, not reason, that receives the Word. The distinction between the two spheres of knowledge, with its accompanying distinction between two organs of knowing, is rigidly maintained. More will need to be

32. W.A., 44, 376.1 (this is the *initium operationis divinae,* God's *ratio gubernationis*); 12, 412.12 ff.; 10 (part I, sec. 1), 504–519.

33. See esp. W.A., 10 (part I, sec. 1), 506.7; 507.14; 506.14; 506.21; on the Gospel for New Year's Day, Luke 2:21.

34. *Ratio* is explicitly contrasted with *obedientia* in Luther's comments on several biblical passages, esp. Genesis 17:23–27, 1 Samuel 15:22, and John 13:6 ff. See, for example, W.A., 42, 669 ff.

said . . . concerning the two spheres of knowledge, for Luther virtually identifies them with theology and philosophy. But . . . we ought to ask two further questions: (1) Did Luther believe that a proposition could be true in one of the two spheres, and not in the other? and (2) Did he allow no place for reason in the domain of theology, even the reason of the "regenerate" believer?

In relation to the question whether fallen man is able to do good, Luther comes close to denying an assertion in philosophy and accepting it in theology. Here is a point where we have to "distinguish the worldly from the spiritual, the political from the theological." [35] When we say that a man, with his natural reason and will, can do no good thing, we must add "theologically speaking" . . . , for in the "political" realm (that is, what we would call "moral philosophy") the statement would certainly not be true. But Luther does not seem to be thinking of a double-truth theory such as we would associate with some of the later nominalists. The assertion "Fallen man can do no good" really has a different *meaning* in theology from what it has in philosophy, since it refers to different sorts of "good" in each context. [36] . . .

The second question, whether Luther did not find any place at all for the exercise of reason in the domain of theology, demands careful consideration, since it is at this point that he has been most seriously misunderstood. In the main, Luther's advice to the Christian on how to handle reason is, as we would now expect: blindfold it, sacrifice it, drown it in baptism. When a man is tempted to listen to the seductive voice of reason, the best thing he can do is close his eyes and hold on grimly to faith. [37] Fortunately, this is not Luther's only counsel. Occasionally he even seems to speak of faith as continuous with reason, as though faith merely *added* *to* the knowledge that we already have through natural reason. But this is, I think, only in regard to a specific issue in which, according to Luther, natural reason does have a certain amount of

35. Tr. 6, no. 6682 (esp. 117.23 ff.).
36. In addition to Tr. 6, no. 6682, see: W.A., 42, 106–107; 10 (part I, sec. 1), 326.7 ff.; 42, 128.38 (on the corruption of reason by the Fall); 40 (part I), 294.16.
37. W.A., 12, 635.5 ff.; 44, 377.10.

206 B. A. GERRISH

insight. For when Paul wishes to defend himself against the charge
of antinomianism, he makes his appeal first to "natural reason" ("I
speak after the manner of men"—Romans 6:19). Even reason
teaches that we must shun evil and do good, and rulers are following reason's guidance when they establish laws for restraining
wrongdoing. "Although the gospel is a higher gift and wisdom
than human reason, it does not alter or tear up man's understanding: for it was God Himself who implanted reason in man." But
reason falls short at two points: it cannot understand why laws
are not naturally fulfilled, and it fails to do anything about it.
The best it can do is restrain evil by laws and punishments; but
it cannot uproot it, because it has no control over the inward
thoughts from which evil works proceed. But we have a doctrine
not to be learned from human reason: and this reveals both the
source of evil (i.e., sin) and how to restrain it (i.e., by grace). So
then, we assist reason. Paul makes use of the law and of reason's
teaching on good works, but he goes beyond them.[38]

Of even greater importance are the passages (and there are many
of them) in which Luther makes room for the possibility of
reason's being regenerated. Asked whether the "tools of learning
. . . and of nature" were of service to the theologian, Luther, mentioning particularly languages, replied: "A distinction has to be
made between the abuse of a thing and the thing itself." The value
of these tools lies in their ability to make things clear (this being
their proper use). But in themselves they do not guarantee sound
results: they do Erasmus and his sort no good at all, for though
the Erasmians have the linguistic skills, yet they make the most
pernicious errors. And what of the "light of nature" (reason)?
Again, Luther's reply is "I make a distinction. . . ." Obsessed by
the Devil, reason is bad; illuminated by the Spirit, it is good. The
essence of the "distinction" lies in a contrast between *ante fidem*
and *post fidem,* between a use of reason "before faith" and a use
of reason "after faith." The result of illumination by faith is that
reason begins to work with an entirely new set of presuppositions,
no longer those derived from experience in worldly affairs, but
those which are revealed in the Scriptures. "Without faith, reason

38. W.A., 22, 105 ff. (seventh Sunday after Trinity, on Romans 6:19–23).
See esp. 108.12, the sentence I have translated.

is no use and can do nothing. . . . But, when illuminated, reason takes all its thoughts from the Word." In short, its value lies in the interpretation and clarification of the sacred text. The substance of reason remains, only the "vanity" is purged away.[39] If reason before faith is darkness in Divine matters, yet in a believer it may become an "excellent instrument of godliness." The same holds for all the *naturalia* (endowments of nature): though in the ungodly they may serve in the cause of ungodliness, yet in the godly they may serve in the cause of salvation. . . . An eloquent tongue moves a man to faith; similarly, reason makes discourse clear. Reason, in fact, must be transformed—slain, but raised to newness of life, like our bodies at the Last Day. Reason is not the same after faith as it was before. All things are changed, and this is "regeneration through the Word": the same faculties remain (*membra*: Luther is still thinking of the parallel with our resurrected bodies on the Last Day) and the same person; but regeneration through the Word transforms the faculties and fashions a different person from the one who was born of Adam.[40] . . .

The main features of Luther's teaching on reason are, then, by no means abstruse or hard to determine. To be sure, inconsistencies remain, and it is another question whether Luther's position is defensible. One thing is certain: many of the time-honored lines of criticism are beside the point. It is not sufficient to say, "Luther was an irrationalist: he attacked reason," and leave it at that. One must stop to inquire *why* he attacked reason, *in what respects* he attacked reason, and *what he meant* by "reason." And a careful scrutiny of the sources makes it plain that the crucial issue concerns Luther's fundamental dualism. To sum up, Luther distinguishes between two areas of human experience, two directions toward which man faces. Man lives in relation with his fellow men (*coram hominibus*) and also in relation with God (*coram Deo*). He has to do both with the created order and with the Creator Himself. His life is lived in two distinct spheres: the one is natural, temporal, earthly; and the other is spiritual, eternal, heavenly. Outwardly, he is related to the world; inwardly, he is related to God. In all his dealings with the world, man's guide is

39. W.A. Tr., 1, no. 439.
40. Tr., 3, no. 2938a (cf. *ibid.*, b); 6, no. 6741.

reason: the world is the kingdom of reason (*regnum rationis*), and by his God-given understanding and wisdom man is able to subdue the earth and have dominion over the beasts of the field. In his dealings with God, however, only faith can be man's guide, specifically, faith in "the Word" or in Christ:[41] The spiritual sphere is the kingdom of Christ (*regnum Christi*). By judicious use of his natural capacities a man may acquire a certain outward or civil righteousness in the *regnum rationis*; but righteousness in the *regnum Christi* is acquired only by faith—indeed, not so much acquired *by* faith as given *to* faith, for here righteousness is not "active," but "passive." Reason illuminated by faith has some grasp of spiritual matters, and works inspired by faith are pleasing *coram Deo*. But if unregenerate reason presumes to pronounce on Divine affairs, it shows itself to be utterly out of place and stone-blind; and if works are performed apart from faith, they are not accepted by God. "Civil righteousness" can in no wise justify a man before God.

If, then, we are to do justice to the complexity of Luther's thought, we must carefully distinguish: (1) natural reason, ruling within its proper domain (the earthly kingdom); (2) arrogant reason, trespassing upon the domain of faith (the heavenly kingdom); (3) regenerate reason, serving humbly in the household of faith, but always subject to the Word of God. Within the first context, reason is an excellent gift of God; within the second, it is Frau Hulda, the Devil's Whore; within the third, it is the handmaiden of faith. And if "we find no more precise discussion of the activity thus attributed to reason in the lives of the regenerate" (reason in the third sense), this is not . . . merely because its function has become purely formal, that is, to deal in thought and speech with the material presented to it by faith and the Word; it is also because reason, when regenerate, is virtually absorbed into faith, becoming faith's cognitive and intellective aspects. Because reason belongs to the natural sphere, Luther will not allow

41. Luther uses "the Word" to refer both to Jesus Christ and to the Scriptures, which bear witness to Him. Sometimes (perhaps most characteristically) "the Word" means for him "the Gospel concerning Jesus Christ." See, for example, the *Treatise on Christian Liberty,* Philadelphia edition, II, 315.

that it is competent to judge in matters of faith; and yet, because faith comes through the hearing and understanding of the Word, Luther found himself bound to concede that reason—man's rationality in the broadest sense—was, when regenerate, faith's indispensable tool. We cannot, I think, deny that Luther's understanding of the place of reason is perfectly intelligible, sometimes well argued, even if we neither like it nor are willing to accept it.

HEINRICH BORNKAMM

Luther's Translation of the New Testament

IN DECEMBER, 1521, LUTHER HAD SECRETLY LEFT the Wartburg for a short sojourn in Wittenberg, where he wanted to check the turbulent innovations that had been introduced and work toward moderation. Upon his return to his quiet asylum he embarked on a momentous undertaking, which his friends had earnestly enjoined upon his conscience: the translation of the Bible. It was self-evident that he, as an individual and with the few aids at his disposal at the Wartburg, could consider only the translation of the New Testament, not that of the entire Bible. Yes, if he could live in hiding in Wittenberg and there enjoy the assistance of his friends, he would come at once and begin with

From Heinrich Bornkamm, *Luther's World of Thought,* translated by Martin H. Bertram (St. Louis: Concordia Publishing House, 1958). Copyright © 1958 by Concordia Publishing House, pages 273–83. Reprinted with permission of the publisher.

the Old Testament! He asks the Wittenbergers to consider this thought "that it may result in a translation worthy of being read by Christians. I hope we shall present our Germany with a better one than that of the Latins." [1] It was the love for his people that pressed the pen into his hand for this great work. This was the motive he also mentioned in a letter, dated November 1, to the Strasbourg humanist Gerbel for the German essays written at the Wartburg: "I have been born for my Germans; them I also want to serve." [2]

All his previous work impelled him with inner logic to the translation of the Bible. Through the Bible alone he had become what he was. Through it he had learned to rout Scholastic theology, and in it he had rediscovered the core of the gospel. The Bible was his only friend in his lonely hours, the sole weapon in his conflict against a thousand-year-old system. If he had a right to believe that up to this time he had won all his oral and literary skirmishes, he had to tell himself that he was indebted to the Bible for these victories. Though the plea of his Wittenberg friends gave the final impulse, yet he carried out his very own work, his *opus proprium*. With this work he not only revealed to his people the source of his life, but in it he also found the fullest justification for his previous actions. Henceforth everybody could and should judge for himself and thereby exercise the first duty and the foremost privilege of the universal priesthood; for this was precisely what Luther had discovered in the Scriptures as the basic essence of the church.

Even though Luther confined himself first to the translation of the New Testament, his task was by no means an easy one. The second edition of the Greek text by Erasmus (1519), to which the great humanist had appended his own Latin translation and his detailed explanations (*annotationes*), was the basis for Luther's undertaking. Some have maintained that Luther could not have used this text of Erasmus, since in several passages he failed to avail himself of hints that were helpful for a proper understanding of the text.[3] Although this in itself is true, the explanation is to

1. January 13, 1521, to Amsdorf: Letters, 2, 423, 48. To Melanchthon: 427, 128.
2. Letters, 2, 397, 34.
3. Wilhelm Walther, *Luthers deutsche Bibel* (1917), pp. 58 f.

be found in the great haste (concurrently with his work on the
book of Advent homilies he completed the translation of the New
Testament in the incredibly short span of eleven weeks), which
precluded a constant consulting of Erasmus's translation and particularly of his annotations. However, many passages prove beyond all doubt that Luther did use this exegetical aid, which at
that time was the most modern work of this kind. Furthermore,
his intimate acquaintance—dating back to his lectures on the
Epistle to the Romans—with the edition of Erasmus, which first
appeared in 1516, would make it seem incomprehensible if he
had forgone its help for the difficult work of translating. To be
sure, in the beginning this help of Erasmus was surely not available in its entirety to Luther at the Wartburg; at first he had only
the reprint of the Greek text (without translation and annotations). Gerbel had published this in 1521 and presented it to him,
or, as Luther expressed it, had brought it to him as a wife who
bore him sons (his Wartburg literary work).[4]

Thus in addition to the Vulgate, the use of which can often be
established, Luther had a second Latin translation of the New
Testament available: that of Erasmus. The very fact that Erasmus's
Latin translation was printed in columns parallel with the Greek
text makes it self-evident that Luther's eyes must have rested on it
continually. Furthermore, one would overestimate Luther's knowledge of Greek if one believed him capable of translating the New
Testament, with all the difficulties of Hellenistic Greek, in such a
short time without the aid of other translations. After all, he had
been schooled in the Scholastic tradition, not humanistically; and
despite his Greek studies, which he did not pursue more seriously
until 1518, he always retained a greater familiarity with the Latin
Bible. A study of Luther's knowledge of Greek reveals that in
spite of the strong stimulation given by Melanchthon, he never
attained the mastery of Greek his philologically trained contemporaries possessed. And this made the constant use of the two
Latin translations he had before him—he knew most of the Vulgate by heart—natural and imperative.

An impression of the use Luther made of the patterns before
him can be gained by comparing a rather long passage of his

4. November 1, 1521: Letters, 2, 397, 41 ff.

own translation word for word with that of his predecessors. To pick words and phrases here and there suggestive of the one or of the other Latin translation does not enable one to penetrate into the live process of translating. But if one follows sentence by sentence Luther's translation through a whole New Testament book, e.g., the Epistle to the Romans, one perceives with what mobility he selected expressions from this or that pattern. We are far from being able to explain all these decisions; one must often assume that a familiar phrase of the Vulgate simply flowed into his pen or that in his haste he did not consult the annotations of Erasmus. Romans 9:28–31 presents three classical illustrations that show how he could use them and immediately afterward disregard them. Nevertheless, one can see very clearly how diversified his procedure is. Often he translates the Greek text in accordance with the Vulgate, sometimes despite an express warning in the annotations, sometimes also in such a way that he instinctively corrects the faulty Greek text of the Erasmus edition. But as a rule he heeds the suggestions of Erasmus and corrects the Vulgate in conformity with them, at times even where Erasmus himself had not yet embodied his suggested corrections in his own translation. Often, however, Luther translates very freely, sometimes according to varying impulses and stimulations, sometimes also according to his own understanding of the Greek text. . . .

Even though Luther always had recourse to the two Latin copies for an understanding of the original text, he was nevertheless entirely dependent on himself for the task of pouring the New Testament into a true mold of the German language. Even if one of the medieval German translations had been available, it would have helped him but little. These vernacular translations were all based on the Vulgate, consequently on a text that he was obliged to correct in innumerable passages. Moreover, they adhered too literally and clumsily to the wording of the text to serve him as a pattern. No matter how highly we may evaluate several of these translations as accomplishments in their day, the disparity between them and the more refined linguistic sense of the early sixteenth century, and, above all, between them and Luther's conception of a good translation, was nonetheless too great to ascribe to them a vital influence on Luther. . . . Naturally,

Luther was acquainted with such older German translations as
the Zainer Bible from former years. Sections from these Bibles,
such as pericopes and plenaria, were often used in sermons and
prayers as well as in classroom instruction and in pastoral minis-
trations. Recollections of these passages, their frequent general
correspondence to the Vulgate, and the limited number of possible
translations explain the various similarities. But it is significant
that such agreements are not traceable to any one printed edition
or manuscript; they point to the various medieval German translations. Consequently, they reveal the traditional diction used in
the church, not a literary dependence and connection.

If we are impressed by the difference between the eaglelike
flight of Luther's language and the diction of his medieval predecessors, our admiration increases as we observe how in his translation at the Wartburg he has grown above his former stature; for
this was not his first translation of Bible passages into the vernacular. His German writings, sermons, and postils abound in biblical
quotations that he himself translated. It is astonishing how Luther
ignored these, even those used in a very recent Christmas homily,
and how his uniform feeling for language created the entire New
Testament anew. His former attempts still betrayed the idiomatic
hue of the ancient language in many spots, especially of the Latin;
but now everything is thoroughly German. Now he relates in the
imperfect tense, no longer in the perfect; he places the predicate
(aside from well-considered exceptions) at the end of the sentence,
and he resolves noun combinations into sentences, e.g., Matthew
12:34: *Aus Überfluss des Herzens redet der Mund* (*Postille*); *Wes
das Herz voll ist, des gehet der Mund über* (New Testament).[5]
Romans 8:7: *Die Weisheit des Fleisches ist Gottes Feind* (*Postille*);
Denn fleischlich gesinnet sein ist eine Feindschaft wider Gott
(New Testament).[6] Almost all foreign words are eliminated, etc.

Even if all this demonstrates conscious and methodical work,
of which he later gave a somewhat detailed account, especially
in his *Sendschreiben vom Dolmetschen,* nevertheless his essen-

5. Authorized Version: "For out of the abundance of the heart the
mouth speaketh." [ed.]
6. Authorized Version: "Because the carnal mind is enmity against God."
[ed.]

tial attainments were born instinctively from the depths of a great poetical heart. Gifted with a language that adapts itself to any mood, to the tenderness of the Christmas story as well as to the terrors of the Apocalypse, Luther does not work according to rules but according to inner laws. The incredible accuracy of expression with which he reacts to the depths of a text stems not merely from alert reflection but rather from a superconscious clear-sightedness. He hears and sees sacred history as though it were taking place at the present time; he transmits its sounds in such a way that the silent reader can hear it as living, spoken words. By means of sentence structure and meaningful punctuation he makes the Bible a book to be heard, not to be read. With deepest sensitiveness he discovers poetical passages and responds to them with the poetical resources of the German language, with alliteration and rhythm. His use of the vowels merits a special study. And still, there is more at work here than the genius of a poet. His newly created biblical language, with which no translation on earth can compare, succeeded not only because he felt his way into it with perfect skill but because in countless hours the Bible message had reached into his own life. He read Holy Writ "as though it had been written yesterday," [7] as though its words of admonition and of consolation were addressed by God to him alone. Yes, his amazement at the fact that God is speaking and revealing the innermost recesses of His heart through the medium of the Word gave Luther full freedom to evolve his own language. His work was not merely the product of poetical intuition; no, in it we hear human words born from the Word of God. Luther did not beget this work during the quiet winter months at the Wartburg; he conceived it.

Thus Luther's work grew completely from his new understanding of the gospel. It could not be otherwise. One clearly feels his heart vibrating to the gospel's consoling message, pervading all his work like a soft undertone. He is resolved to preserve the gospel in its purity and to protect it from misinterpretations. For this reason he translates the term "the righteousness of God" (*die Gerechtigkeit Gottes*), which had proved so ambiguous in his own experience, with "the righteousness which is valid before

7. Sermon (1523), 12, 444.20.

God" (*die Gerechtigkeit, die vor Gott gilt*). By inserting the word "alone" (*allein*) twice in harmony with the context he engraves the Pauline meaning sharply: *Auf dass er [Gott] allein gerecht sei* (Romans 3:26); *dass der Mensch gerechtfertigt werde ohn Zutun der Werke des Gesetzes* (since 1527: *ohne des Gesetzes Werke*), *allein durch den Glauben* (Rom. 3:28).[8] In place of *aus den Werken* he says, more pregnantly, *aus Verdienst der Werke* (Romans 9:12, 32; 11:6). His effort to preserve the ring of the evangelical message is manifested most clearly in the painstaking care with which he reproduces one and the same word with consistent modifications. Thus he retains the word *gerecht* as an attribute of man only when it pertains unmistakably to God's gift of unmerited grace; otherwise he replaces it with the word *fromm,* a term replete for him with the content of the gospel and devoid of any intimation of human attainment. Luther carefully divides (perfecting the division in subsequent revisions) the rather common New Testament word group σῴζειν, σωτηρία into expressions of saving, helping, preserving, on the one hand, and, on the other hand, into *selig machen, selig werden, Seligkeit* (to save, to be saved, salvation), achieving for the noun σωτηρία an especially ingenious differentiation: *Heil* for God's great deed for mankind, *Seligkeit* for its effect on human hearts in this life and in the life beyond. With keen discernment he avoids the term *Kirche* and chooses the word *Gemeine;*[9] thereby he wished to avoid any transmission of the erroneous Catholic concept of the church to the days of primitive Christianity.

Luther's translation of the Bible supplied the evangelical movement with the inexhaustible source of its message and the German nation with a perennial fountainhead for its new language. A wonderful providence had placed Luther, the greatest sculptor of the German language, into an area where a universal German language had long been in the making and could grow only at that time: the eastern German territory. Through the agency of the

8. Neither the translation of the Authorized Version or the Revised Standard Version of the English Bible inserted Luther's *allein* (alone, only) into the text.

Authorized Version: "Therefore we conclude that a man is justified by faith without the deeds of the law." [ed.]

9. Community. [ed.]

political and economic power of the extensive Wettin dual state, culturally of greater importance to Germany than the mighty Habsburg territories situated on the fringe of the empire, the unifying language of the Saxon chancellery radiated its influence also into most of the other German states. Luther was cognizant of this development: "I use the speech of the Saxon chancellery, which is accepted by all the princes of Germany." He knew that the methodical efforts to achieve a uniform German language were of recent origin; they dated from his own days. Emperor Maximilian and Frederick the Wise, he said, "have thus merged all languages into one." [10] By adopting this dialect natural to him, he could hope to be intelligible to most Germans. But by this very act he, as no other German, opened the portals of the future for this High German dialect. . . . Luther's language of the Bible and the resulting sermonic language of the Reformation were not only universal inasmuch as they spanned the farthest dialectal areas but also inasmuch as they became the language of the people, the language used in the studies of the scholars, and the language spoken in the huts of the unlearned. By reason of their unparalleled dissemination through the printed page they reached all strata of society. Whatever stock of raw material Luther received from his adoptive dialect he gave back after qualifying it for the greatest role in the history of the German language. For not until there was a union of subject matter and genius was the common language of all Germans born.

10. *Table Talk* (1532), 2, 2758.

FRIEDRICH BLUME

Luther the Musician

LUTHERAN CHURCH MUSIC is no separate species of music. It did not grow autonomously from some substance or principle belonging only to itself, nor, once it had appeared, did it shut itself off from other species of music. It drew its strength from the soil of a highly developed, nationally oriented art. The tempest of the new spirit that arose in Wittenberg assimilated effectively all that contemporary art and learning had created in all fields, even if, like some streams of humanism, it was hostile to such creations. Thus the reform movement also ingested the musical culture of the period. Quite consciously, it accepted what existed in order to use it for its own purposes. Thus Luther thought

From Friedrich Blume, "Die evangelische Kirchenmusik," *Handbuch der Musikwissenschaft* (Potsdam: Akademische Verlagsgesellschaft Athenaion, 1931). Translation copyright © 1973 by H. G. Koenigsberger, pages 1–21.

of all the arts and thus, especially, he thought of music. "Music in the service of Him who has created it"; variations on this idea appear frequently in Luther's writings and pronouncements.

As the new teaching accepted and made use of existing music, Lutheran church music grew one of its strongest roots: its relevance for its contemporaries and its modernity. It is characteristic, both for Luther's practical view of the world as well as for his conception of the ends of church music, that he would have nothing to do, either with experiments or with pedantic theoretical regulations; nor did he, as Calvin did in his puritanical narrow-mindedness, restrict music to the most primitive singing in unison; rather, he deliberately and consciously used contemporary music for the service of his cause. For in this way Lutheran church music received its second strong root, its close connection with popular culture and its national character. German music around 1520 was an independent art, with considerable stylistic differences from that of the other European peoples. It had grown from the German song and it was at its best and most original in the invention and handling of song. And this German song was at that time very much a part of popular culture. Taking over this tradition assured both the close contact with the whole German people and, through acceptance of the sophisticated tradition of the artistic development of the song, also the close contact with the educated sections of the nation. Luther, moreover, with his healthy respect for the musical needs of the young church, did not commit the mistake of courting an easy popularity any more than he fell into the trap of engaging in dim experiments or accepting puritanical narrowness. By not committing church music purely to song and its artistic possibilities but by anchoring it firmly in the liturgical traditions of the pre-Reformation service, Luther provided it with a third root from which to draw its strength: its traditionalism and its liturgical character. He wanted to keep whatever religious content the Catholic Church had enshrined in its ceremonies, only modifying and developing these according to his own conceptions. Just as his doctrine was originally intended not for the foundation of a new church but for the reform of the old, so also he did not intend to create a new form of musical church service but only a modification, in his spirit, of the traditional service.

On these foundations Lutheran church music quickly reached its highest development. Soon it became the core of all German music. Its great achievements attracted the finest spirits of the time, even those of the opposing camp. It concentrated within itself the artistic forces of the whole period of the Reformation. It assimilated the new musical influences that made themselves felt toward the end of the century and which heralded the baroque. It could even press the strongly secular tendencies of the late baroque into its service. Its vitality had tenacious roots. But in the course of the centuries these roots died, one after another. First, the liturgical component of Lutheran church music disappeared as, gradually, the strict ritual of the church services was loosened; for, with the splintering of the territorial churches, it declined from a universal form to a merely local arrangement: the essential elements of the form of the church service, the singing of the minister, the chorale of the congregation, and the more elaborate composed music (*Kunstmusik*), these were changed—a process that started as early as the sixteenth century and continued for a long time. When the flowering of German civic culture came to an end, when Italian art flooded Germany, when the Thirty Years' War destroyed national consciousness and paralyzed national power, the second basic force of Lutheran church music died, its intimate contact with the people: Lutheran church music became a matter for the educated classes. But it still remained alive and up to date; it could still harness the artistic movements of its time to its service; its vitality was not yet spent.

But when the Lutheran Church itself more and more gave up its Lutheran tradition, when men of the Enlightenment thought that Luther could be of no further "use," and when a rationalistic theology dissolved all forms and ceremonies of the church service, when all the arts fled the church, or when they invaded it in purely secular forms, then the time had come for even the vital modernity of Lutheran church music to die. Bach's late cantatas, the last testimonies of the spirit of a vanished age, confronted a time that neither understood nor valued them. Lutheran church music had lost its last root and appeared, from then on, no longer as the core and summit of German music but as a minor field of activity, the playground for small minds.

At the beginning of the history of Lutheran church music there stands the figure of Martin Luther. Nothing could be more wrong than to see in him an enthusiastic musical dilettante in the modern fashion, as has often been done by investigators endowed more with enthusiasm than with knowledge of the subject. In Luther's day, music was part of man's daily bread. It accompanied the course of the year, as much as that of each day. It was an inalienable part of life. Church and secular festivals, baptism and burial, feasts and family prayers were saturated with music. One must rid one's mind of the modern idea that in these cases music was only an ornament, a "beautification" of life. Music, and in each case quite definite types of music, were indispensable parts of both divine service and secular festivity. The mass or the vespers were as unthinkable without music as was the dance. In the communal existence of the congregation even the layman was musically far more educated and, indeed, filled with music than at any later period. And anyone who, like Luther, had gone through a humanistic *gymnasium* and through a monastery received a degree of musical education that is inconceivable today. There is, therefore, no good reason to doubt Luther's own musical activities nor his musical productivity.

To understand Luther's own attitude toward music it is necessary to distinguish between two points of view: his purely personal, emotional relation to music and his attitude to music as a practical theologian, organizer, preacher, and teacher. He did not himself consciously distinguish between these two viewpoints. His fundamental feeling for music remained the same, but its effects tended in two different directions. It is well known that Luther was a great lover of music. It represented for him not only an aesthetic enjoyment but also an inner uplifting, a freeing of the soul, a giving of thanks and a sacrifice to God. Many and oft-quoted sayings testify to how closely he felt bound to music.

"Music is a beautiful and lovely gift of God. It has often awoken and moved me so that I felt the desire to preach," he said in his *Encomion Musices* of 1538, and here he reflects Augustinian ideas. In the same place he continues: "Music is the queen of all emotions of the human heart . . . nothing on earth has greater power than music to make the sad joyful, the joyful sad, the despondent courageous, to incline the arrogant to humility and to lessen envy and hatred."

His favorite composer was Josquin des Prés. This is remarkable in many respects, for, in the first place, Josquin's music was not yet well known in Germany during Luther's lifetime and, in the second place, it stood in strong contrast to the type of music that was practiced in the reformer's circle. Of this "very special master" Luther said that music came to him "joyfully, willingly, gently, and delightfully as the song of the finch," and "he is the master of the musical notes which have to do what he wants them to do; the other musicians have to do what the notes want." These two very perceptive remarks show how well Luther understood the difference between German and all-European music of which Josquin was, at that time, the uncontested master, and that he appreciated not only the style of the German song. His remarks, moreover, show that he accepted Josquin's music not as a specifically Catholic form of expression but one that was natural and individual, that is, as the art of an educated religious person. Thus he opened the door to the polyphonic music of the motets and masses of his day, without regard to the composer's confessional affiliation.

But what Luther and other educated persons could understand was not equally comprehensible to the congregation. Moreover, the congregation could take no active part in the traditional forms of elaborate Latin music. Yet it was this participation which was especially important for Luther. The congregation remained a congregation of lay people facing the priest as the only active member—instead of being itself a congregation of priests. Luther found a way out of this difficulty by giving the congregation the opportunity of taking an active part in the service through its singing. It followed that this singing had to play an important educative role. This explains why a large part of Luther's remarks about music show a highly pedagogical orientation.

His well-known words about the education of teachers and ministers point clearly in this direction. "A schoolmaster must be able to sing, otherwise I won't look at him. And a young fellow should not be directed toward the preacher's profession unless he has been proven in the school of music." Luther always expected a decisive moral effect of music on men. "Music is a half discipline and trainer that makes people more mild and gentle, modest and reasonable." More specifically, music was to have an educative effect on the congregation in the sense that it allowed the congregation to participate in declaring the Word of God and of offering a sacrifice to God. The chorale in the German language was to make this possible. "I wish we had many German chorales which people could sing with the mass or with the gradual and also with the Sanctus and the Agnus Dei. But we lack German poets, or we don't know them at present, who could write us pious and intelligent hymns, as Saint Paul calls them, so that one could use them in the congregation." Thus he wrote in the *Formula Missae* of 1523. Since there were no hymns, Luther himself undertook to fulfill his obligations as a teacher by writing them. His special concern was always for young people. It was his ardent endeavor that young people should be educated by music to knowledge of the Word of God and its pure teaching. For them Luther wishes for the writing and practice of part songs, and for the first book of part songs of the Lutheran Church, which Johannes Walther published in 1524, he wrote the introduction: "And thus, to make a good beginning and as an example to others who can do it better, I have brought together some spiritual songs in order to bring the holy gospel, which by God's grace has now risen again, into common knowledge. . . . And they have been edited in four voices, from no other cause but that I wish that young people, who must be educated in music and other good arts, should have something better than love songs and immodest songs. . . . And I also do not think that the gospels should overthrow and destroy all the arts, as some pseudotheologians would have it, but I would like to see all the arts, and especially music, in the service of Him who has given and created them."

For Luther, music was not an end in itself, any more than all the other arts and sciences. Its end, just as that of language, was rather to make young people mentally alert and receptive to the Word of God. It is nowadays a common misconception to think that Luther meant only to achieve the active participation of the uneducated, of the congregation as a whole, in divine service, and that in consequence he insisted on the exclusive use of the

German language. On the contrary, he himself set his face quite firmly against such an interpretation. As early as the *Formula Missae* of 1523, he divided church service into a service for chapter houses and cathedrals, on the one hand, and for small towns and country congregations, on the other. The large churches, which could make use of school and cathedral choirs, were to celebrate the main parts of the mass and of matins in Latin, while only the small churches were to use a simplified service entirely in German. He put this even more unequivocally in his *German Mass* of 1526: "For I do not wish to let the Latin language disappear from church service; for I am above all concerned with our youth. If I had my way, and if Greek and Hebrew were as common among us as Latin, and if they had as much fine music and song as Latin, then we should on alternate Sundays celebrate mass, sing, and read in all four languages, German, Latin, Greek, and Hebrew."

In the field of song, as in all fields of music, creative activity linked up with what already existed: the liturgical singing of the old church, the folk song, and the pre-Reformation German spiritual song—the ancestry from which developed the Lutheran chorale. They were the sources both for text and melody, but not necessarily in such a way that word and melody always remained together when the Lutheran church took them over. Frequently, old melodies were used for new or simply translated texts; in other cases, the text later acquired a new melody. In some cases again, an "improved" text was, from the beginning, linked with a new melody. These circumstances make a clear view of the Lutheran chorale very difficult, especially as the chorales that were taken over from older models were, quite early on, mixed together with others that had been written quite independently of the old examples and, in their turn, were provided with traditional or new melodies—a development that appeared already in the case of Luther's psalm compositions.

As a kind of bridge between the group of liturgical pieces, such as hymns and sequences which possessed a song-like character even in their original form, and the second group of the Lutheran chorales, there appeared another, quite large group. This consisted of pieces in the style of folk songs derived from Latin or from mixed Latin and German nonliturgical pieces which the congre-

gations had sung even in pre-Reformation church services. Some
of these even went back to the time of the troubadours. It was
precisely their popular origin and character that made them particularly suitable for Luther's purposes, and, in consequence, this
type of song achieved for a long time a special and widespread
popularity. This may also have been due to the fact that they
were regarded primarily as children's songs. Their many editions
for several voices prove this popularity.

Closely related to these mixed-language songs were the spiritual
songs in German composed before the Reformation. In most cases
their origin is unknown; but undoubtedly many derived from
the musical culture of the high and even of the early Middle
Ages. The medieval lays (*Leisen,* the word derives from the cor-
rupted refrain of *Kyrieleis,* which was added to many songs) were
further developed during the Crusades and in the spiritual minne-
song. Among this group are some of the strongest and most beautiful melodies to have survived through the centuries and even to
the present.

In this context there is one special group of old spiritual songs
in German, the songs in praise of the Virgin (*Marienlieder*).
Luther did not prohibit the veneration of the Virgin and of the
saints. He kept the principal Marian festivals, and the Lutheran
Church used Marian texts, at any rate in Latin, for a long time.
On the other hand, the German songs in praise of the Virgin
were not taken over unaltered but, from the beginning, they
were "improved in a Christian form."

With this type of song we have come to another group of
German songs that played an important role for the Lutheran
Church, the "parody" songs. Up to now, it has been a question
of only lightly modified song traditions. Here, by contrast, only
the melodies and the general pattern of the text were taken over,
and the text itself was completely recomposed, in the old pattern
but in a Protestant sense. The technical term for this reworking
of the text is *contrafactum* (*Kontrafaktur*), or parody. Formerly
there were doubts whether, during the Reformation period, secular
melodies with new religious texts were used in Lutheran churches.
But more recent investigations leave no doubt of this fact and
contemporary documents prove it. Luther said: "There is no reason

why the Devil should keep all the beautiful melodies for himself."
It would indeed have been remarkable if the Lutheran Church
had been offended by such a religious-secular musical community,
at a time when no one thought anything wrong with using secular
melodies for French and German masses and for the liturgy.

Luther's chorales, which he himself published in a series of
hymnals, soon became the core of Protestant hymnology. There is
no hymnal of the sixteenth and seventeenth centuries that does
not contain them. Only in the eighteenth century some were left
out. They became the models for "those who could do it better."
In numerous letters, writings, and introductions to hymnals, Luther
made the request that others should follow him. But there were
none who could do it better. Some chorales of his time do indeed
reach his level, but none surpassed him. Chorales flowed in a
mighty stream from his devoted heart, announcing the truth of
the gospel and winning victories for the new teaching such as
no sermon or tract was capable of doing. The Jesuits said, with
justice from their point of view, that Luther's chorales had
"damned more souls than his writings and speeches." The deep
significance of these chorales cannot be estimated too highly.
They constituted the Word of the Bible in poetic form, not just
edifying thoughts or prayers, such as the German hymns of the
Catholic Church. Not only did they possess a religious content
but they instilled in the layman the very words of the Bible or,
at least, of the nonbiblical liturgy. The Psalm compositions are
really the Psalms, not just borrowings or paraphrases (so that they
came justly to be called "German Psalms"). It is the basic principle of the Lutheran chorale that it is itself biblical text, not its
substitute, that it is part of the liturgy, not an appendage to it.
This fundamental fact becomes musically important in that the
melodies, together with the texts, now took on a kind of liturgical
and, hence, sacrosanct character. Just as in the Catholic Church,
where ritual chant raised Gregorian melodies to the status of a
basic part of the liturgy, so in the Lutheran Church, chorale melodies, within a short period of time, attained the status of a liturgical tradition that became inalienable and untouchable by individual preferences.

Bibliography*

GENERAL HISTORY OF THE REFORMATION

There are many excellent modern histories of the Reformation. I have included here those which are at once authoritative, up to date, and well written. Elton gives the most detailed and most readable political history of the period. Koenigsberger and Mosse as well as Dickens include a wider context of social and cultural history together with political and religious developments. The former work covers all of Europe throughout the sixteenth century and provides systematic information on sources and bibliography. The latter book, alone of this group, is superbly illustrated. Chadwick emphasizes the religious side, and the New Cambridge Modern History contains authoritative chapters on nearly all aspects of the history of the period.

* The books from which extracts and chapters have been reprinted are all well worth reading in full.

Chadwick, W. O., *The Reformation* (London, 1965).
Dickens, A. G., *Reformation and Society in Sixteenth-Century Europe* (London, 1966).
Elton, G. R., *Reformation Europe* (New York, 1966).
Koenigsberger, H. G. and George L. Mosse, *Europe in the Sixteenth Century* (London and New York, 1968).
The New Cambridge Modern History, Vol. II, edited by G. R. Elton (Cambridge, 1958).

BIOGRAPHIES OF LUTHER

Of the almost innumerable biographies of Luther, Bainton's has become a classic, being distinguished by both impeccable scholarship and sympathetic insight. Dickens makes use of more recent scholarship, both his own and that of others. Rupp is particularly good on Luther's religious and theological development in the early and formative parts of his career.

Bainton, R. H., *Here I Stand* (New York, 1955).
Dickens, A. G., *Martin Luther and the Reformation* (London, 1967).
Rupp, E. G., *Luther's Progress to the Diet of Worms* (London and Greenwich, Conn., 1951).

LUTHER'S THEOLOGY

From an enormously vast and still growing field, I have selected those works that would interest students of history rather than students of theology. Carlson provides a historiographical survey of the fundamental advances in Luther studies, which were begun in Scandinavia some fifty years ago. Pelikan concentrates on Luther's ideas about the church and its institutions. McDonough's is a Catholic theologian's account of Luther's doctrine of the gospel and the law. Bornkamm includes Luther's views on the whole physical and intellectual world around him. Althaus gives a useful modern compendium of the principal tenets of Luther's theology.

Althaus, P., *The Theology of Martin Luther,* translated by R. C. Schultz (Philadelphia, 1966).

Bornkamm, H., *Luther's World of Thought,* translated by M. H. Bertram (St. Louis, 1958).

Carlson, E. M., *The Reinterpretation of Luther* (Philadelphia, 1948).

McDonough, T. M., *The Law and the Gospel in Luther* (Oxford, 1963).

Pelikan, J., *Spirit versus Structure: Luther and the Institutions of the Church* (London, 1968).

LUTHER'S WORKS

The standard edition, described in the chapter "Luther's Words" is the so-called Weimar edition (*Weimarer Ausgabe*): *D. Martin Luthers Werke: Kritische Gesamtausgabe* (Weimar, 1883–   ). The most comprehensive English translation is *Luther's Works: American Edition,* edited by Jaroslav Pelikan and Helmut T. Lehmann (St. Louis and Philadelphia, 1955–   ). Magnificent as is this enterprise, it is sometimes more satisfactory to use different translations of separate works, such as: *First Principles of the Reformation* (the Ninety-five Theses and the three pamphlets: *Address to the Christian Nobility of the German Nation, The Babylonian Captivity of the Church,* and *The Liberty of a Christian Man,* translated by C. A. Buchheim [London, 1883]) or *Luther and Erasmus: Free Will and Salvation* (Erasmus: *De Libero Arbitrio*; Luther: *De Servo Arbitrio*) translated and edited by E. G. Rupp and P. S. Watson (London, 1969).

Contributors

FRIEDRICH BLUME is professor of musical sciences (emeritus) at the University of Kiel. He edited and made many contributions to the fourteen-volume dictionary of music, *Die Musik in Geschichte und Gegenwart* (1949–1968). His other publications include *Two Centuries of Bach: An Account of Changing Taste* (1950), *Renaissance and Baroque Music* (1967), and *Classical and Romantic Music* (1970).

HEINRICH BORNKAMM is professor of historical theology (emeritus) at the University of Heidelberg. His publications include *Luther und Böhme* (1925), *Das Wort Gottes bei Luther* (1933), *Luther's World of Thought* (1947, 1958), *Luther und das Alte Testament* (1948), *Grundriss zum Studium der Kirchengeschichte* (1949), *Martin Bucers Bedeutung für die europäische*

Reformationsgeschichte (1952), and *Luther im Spiegel der Geistesgeschichte* (1955).

GERHARD EBELING is professor of theology and hermeneutics at the University of Zürich. His publications include *Untersuchungen zu Luthers Hermeneutik* (1942), *Die Geschichtlichkeit der Kirche* (1954), *Was heisst Glauben?* (1958), *Das Wesen des christlichen Glaubens* (1959), *Gott und Wort* (1966), and *Frei aus Glauben* (1968).

FRIEDRICH ENGELS (1820–1895) was a friend and collaborator of Karl Marx. He spent most of his adult life in England and in 1870 became secretary of the First International. His publications include *The Condition of the English Working Class in 1844* (1845, 1892), *The Communist Manifesto* (co-authored with Marx) (1848), *Anti-Duehring: Socialism Utopian and Scientific* (1878), *Dialectics of Nature* (1940), and *The Origin of the Family, Private Property, and the State* (1884, 1902).

ERIK H. ERIKSON is professor of human development and lecturer in psychiatry at Harvard University. He is a Fellow of the American Academy of Arts and Sciences. His publications include *Childhood and Society* (1950, 1964), *Insight and Responsibility* (1964), *Identity: Youth and Crisis* (1968), and *Gandhi's Truth: On the Origins of Militant Nonviolence* (1969).

LUCIEN FEBVRE (1878–1956) was professor of the history of modern civilization, Collège de France. Together with Marc Bloch, he founded the journal *Annales: Histoire, Economie, Société* in 1929. His publications include *Philippe II et la Franche Comté* (1911), *Le Problème de l'incroyance au XVIe siècle* (1942), and *Autour de l'Heptaméron* (1944).

B. A. GERRISH is professor of theology and reformation history at the Divinity School, University of Chicago. His publications include *The Faith of Christendom: A Source Book of Creeds and*

Confessions (1963) and the edition of *Reformers in Profile* (1967).

BENGT HÄGGLUND is professor of systematic theology and history of theology at the University of Lund, Sweden. His publications include *Die Heilige Schrift und ihre Deutung in der Theologie Jann Gerhards* (1951), *Theologie und Philosophie bei Luther und in der Occamistischen Tradition* (1955), and *History of Theology,* translated by Gene J. Lund (1968).

LENNART PINOMAA is professor of theology (emeritus) at the University of Helsinki. His publications include *Der Zorn Gottes in der Theologie Luthers* (1938), *Der existentielle Charakter der Theologie Luthers* (1940), and *Die Heiligen in Luthers Frühtheologie* (1959).

LEOPOLD VON RANKE (1795-1886), the leading German historian of the nineteenth century, did much to establish modern scholarly methods in the study and writing of history. He became professor of history at the University of Berlin in 1834 and was ennobled in 1865. Most of his research focused on the early modern period. While many of his works have been translated into English, these translations have largely been mediocre and thus give little indication of Ranke's magisterial German style. The following are some of his works (the first dates within the parentheses are those of the first German edition; the second of the first English translation—not always of the whole work): *History of the Latin and Teutonic Nations* (1824, 1887), *History of England* (1859-1869, 1875), *Civil Wars and Monarchy in France in the Sixteenth and Seventeenth Centuries* (1852-1856, 1852), *The Popes of Rome* (1834-1836, 1840), and *History of the Prussian Monarchy* (1847-1848, 1847-1848).

GERHARD RITTER (1888-1967) was professor of modern history at the University of Freiburg. He participated in the June 1944 resistance plot against Hitler. His publications include *The German Resistance* (1954, 1958), *The Corrupting Influence of Power* (1948, 1952), *The German Problem* (1962, 1965), *Fred-*

erick the Great: A Historical Profile (1936, 1968), *The Schlieffen Plan* (1956, 1958), and *The Sword and the Scepter: The Problem of Militarism in Germany* (1955, 1969).

GORDON RUPP is a Fellow of the British Academy and Dixie Professor of ecclesiastical history at the University of Cambridge. He is also principal of Wesley House, Cambridge. His publications include *Studies in the English Protestant Tradition* (1947), *Some Makers of English Religion* (1957), *The Old Reformation and the New* (1967), and *Patterns of Reformation* (1969).

H. G. KOENIGSBERGER served in the Royal Navy in 1944 and 1945 and then went on to receive his Ph.D. from Cambridge University in 1949. Since then he has been a visiting lecturer in history both in the United States and abroad. In 1966 he became Professor of Early Modern European History at Cornell University. He is joint editor of *Cambridge Studies in Early Modern History* and his publications include *Estates and Revolutions: Essays in Early Modern European History, The Hapsburgs and Europe, 1516–1660, The Practice of Empire, Europe in the Sixteenth Century* (with G. L. Mosse), and *Diversity of History: Essays in Honor of Sir Herbert Butterfield* (edited, with J. H. Elliott).

AÏDA DIPACE DONALD holds degrees from Barnard and Columbia and a Ph.D. from the University of Rochester. A former member of the History Department at Columbia, Mrs. Donald has been a Fulbright Fellow at Oxford and the recipient of an A.A.U.W. fellowship. She has published *John F. Kennedy and the New Frontier* and *Diary of Charles Francis Adams.*